Strategy and Planning

CBI Series in Practical Strategy

Strategy and Planning

A Manager's Guide

David Hussey

JOHN WILEY & SONS, LTD
Chichester • New York • Weinheim • Brisbane • Singapore • Toronto

First edition published by Pergamon Press under the title *Introducing Corporate Planning* in 1971. Second edition 1979. Third edition 1985. Fourth edition 1991.

Other Wiley Editorial Offices

John Wiley & Sons, Inc., 605 Third Avenue,
New York, NY 10158-0012, USA

WILEY-VCH Verlag GmbH, Pappelallee 3,
D-69469 Weinheim, Germany

Jacaranda Wiley Ltd, 33 Park Road, Milton,
Queensland 4064, Australia

John Wiley & Sons (Asia) Pte Ltd, 2 Clementi Loop #02-01,
Jin Xing Distripark, Singapore 129809

John Wiley & Sons (Canada) Ltd, 22 Worcester Road,
Rexdale, Ontario M9W 1L1, Canada

Library of Congress Cataloguing-in-Publication Data

A catalogue record for this book is available from the British Library

British Library Cataloguing in Publication Data

A catalogue record for this book is available from the British Library

ISBN 0-471-50006-2

Typeset in 11/13 pt Times by C.K.M. Typesetting, Salisbury, Wiltshire.
Printed and bound in Great Britain by Biddles Ltd, Guildford and King's Lynn.
This book is printed on acid-free paper responsibly manufactured from sustainable forestry, in which at least two trees are planted for each one used for paper production.

Contents

Series Foreword

The aim of this series is to provide managers with books on strategy, strategic management and strategic change, which are helpful, practical, and provide guidance for the practical application of sound concepts in real situations. It is thus very welcome that a number of the books in the series should be selected for publication under the logo of the CBI, whose member organisations are very much concerned with the topics covered in the series.

In the mid 1960s when the subject of planning began to emerge, the whole literature could have been listed on one or two sheets of paper. It was easy to decide which books to read, because so few were available. This state of affairs changed rapidly, and the scope of the subject has moved from a focus on formal planning to a broader view which merges with the literature of leadership, change management, strategic analysis, and organisation. Modern writing sees the organisation and its strategies in an integrated way, and there are many, often conflicting, theories about the "right" way to formulate strategies and practice strategic management.

Management usually does not take an academic interest in theories, but is concerned about what works best in the situation in which it operates. Hence this series. Each book is conceptually sound, and gives proper acknowledgement to the originators of concepts and ideas, but the emphasis is on using the concepts or methods, rather than academic argument. Hence, too, the choice of the six subjects initially offered under the auspices of the CBI.

There are two books which offer complementary overviews of strategic management. McNamee's *Strategic Market Planning* follows the author's belief that enduringly successful firms are those that understand most clearly, and then serve most effectively, the markets they address, and offers a blue print for this. Hussey (*Strategy & Planning*) provides essential, up to date, information for managers and practitioners of strategic management who require a practical view of the whole subject.

Segev writes on business unit strategy, and its emphasis is on analytical method for businesses that focus on one industry or product/market grouping. The remaining three books deal with specific aspects of strategy which are topical concerns for many organisations. They cover the subjects of virtual organisations (Hedberg et al), the related but different subject of multinational strategic alliances (Mockler), and competitor analysis, (Hussey & Jenster).

The emphasis of all the books is on practical application. The aim is to give the reader clear guidance on how to make the subject of the book work in his or her own situation, while at the same time taking care to ensure that the books do not over-simplify situations. Check lists and questionnaires are included when they aid the aims of the book, and examples are given. The experience of the author in actually applying the concepts, rather than just knowing about them, is intended to show through the writing.

The books are written by authors from Denmark, Israel, Sweden, the UK and the USA, which brings an international flavour, as well as helping to make complex matters understandable. We hope that it will become a catalyst that helps managers make a difference to the strategic performance of their organisations.

David Hussey, Series Editor
Visiting Professor in Strategic Management,
Nottingham Trent University
Managing Director, David Hussey & Associates

August 2000

Preface

The first edition of this book came out in 1971, and was based on my experiences in strategic planning inside various organisations. It was written more than a year earlier, and was lucky it came out at all, as it was a period before easy access to fast copiers, and certainly before PCs and word processing, and the manuscript only just survived a fire in the publisher's office. I eventually received one copy of the typescript back from the publisher, scorched and singed. But the book eventually appeared, and has gone through several editions. There is a family resemblance in this new edition to its predecessors, but like any child it is not identical to its parent.

The changes have been made because the whole subject has changed, and because my experiences have enlarged. The topic has gone through the change of name sequence which sometimes passes for evolution. I was very modern in the first edition, as I used the stage 2 name instead of the original long range planning. Stage 3 was strategic planning, stage 4 became strategic management, which we all seem to like because we have used it for some 25 years. The explosion of the literature has been enormous, and I suppose we could claim to have arrived, as it is now no longer possible for any one person to read every book and every article that comes out. But with that explosion has come a development of methods, tools and techniques, which are intended to help make sense of strategy in an increasingly complex and fast changing environment.

I have changed because in 1976 I gave up my claim to be the only person in the world who wrote about corporate planning and actually was a planning manager (the rest were consultants and academics), and moved into management consultancy myself.

This gave me access to many more opportunities for experience, although I should stress that the style of consulting was usually in a skills transfer mode, where I would help managers to apply the appropriate methods and draw conclusions for themselves. So the practical application concern of the book continued, reinforced by my day-to-day work.

This new edition has a change of focus from the original. The priorities are strategic thinking, strategic planning, and as an option, the strategic management process. Although part of the scope is unchanged, the book no longer assumes that the best way to develop strategy is to do it within a corporate-wide process. It recognises that for some people the priority is the strategy itself (which in one sense was always the priority of a process), and that just thinking this through on an ad hoc basis can have value. However, some readers will also want to prepare a written strategic plan either because of their own perceived needs, or because some outside agency like a head office or a bank insists. Those who do not wish to set up a continuous process of planning may not wish to read the last chapter which explores this issue.

The various editions of the book have always been written for managers and practitioners as the prime audience. What the reader will find is an approach which is rooted in reality. I have used the methods, techniques, and concepts in a variety of situations, so I am not offering new theories, or methods which I cannot personally endorse. I know that the world of text books and the realities of organisational life do not always seem to be the same. I hope that new readers will find the book useful.

It was Professor Bernard Taylor who in 1969 suggested I write this book, at a time when there was little published and I was compelled to be original. I owe a debt to Bernard, and a subsequent debt to all the colleagues, clients, and writers on strategy who have helped me shape my thinking.

About the Author

David Hussey is a well-known international authority on strategic management, with experience as both a practitioner in and a consultant to major companies from many industries, including 18 years spent with Harbridge House. He is author or editor of over 25 books on strategy or management development. One of the founders of the Strategic Planning Society, and a director of the Japan Strategic Management Institute, he is currently visiting professor in strategic management at Nottingham Business School. He is also editor of *Croner's Journal of Professional HRM* and former editor of the *Journal of Strategic Change*.

1
Modern Concepts of Strategic Management

Strategic management has evolved from a variety of related approaches, a point to which I will return later in this chapter. As it has evolved it has spawned different, schools of thought, not all of which live happily with each other. Some of these are about the process through which an organisation develops and implements its strategies, while others argue for particular methods of determining strategy. There is at least one common link between all the approaches: a focus on strategy.

Three terms should be defined. I see *strategy* as the means by which an organisation moves to attain its long-term aims. *Strategic planning* is the detailed specification of both the long-term aims and the strategy for achieving them. *Strategic management* is the process by which the long-term aims, the strategy, and its implementation are managed: it is thus as much concerned with the human aspects of management as it is with markets, factories and finance. The three concepts are intricately bound together. For example a strategy which is formulated without any thought about how it can be implemented is unlikely to succeed. Strategic planning is more than just writing down the strategy: it should give consideration to the culture, structure and systems in the organisation, so that every element of the organisation can be mobilised to make the strategy effective. Strategic management encompasses both strategy and strategic planning, but means something more: it is the way in which strategy becomes the driving force of the organisation.

A key element, if a strategy is to be effective, is a long-term view.

This does not mean that a strategy should be expected to last forever, but it does mean that every strategy should move the organisation towards its long-term aims, and that the organisation should be in a better position to achieve these aims at the point where a strategy has to be fundamentally changed, or even abandoned. Concepts of vision, or strategic intent, objectives and goals which expand this idea of long-term aims will be discussed in a subsequent chapter. Although it will vary between organisations, we can put one plank down here, which is that for a commercial organisation the long-term aim will include some notion about increasing shareholder value: for a public sector organisation or charity the notion may be one of increasing stakeholder value.

A future orientation is important, and some would argue is the most important aspect of strategy. For example Hamel and Prahalad, 1994, argue for:

> "... a view of strategy quite different from what prevails in many companies. It is a view of strategy that recognizes that a firm must unlearn its past before it can find the future. It is a view of strategy that recognizes it is not enough to optimally position a company within existing markets; the challenge is to pierce the fog of uncertainty and develop great *foresight* into the whereabouts of tomorrow's markets. It is a view of strategy that recognises the need for more than an incrementalist, annual planning rain dance; what is needed is a *strategic architecture* that provides a blueprint for building the competencies needed to dominate future markets."

These thoughts are not completely new. Drucker, 1964, said:

> "But tomorrow always arrives. It is always different, and then even the mightiest company is in trouble if it has not worked on the future. It will have lost distinction and leadership—all that will remain is big company overheads. It will neither control nor understand what is happening; not having dared to take the risk of making the new happen, it perforce took the much greater risk of being surprised by what did happen. And this is a risk that even the largest and richest company cannot afford and that even the smallest business need not run."

TOWARDS THE FUTURE

The modern business operates in an environment of continuous change. Nothing is static. Complexity is one of the dominant consequences of the change-causing issues which businesses face as we move into the millennium. What are some of these issues?

- *Intensifying competition.* The world has become more competitive, and competition is more global. Few companies can now afford to think only of their domestic market, because to compete against global competitors they have to achieve the scale of operations of those competitors. Japanese companies led the world in thinking of markets in global terms. The new conditions require organisations to be more global, and this is likely to be as difficult for Japanese firms as it is for many insular US businesses who are waking up to the fact that the US market, large as it is, will no longer insulate them from the new competitive arena. For UK firms it is the threat and opportunity of the new European monetary union.
- *New technologies.* Only the brave would try to predict the specific direction of new technology. What is clear is that the continued development of computers, and the merging of computer technologies with those of video, television, and telecommunications will change further the way in which the world operates, as well as creating many new products and markets.
- *Smaller more flexible organisations.* Partly because of the need to be cost effective in order to compete, there will be a continuation of the trend to reducing the number of people in organisations, while increasing the overall volume of business. Flexibility remains one of the key issues for survival and development.
- *The power of information.* Ten years ago it was not infrequent to hear managers complain that a decision was difficult because of lack of information. Now the probability is that there is so much information that a decision is difficult because of the need to absorb and use the right information.
- *The power of customers.* Customer expectations continue to rise, requiring more attention to service and quality. This is perhaps one of the lessons of *In Search of Excellence* (Peters and Waterman, 1982) which continues to be valid, and which will increase in intensity. Allied to this are the drives to total quality management.
- *Demographic trends.* In the USA and much of Europe there is an ageing population structure. This is not true of Africa and much of Asia. The implications for Europe are a shortage of school

leavers, which ties back to the need for smaller, leaner organisations mentioned above. It also leads directly to the next trend.
Population growth in the poorer countries of the world, already
outstrips that of the richest, and the gap between rich and poor
may be expected to become a more dominant issue in the future.

- *Diversity*. One trend that has received little attention so far is
  the need to learn how to manage a much more diverse body of
  employees. In the USA the traditional white male has always
  been in the majority in management. Forecasts are that this
  supremacy is disappearing, and that women and the other
  ethnic groups will collectively remove this dominance. In the
  UK the recommended solutions to the shortage of school
  leavers include more flexible working conditions to attract
  women with children back into the workforce, and an increase
  in part-time jobs for retired people. Add to this the need for
  most companies to begin to think of their employees on a
  European rather than a British basis, and more issues of
  diversity begin to emerge. Successful management will require
  greater flexibility, and a greater cultural sensitivity as we move
  into the future.
- *Shortening product life cycles*. The pace of technological change
  will continue to accelerate. One implication is a shortening of
  product life cycles. This has many implications for management, one being the need to reduce the lead time in the
  development of new products.
- *New alliances*. Strategic alliances are buzz words which
  appeared in the chairman's statements of a very large number
  of companies throughout the 1990s. Fed by a fear of being left
  behind in the scramble for global scale, organisations seek alliances rather than attempt to acquire or set up in a crowded field.
  At the same time, the need for flexibility has led to a different
  type of alliance between buyers and suppliers, as outsourcing
  has become an action of considerable importance. The management of strategic alliances will be one of the challenges through
  the next decade.

Change is not new to business, but each decade seems to bring an
increase in the strategic stakes. The price tickets to pay in many
industries are tending to become larger, and the implications of
failure much more serious.

For many companies any change is, if noticed, regarded as a threat, and too often is completely unobserved until it begins to attack profits. The forward-looking company sees opportunity in the new patterns which will emerge in the future, the chance to adapt the organisation to make additional profits from innovatory measures. Indeed it may actively seek to create change to its own advantage, and to mould some of the trends into the direction it would like to see them go. It does not stand and bewail the buffets of any unkind fate, or look back to history at its past glories. Although it is not possible for every organisation to reinvent its industry, as Hamel and Prahalad, 1994 suggest, innovative strategic thinking is important for all.

WHAT REALLY HAS HAPPENED?

One reason why new ways of applying strategic management are regularly published is that not all organisations have achieved the degree of strategic success that past concepts have promised. As an example, numerous research studies over some 30 years show that around 50% of acquisitions and mergers fail. The popular Business Process Re-engineering initiatives have disappointed more organisations than they pleased (for example, see Hammer and Champny, 1993) and some studies show that many organisations which downsized fared worse than those who did not (for example, Meuse et al., 1994 and Wyatt Co, 1994). It has been suggested that in uncertain situations, organisations often copy each other's actions as this makes them feel more secure. But what perhaps is really significant is the fashion element in strategic moves, and mimicking others seems to be a permanent condition in much of the business world.

In the 1960s and much of the 1970s the conventional wisdom was diversify. It was as a result of this that corporate raiders were able to buy companies to break them up, as the value of the individual parts was greater than the whole. Imperial Group was one such organisation, which was purchased by Hanson, whose subsequent sale of much of the organisation meant that the retained cash-generating tobacco business was gained at much less than its real value. In the 1980s the fashion was to strip down to core businesses. Vickers, for example reduced its 35 business units to 6 core activities, which were further reduced through the decade. The Rolls-Royce car division has been sold recently, leaving the organisation as a focused defence manufacturer. The core of the 1990s is slimmer than the core of the 1980s. To some extent the gradual narrowing of focus was an evolutionary strategy, and there is a good argument for this approach which I will return to later in this chapter.

In the 1970s it was considered a good strategy for airlines to own hotels: in the 1980s many airlines sold off hotels to concentrate on the key airline business. Many financial service companies followed Lloyds Bank into the estate agency business in the late 1980s, often paying a premium to acquire chains of estate agents. Large losses were made, and in the 1990s the conventional wisdom was that this was a bad strategy, and many, including Prudential, cut their losses and divested the activity.

Sometimes a strategy will deliver good results in the short term, but will leave the organisation weaker thereafter. Good examples are retailers such as Next and Burton, which in the late 1980s followed a strategy of expansion and acquisition, and seemed to be doing well. By the 1990s such companies faced major difficulties, and had to re-structure themselves, and sell off many of the acquisitions they had recently made. Some did not survive.

One of the success companies of the 1980s was the Ratner Group. This retail jewellers was started in the 1940s, and gradually built up by 1983 to a chain of 130 shops with earnings per share (EPS) of 2.4p. In that year Gerald Ratner became managing director, and by 1990 EPS reached 26.9p. The financial year ended in January, so 11 trading months were in the previous calendar year. Growth was phenomenal: 1990 pre-tax profits of nearly £121 million compared with 1984 sales of under £28 million. There was a reduction in EPS in financial year 1991, and after that it moved into massive losses. It took until financial year 1998, under a different management and with the name changed to Signet, before it appeared to be back on an even keel, but at a far lower level of profitability.

Growth began with an innovative strategy to change the cheap end of the UK retail jewellery market, and much of the expansion of the overall market was the result of this strategy. Systems and procedures were developed which reinforced this strategy, and the number of outlets was expanded. Novel marketing methods, for this market, were used, and manufacturers were persuaded to develop products such as hollow gold jewellery which could be sold for low prices. The growth engine began to turn.

The next stage was to fuel growth by acquisition of other chains of jewellers, including Zales, H. Samuel and Ernest Jones. These traded in different segments of the market, which Ratner Group recognised, but the Ratner systems gradually eroded the differentiation from the Ratner stores' bargain image. There were immediate benefits from buying economies, elimination of separate head offices, and reduced distribution costs, but in my opinion a failure to exploit the different segment positions was one factor which contributed to the collapse.

Ambitions grew, and after a few years as managing director, Gerald Ratner turned his attention to the US market, and started to build a position there through an acquisition strategy. It is interesting to question what synergy could result from such a strategy, but initially this too was successful, and was largely financed by cumulative preference shares and debt. The last of these acquisitions took place in October 1990 and cost £426 million. Press reports suggested that there were unexpected problems with this purchase, but my view is that the main problem was timing, in that the recession had already started.

In 1988 Ratner bought the Zales and Salisbury chains from Next, which had outbid Ratner for its previous owners Combined English Stores in 1987. This group included retail chains in fashion clothing and sweets, chemists, and the holiday firm Eurocamp. The Salisbury chain sold leather and fancy goods, and proved to be a drain on profits until eventually sold in 1985: the capital loss on disposal was over £87 million. The purchase of Salisbury was another shift of strategy, although whether it was unplanned opportunism, or part of an intention to build a large retailing empire is unclear. Press reports had suggested that the Ratner Group was interested in buying Dixons, the consumer electronics retailer.

Gerald Ratner achieved unwelcome publicity in April 1991 when jokes he made about the Ratner products were widely reported in the mass media. It would be wrong to blame the company's problems on this, although it must have had some adverse effect of sales through those shops bearing the Ratner name. Similarly it would be superficial analysis to argue that the problems were the result of the recession, although this too contributed. I would suggest that the cause lay in the company's strategy, and the implementation of that strategy. As the strategy moved away from the innovative actions the company had taken to redefine its industry, the company's vision became less focused and more opportunistic, and no longer had such a clear fit with the business environment and the company's own competencies. I suspect that there was also a fashion element in some of the actions: if Next and other retailers were building broad-based businesses by acquisition, should not the Ratner Group follow suit?

One of the difficulties in assessing a strategy is that companies can make good profits for some time after the strategy they have been following has passed its sell-by date. The parallel with supermarket food is quite close. We can probably eat a food product a day or two after expiry date, provided it is not obviously bad, without suffering ill effects. A day or two later, when the food has gone off, we could become ill or worse. But the sell-by date does not give complete protection either, and only a fool or a starving person would insist on eating something just because the label says it is fine, when our eyes, nose or tongue tells us it is tainted.

Rushing on with a strategy when common sense says it can no longer deliver its promised benefits is akin to eating tainted food. However, a more common mistake is to assume that continued current profitability means that the sell-by date has not been reached. For example, many of the companies chosen as excellent in the Peters and Waterman, 1982 study have since fallen from grace. A more striking example is Xcrox, which was chosen as one of the nine successful companies whose approach to strategy formulation was studied by Quinn, 1980, from which he derived his theory of logical incrementalism. Hamel and Prahalad, 1994, use Xerox of the late 1970s as an example of a company which did not have a sound strategy, in that it did not at that time recognise the threat from Canon and other Japanese companies to whom it surrendered a considerable market share. "In fact", say Hamel and Prahalad, "Xerox has probably, left more money on the table, in the form of under exploited innovation than any company in history." Despite becoming a superb example by the 1990s for cost reduction, quality improvement, and customer service, it has still not recovered much of what it lost. Why did it not change strategy earlier? Because it was still growing and making good profits. The flower of current success was maturing the seeds of potential future failure. And all this begs the question of why the approach to strategic thinking it was using in the 1970s should be held out as an example everyone should follow.

MORE ABOUT FADS AND FASHIONS

Hillmer and Donaldson, 1996, listed five fads which many organisations follow, which were false trails and led to the trivialisation of management. Of the fads, four are relevant to our present discussion: the fifth concerns the nature of the board which is of less interest here. The four fads are:

- Organisations should be flat.
- Actions are better than deliberation, intuition is better than analysis, decisions will emerge from the action.
- If a problem arises it can be quickly fixed by using a technique.
- A corporate clan culture will mean that everyone will always know what is the right thing to do, so rules and procedures are not necessary.

The issue is that these fads do not lead to automatic success: neither do they explain the success of the best performing companies. Some of the actions may be right for some companies at a particular point in time, but this does not turn them into miracle cures. To discuss each of these fads would be to either repeat things already mentioned, or to pre-empt things that will be covered later in this chapter, so I will restrict comments to just one of them: techniques.

Of course there are numerous techniques that can be helpful. They do not solve problems, but if chosen appropriately and used correctly they can give insight which can help managers to make better decisions. Techniques of strategic analysis throw light on certain aspects of a situation, but they leave other aspects in the dark. An analogy I have often used is that of a toy, the kaleidoscope. Every time it is held to the light something different is seen, but the basic situation has not changed. It remains a combination of mirrors, glass to let in light, and coloured shapes which move by gravity into different positions. Each technique, like each view through the kaleidoscope, may help us understand things a little better, but no single technique will ever reveal everything.

Five common failings in the use of techniques are:

1. A belief that a technique is all that is needed to solve the problem.
2. An inappropriate technique is chosen, because it is fashionable.
3. Too much reliance is placed on one technique, when a combination would give more insight.
4. The technique is misused (my experience has been that many techniques are not applied correctly, and rubbish in means rubbish out with interest).
5. The flat earth syndrome.

The flat earth syndrome can more elegantly be called the boundary of perception: it is what managers believe to be the basic situation rather than what that situation really is. Medieval man knew that the world was flat, like a plate, and therefore the sensible people developed logical strategies that fitted this certain knowledge. One such strategy was not to sail too close to the edge, because you would fall off. Reality, as we now know, is somewhat different, and the strategy neither logical nor sensible. Our forefathers knew that malaria was caught by breathing the miasma from marshes, so they took appropriate and unsuccessful action to avoid it. The British motor cycle companies in the 1960s and early 1970s knew how their business worked, and when Honda applied different ideas they cried "dumping" and never addressed the fundamental issue that this new competitor had a superior competitive strategy. Techniques are often used in a way that confirms prejudices, and imprisons the organisation: they should be used to help free thinking, not to constrain it.

Fads and quick fixes are chosen by managers because they feel a need to be seen doing something. The problems themselves may be complex and hard to deal with, but there is a personal security in being "modern", following the fashion, and being able to quote the latest guru. There is no corporate security in these unthinking copycat approaches.

Hilmer and Donaldson argue that the false trails "... encourage managers to do the wrong things for their specific situation—to train for swimming when the race is to be held on land." Secondly even when the trail goes "... in the right direction, its prescriptions implicitly encourage poor implementation". The reason is that the quick fix is expected to yield quick results, and managers do not persevere long enough when benefits do not flow quickly.

FIVE ESSENTIALS FOR STRATEGIC SUCCESS

Figure 1.1 emphasises the five elements that an organisation must have if it is to achieve lasting strategic success. It is not a step-by-step model, in that the need for each of these five elements occurs and recurs as a strategy is developed, formulated, and turned into action. All the elements are critical, although their importance relative to each other will vary. No approach can guarantee that strategies will always be successful, because by definition something determined today will be affected by external events that happen in

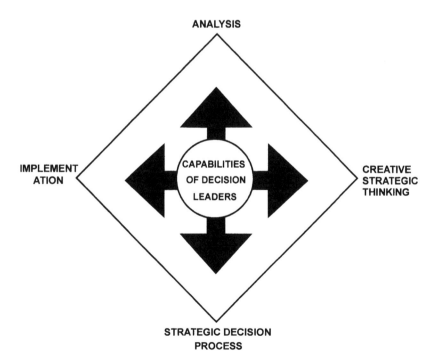

Figure 1.1 Critical factors for strategic success. (From Hussey, D. E., 1997, Strategic management: past experiences and future directions. *Strategic Change*, Vol. 6, no 5).

the future, and even the most meticulous study will not foresee everything. Figure 1.1 does not offer a quick fix solution. Adverse circumstances may occur in the future. It is a bit like walking on a crowed city street; we cannot always avoid being jostled and bumped: but that is no excuse for walking with our eyes shut! A sound basis for strategy is a way of keeping the company's eyes open.

Figure 1.1 recognises that strategy cannot be successful until it is implemented, and that the whole process is a mix of the "hard" and "soft" aspects of management. As the model is explored, attention will be drawn to some of the different schools of thought about strategic management.

Analysis

It seems to be a self-evident truth that information should be collected and analysed at various stages in the strategic management process, and that if this is neglected or done badly the strategic decisions taken may be flawed. There are many points in the overall process where analysis is required, but for our purposes four are distinguished:

- *As a basis for strategy formulation*: many authors have identified ways of analysing a situation, including Ansoff 1965, who laid the foundation for the analytical approach to strategy; The Boston Consulting Group through the 1970s, whose concepts of portfolio analysis and the experience curve will be found in Stern and Stalk 1998; Porter 1980, 1985, who gave us a structured approach to industry and competitor analysis; and the PIMS organisation whose data base relates strategic decisions to outcomes (see Buzzell and Gale, 1987). Many analytical approaches will be discussed in later chapters.
- *The evaluation of strategic options*: even a strategic option which everyone is enthusiastic about should be analysed. There are a number of aspects to this, including the fit of the option with the rest of the corporate strategy, the assessment of the expected results, and the financial analysis of the option, preferably using discounted cash-flow techniques.

- *Development of an implementation plan for the strategy*: which usually takes the organisation into a different and quite detailed series of analytical steps.
- *Reassessment of the option in the light of its outcome*: monitoring and controlling is an important aspect of implementation, which may throw up a need for further analysis if results are better or worse than expected.

Analysis is always important, although there are several schools of thought about whether a good strategy will arise from a detailed and formal process. This is something we will touch on when we look at another element of Figure 1.1. However, it would be naïve to believe that the analytical process is always objective, for it is nearly always affected by behavioural issues. The choice of information to collect and analyse is affected by the boundaries of perception mentioned earlier: after all which of our early explorers would have made a study of the mosquito, when the cause of fever was "known" to be the miasma from the swamps? Similarly the results of an analytical exercise can be interpreted according to what the analyst expects to find. It is also not unknown for data to be tweaked to give the result that everyone "knows" is correct. Objectivity is desirable, which is why outside eyes, such as those of a management consultant, can sometimes help.

Creative strategic thinking

My personal view is that the best analysis in the world is unlikely to, by itself, deliver the best strategy in the world. It needs a spark of creativity. The creative input can come before the analysis, in which case the analytical task is to confirm that it is as bright an idea as it first seemed, or it may come when the situation has been analysed, so that it moves from a clear understanding of the situation.

Ohmae, 1982 suggests that analysis is the craft of strategy, and creative strategic thinking is the art. Mastery of the craft enables the artist to paint a masterpiece, but without the creative genius the result will be ordinary rather than excellent. Of course Kenichi Ohmae may never have visited the Tate Gallery in London, where the technical mastery in some of the modern sculpture is the ability to use an electric saw to cut a cow in half, or a wheelbarrow to bring in a pile of house bricks, but not all of us see the creative genius in these "masterpieces" either. Ohmae stresses the importance of insight and intuition in conjunction with analysis.

Hamel and Prahalad, 1994, as mentioned earlier see the need to recreate the firm and reinvent the industry, which is clearly an exercise in creative strategic thinking. They tie this to the need to identify and obtain the core competencies needed to make this happen, which of course requires analysis and implementation.

Farrell, 1993, reaches the need for strategic creative thinking by a different route, entrepreneurship, which he feels has been lost in many US and European firms, driven out by corporate systems. He also stresses another important factor in setting a good strategy: common sense.

Strategic decision process

The third element of the model is the process by which strategic decisions are reached. Initially the planning literature implied that there was only one correct way, which is objective analysis, followed by a firm plan to achieve pre-decided objectives. Generally, the early authors argued for the involvement of line managers in the planning process, on the theory that this would build commitment to the plan, and therefore they would implement it. The rational planning school owes much to Ansoff, 1965, but was embellished and developed by numerous authors, including Steiner, 1969. There is still relevance in many of the early ideas, but one of the flaws that developed in many organisations was that the "pass the hat round" approach to strategy, which was the form of process used by many, resulted in volumes of paper without necessarily developing appropriate plans, so that many strategic decisions were taken outside the "plan". Ansoff through the 1980s and 1990s developed a contingency approach to the strategic decision process. He argues (Ansoff, 1990 is a typical reference) that the process chosen should be different depending on the degree of environmental turbulence that the organisation is facing. His analysis matches five degrees of turbulence to five different approaches to determining strategy, and the research he and his colleagues have undertaken demonstrates that a mismatch has an adverse impact on results.

However, this is not the only view of the decision process. Another school of thought, currently led by Quinn, 1980, and Mintzberg, 1985 (these are by no means a complete reference to their work), argues that the process of strategic decision making should be incremental, and that strategy emerges instead of being found from a deliberate planning initiative. There are some truths in all these approaches, and it is not hard to see how choosing an inappropriate process for the organisation could damage the organisation. The appropriate process is related both to the degree of environmental turbulence, and to the culture of the organisation.

Implementation

In many organisations implementation is the Cinderella of strategic management. There may be a carefully thought-out strategy, but if it is not implemented properly, management is left not knowing whether the strategy has succeeded or failed. Inadequate attention is given to implementation in most organisations, the assumption often being that once the strategy has been decided it will happen as a matter of course. In reality there may be numerous tasks, large and small, on the path to implementation, and in some situations changes are needed to the organisation and its processes before implementation is possible. Examples are a culture that is opposed to the strategy, or a reward system which encourages behaviour which is different from what is needed in the new circumstances.

The strategic management literature on implementation is sparse, most books giving it scant attention. Although the literature on transformational leadership and change management is relevant, it does not cover everything. For a more extensive treatment of implementation see Hussey, 1996.

Implementation implies an appropriate monitoring and control approach, so that it is possible to know whether the right actions have been taken.

Capabilities of decision leaders

This is really no more than another way of saying that if management is poor or inadequate, the strategic management is likely to disappoint, even if attention appears to be given to each of the other four elements in Figure 1.1. This point does not need labouring, as it is self evident.

PLANNING STRATEGY

Most of this book will be about planning business strategy, although there are chapters on implementation and the strategy process. The implications of Figure 1.1 should be kept in mind throughout, and it is particularly important not to lose sight of the need for analysis and creative thinking.

Figure 1.2 may be used in two ways. Firstly it is a route map of the broad tasks that are required to complete a formal written plan. Secondly, it can be used more informally as a check list to aid thinking about an unwritten strategy.

Many managers, at some time or other in their careers, have to complete a business plan. It may be as their contribution to the annual round of a complex corporate planning process, it may be because a bank or other lender requires it before a loan application can be considered, or it may be that the manager feels the need to think through a strategy as a one-off event and to get the results down on paper. A plan should firstly aid strategic thinking. However another purpose of a plan is to communicate, whether to key managers under you, to your superiors, or to outsiders such as a banker. The step-by-step approach suggested by the diagram can aid both of these purposes.

The middle vertical line of five boxes in Figure 1.2 can be correlated with some very simple questions: simple that is to ask, but rarely simple to answer.

- *Vision*: What are our overall hopes for the longer term position this company will achieve, and that this plan will take us towards?
- *Objectives*: What financial targets are we intending to achieve over the period of this plan?
- *Gap analysis*: What is the gap between where our current strategies are taking us, and where we want to go to?

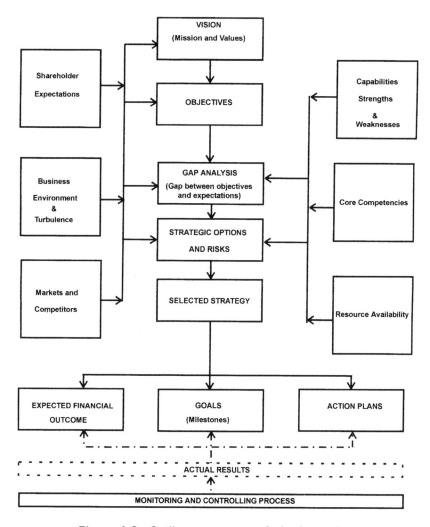

Figure 1.2 Outline components of a business plan.

- *Strategic options and risks*: What are the strategic choices that we face, their likely outcomes, and the risks associated with each?
- *Selected strategy*: What is our chosen strategy?

This then moves into three things developed from the strategy: what we expect the financial results to be, goals which help us measure our progress on the way, and the action plans we need to put in place if we are to implement the strategy. Expectations and actual results are not always identical, so the bottom boxes on the diagram show the need to monitor and control progress against the plan.

The three vertical boxes on the left-hand side represent the external facts and trends which have an important bearing on or strategic decisions, while the three on the right represent the internal facts about our organisation which will either inhibit our choice, or on which we can build our future success.

Of course there is much more to each element of the figure than this brief description can even begin to indicate, and the various chapters that follow will put some flesh on the bones. At the very least more meaning will be given to each element of Figure 1.2, so that you can check its relevance to your own situation. The chapters will also add information on various techniques and methods which will aid progress through the model to the formulation of a comprehensive and integrated plan. The intention is to present a menu of ideas which will help managers to think strategically and to prepare a business plan. But it is a menu. Not everything is right for every situation, and there is no question of trying to force feed the reader with a single dogmatic approach.

You will have to make the choices of what is important for your own situation.

REFERENCES

Ansoff, H. I., 1965, *Corporate Strategy: an analytical approach to business policy for growth and expansion,* McGraw Hill, New York.

Buzzell, R. D. and Gale, B. T., 1987, *The PIMS Principles: linking strategy to performance*, Free Press, New York.

De Meuse, K., Vanderheiden, P. and Bergmann, T., 1994, 'Announced layoffs: their effects on corporate financial performance', *Human Resource Management*, vol 33, no 4, winter, 509–530.

Drucker, P. F., 1964, *Managing for Results*, Heinemann, London.

Farrell, L, 1993, *Searching for the Spirit of Enterprise*, Dutton, New York.

Hamel, G. and Prahalad, P. K., 1994, *Competing for the Future*, Harvard Business School Press, Boston, MA.

Hammer, M. and Champney, J., 1993, *Re-engineering the Corporation: a manifesto for business revolution*, Nicholas Brealey, London.

Hillmer, F. G. and Donaldson, L., 1996, "The trivialisation of management", *McKinsey Quarterly*, no 4. An excerpt from the authors' book *Management Redeemed: Debunking the fads that undermine our corporations,* The Free Press, New York, 1996.

Hussey, D. E., 1996, *The Implementation Challenge,* Wiley, Chichester.

Mintzberg 1985, H., 1985, "Of strategies deliberate and emergent", *Strategic Management Journal,* July/September.

Ohmae, K., 1982, *The Mind of the Strategist,* McGraw Hill, New York.

Peters, T. J. and Waterman, R. H., 1982, *In Search of Excellence,* Harper & Row, New York.

Quinn, J. B., 1980, *Strategies for Change: Logical Incrementalism,* Dow Jones Irwin, Homewood, IL.

Steiner, G., 1969, *Top Management Planning,* Macmillan, New York.

Stern, C. W. and Stalk, G. S., 1998, *Perspectives on Strategy,* Wiley, New York.

Wyatt Company, 1994, *Best Practice in Corporate Re-structuring,* Toronto.

FURTHER READING

Hussey, D. E., 1998, *Strategic Management: From Theory to Implementation,* 4th edition, Butterworth-Heinemann, Oxford.

Joyce, P. and Woods, A., 1996, *Essential Strategic Management,* Butterworth-Heinemann, Oxford.

2
Vision and Purpose

This chapter covers three of the boxes in Figure 1.2, vision, objectives and goals. Although these are derived in different ways, as we have seen, the first two are at the start of the planning process, while goals follow the formulation of strategy: there is a relationship between the three. All have a role in the implementation of strategic plans. Vision drives the objectives, and together they provide a framework for the strategy. In turn goals are derived from the strategy to show where the organisation plans to be at various points in the future, and related to this are individual performance standards, which are not shown in Figure 1.2, but which have a logical fit with the overall concept. Figure 2.1 relates these four topics to each other.

Initially I should like to bundle vision and objectives under the term "strategic purpose", although they will be separated later. Strategic purpose gives something for the strategy to aim at, although it should be regarded as a map grid reference rather than as a target at the rifle range. The organisation will not always find that the shortest distance is a straight line, and may have to make detours to avoid obstacles. But having made the detour it is possible to come back to the grid reference from another direction. Without a defined strategic purpose, it becomes very difficult to measure progress: having detoured, the organisation is likely to remain pointed in the wrong direction.

Strategic purpose may be regarded, when used in the appropriate manner, as the beacon which on a dark night welcomes the fishing fleet into the safety of the harbour: used badly it can become the sweet singing sirens which lure the unsuspecting vessel to flounder on the rocks of disaster.

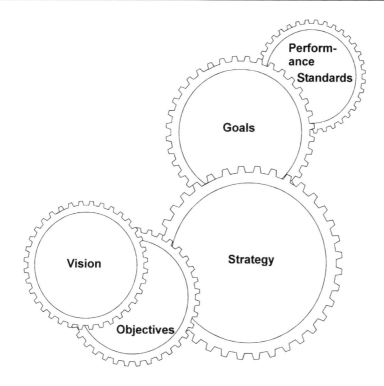

Figure 2.1   The vision driven organisation.

I think it is fair comment to say that some organisations do not have a clearly established and shared strategic purpose. Of course, they must have some purpose, even if it is undefined. A problem comes through the variations of what is perceived by the different managers in the organisation. Often questioning will reveal that this difference may be more than a problem of emphasis: sometimes it means that different managers are pulling in completely opposite directions.

There are advantages if all members of the company at least know what the strategic purpose is. This is more than a problem of communications, because interpretation of the words is based as much on the observed behaviour of top management as it is on a knowledge of the language. From a common ground of under-standing, it is desirable to lead the employees into a shared belief in the significance of the strategic purpose. Apart from the feeling of pulling together and playing a key part which this can generate in a manager or other employee, the shared purpose provides a yardstick against which actions and corporate performance may be measured.

Of course there can be a danger. This occurs when the wrong strategic purpose is set, and the organisation is taken away from the course which would yield the best results. In other words, the company works to the wrong map grid reference, and ends up not in a land flowing with milk and honey, but in a barren plain. So getting the strategic purpose right is a very important part of the chief executive's task.

One of the dangers to avoid is dealing in delusions. It is very comforting, and usually quite meaningless, to define strategic purpose in noble sounding but empty phrases; to deal in platitudes, rather than fact; to use words which leave a pleasant, warm feeling, but which are in fact a lie. Vision statements and objectives, unfortunately, when they are stated are often written in these terms. It may sound very public spirited to claim that the company exists for the benefit of its employees or its customers, but unless the company means to live up to these ideals it can only do harm by so stating them. Self-delusion is no help in strategic management.

VISION

The word vision has come into prominence, although the concept of what it expresses is very old. It is the emotive aspects of the word, as well as its meaning, that have made it so popular. In this context it applies to the totality of the business which is the subject of the strategic plan. When we use the term in a later chapter on change management, the meaning may be more restricted in scope.

Vision is top management's expression of what the organisation is striving to become, and incorporates both the critical values of the firm, and what in earlier literature used to be called mission statements. A vision is semi-permanent. It is likely to outlast any strategic plan that may be prepared, but will not last forever.

It includes a description of the nature of the organisation's business as it is intended to be at some time in the future (the term "mission" is used in some books). First the question "What is my business?" should be asked. A second question is even more important "What should my business be?" Typically the vision embraces a view not only of the evolution of the organisation, but also of the industry, and the unique position the organisation is intending to fill. The values of the organisation are an important component of vision, and the typical vision statement will have some mention of how the organisation will conduct itself in relations to customers, employees, suppliers and the community.

The result is the definition in as concise a way as possible of the type of organisation the chief executive intends to have at some future date.

Unfortunately one person's vision is another's collection of platitudes. As mentioned earlier, it is not what the organisation says about its vision as much as how it behaves that will distinguish the genuine thing from the rhetoric. This is particularly true of values defined in the vision.

The argument for beginning the plan with a definition of the vision, is that the vision probably exists even if it is not defined. There is a concept of what an organisation should be in the minds of every chief executive. For example, there is a very real difference in vision between a conglomerate company which is willing to make an investment in any field, provided it is profitable, and a company operating in one or two industries which would never consider moving into a new area. It may be that the day will come when either company will have to change its objectives, but this in itself is not wrong. There is a similarity with the objectives of a person as he or she matures. As experience and education is gained, and as family and other responsibilities change, a person's concept of his or her ultimate aims changes. So it is with an organisation. There is no reason to expect any vision set today to be the right one for the next hundred years. What is going on inside and outside the organisation may make a new vision desirable.

Of course it is important for vision to be stated in terms that lead the company in the right direction. Too narrow a definition of the scope of the organisation can be stultifying: the wrong map grid reference mentioned earlier. An insurance company might put itself in a strait-jacket if it saw its business as simply the "supply of car insurance". A broader definition "Meeting the protection and savings needs of consumers and businesses" might help the chief executive to see opportunities in different products to those currently in the portfolio. But it is still a bit bland, and would fit most other insurance companies. Now let's imagine that it was us that had the idea of setting up Direct Line, initially offering car insurance to individuals through telephone contact. Our vision would include something broader than our initial product, so we might want to define a broader range of activities than this. But what is special about our vision is that we intend to create a major player in various categories of insurance by changing the traditional way in which the insurance industry has operated. Instead of regional offices, we have a telephone call centre: instead of brokers we sell only in one way direct to the customer. A key part of our vision is that by changing the economics of the industry, we can offer a faster more helpful service to customers at a lower price. Our advertising will be more effective since we can offer these twin benefits, while giving the customer an immediate action that can be taken: phone us. The chief executive's vision would embrace all of this, and possibly more besides, moving a long way from something that could be attached to all other companies. What Direct Line did was, at the outset, unique.

The vision can be used as a motivating agent, to help managers and other employees to see the opportunities, and to stretch beyond the short term. Once people are thinking on the right lines it becomes less easy to overlook the obvious.

The idea of vision is not limited to the centre of a corporate empire. Within the constraints of this vision, it is possible and desirable for a vision to be developed by every subsidiary managing director, and by the heads of the major functions, of the future shape of their activities.

The term strategic intent is sometimes used in the literature. I have been unable to distinguish any difference between vision and this term, so see it as just another way of saying the same thing.

OBJECTIVES

Although the vision is a semi-permanent state, the objectives relate specifically to the life of the plan. So if the plan is intended to cover five years, this is the period for which objectives should be defined. The objectives are expressions of profit targets, although there are various ways in which these can be defined. I have used the plural because there may be different objectives for each year, and for each business unit within the organisation. Profit must be a prime motivation for all companies, except those who are formed as a charity or similar purpose. I have heard managers argue that their objective is to maximise profits. The only problems with this definition are that nobody knows what it really means, and there is no method of telling when it has been achieved. In most cases it also happens to be untrue: no company is prepared to do absolutely *anything* for profit. For example, a company may hold the view that profits connected with the betting industry are immoral, and so would not move into this area whatever the profit potential. Few would now insist on working their employees into a state of complete physical and mental exhaustion, although there are exceptions! In dealings with their customers, most companies are likely to argue that they must act in such a way that the customer is likely to repeat purchases in the future, as they are not looking for high profits that end with the first order, but a source of profits stretching out to some future time horizon. So the definition that "our objective is to maximise profits over the long term" is coined.

Unfortunately, this too is meaningless.

Some organisations express their target in terms of a return on investment ratio. Unless this is linked to a specific figure of required profits this is a poor objective. Return on investment can be maintained while profits shrink, if capital is reduced by the reduction of debtors or inventories, or by the normal process of depreciation. A shrinking target is hardly likely to appeal to the owners of the business, nor does it attempt to provide the organisation with the cash needed for further development.

Return on investment itself can be a mixture of numerous items. Assets may be in the books at various values: at original purchase price, at a revaluation, or depreciated. What the accountants call goodwill—when the acquisition of a business costs more than the value of its assets—may or may not have been written off. None of this renders the concept of return on investment meaningless, provided the company sets itself a series of house rules to work to. This means that the capital employed figures may differ from those in the books: for instance, I think there is a good economic argument for not writing off goodwill in the management control figures. Having set its rules, the company has one of the parameters of its profit target.

In fact this parameter should be defined and expressed in two ways. From the management viewpoint, return on capital employed provides a criterion of effectiveness. The shareholder is more interested in a return on equity capital, and this must also be taken into account. Return on shareholders' capital could drop because of a change in gearing, even though profits were rising: this would affect the dividend earnings per share, which in turn could cause changes in stock market prices.

The second element of a valid ROI objective is a rate of profit growth, on a defined base. So the target might be expressed in terms like these:

> The target for the next 5 years is an annual growth of after tax profits of 5%, provided that a minimum after tax return on capital employed of 10% is maintained. (Note ROI can be calculated before or after tax: for the total organisation the second option is preferable. For internal units of the organisation, a pre tax figure avoids the problem of trying to allocate tax between the various business.)

This example shows the sort of target that can be established, but we still have to think about the things an organisation might consider to arrive at these figures. Whatever target is set, it has to satisfy the people who own the business. So one guideline that should be taken is the return and growth rate which the organisation has achieved in previous years. This provides a baseline. Now if this is below the performance of other similar organisations, and we must accept that it is sometimes difficult to find exactly comparable data, so figures may be approximate, the chief executive may feel that the sights are set too low, and may upgrade the target. Even this improved target may not be thought good enough, and the chief executive may further increase it. Whatever target is set, he or she will want to review it in the light of the corporate appraisal (see the next chapter), to make sure that it is neither below nor above the capacity of the organisation.

In theory objectives can be set which recognise a worsening of performance. This is an action that should be used with caution, as shareholders may not respond well to the implications of this.

Another way of thinking about the profit objectives, which has found favour with many, and is one of the figures now reported in the annual reports of most public companies is based on earnings per share. Earnings per share are the profits attributable to shareholders divided by the number of ordinary shares. This measure has the advantage of relating profits to the shareholders' stake in the company. It could lead to financial policies based on loan finance rather than risking reducing the earnings per share by increasing the number of shares. Overall it is a useful measure, since it is easy to understand, and reflects at least one of the expectations of shareholders.

We have not yet exhausted all the ways in which the objective can be expressed. One criticism of all the measures suggested above is that they relate to accounting profit, whereas a main component of an organisation's ability to prosper is cash. The true value to shareholders of an organisation is not its past profit record but its future ability to generate cash. There are a number of measures that are used to measure economic value, as an alternative to accounting profits, and all relate to measuring future cash flows on a discounted cash-flow basis. Hussey, 1998 gives some brief examples of shareholder value approaches, and there are many books which deal with this complex subject in great detail, such as Stewart, 1991. There is little point in setting objectives in this way until the whole organisation uses a value-based approach.

The company profit target must eventually be broken down into targets for each division (or subsidiary) of the company, and for each profit centre. The chief executive should not make the mistake of setting the same growth and return on capital employed targets for each division. One area of the organisation may yield a 30% ROI, another may struggle to make 10%. One may have fast growth, another may be in a mature market. These varying returns may reflect the differing degrees of risk attached to each business area. It may be very wise to have a low yielding sector of the company, which can be expected to turn in a constant level of profits, and seeking to achieve the total company target through a balance with high yield, but higher risk, projects. But this is moving into the realms of strategy.

Profit centre targets are probably best set by the division controlling them. It may be that only yearly targets are required at this level. It is also possible that a further modification of the ROI concept is desirable. For example, a retailer might operate three shops of identical size, yielding about the same profit. If one was purchased in 1970, another in 1988, and the third is rented, there will be a completely different capital employed structure. It would be necessary for the manager of the 1988 shop to be four or five times as efficient as the other managers, in order to obtain the same ROI. What may be a better motivating target is one which is adjusted for these differences—perhaps all buildings valued on a current basis (including the rented one), and earnings adjusted by a rent/depreciation factor. The reasoning is not, of course, to make the task of the manager of the 1988 shop easier—it must still yield an ROI acceptable to the company! It is to upgrade the targets of the other managers in a fair way.

These specified profit targets at corporate and business unit levels are an essential part of any system of objectives. They are not in the least vague, and are measurable.

GOALS

The next concept, goals, stretches over the whole time span of the planning period and marks the intended achievements along the time lines.

Goals are quantified objectives that provide a unit of measurement, from which the chief executive can confirm that the strategies have been carried out. This means that they can only be set *after* strategy has been decided. They are, therefore, a very different type of objective from the vision and the profit objective which are determined *before* strategy is formulated. It is important to understand this difference. The primary objective, and certain of the secondary ones, are the map grid references that show the corporate target: the goals are the landmarks and milestones which mark the selected path the organisation is to take to reach the reference point. There is a simile with an explorer who knows where he wants to get to, and has the choice of several alternative routes that will take him there (just as the organisation has the choice of various strategies), one of which is better than the others. He will want to make sure that he is on the right track and will identify landmarks that he has to pass by a certain time: on day two he should have reached a range of mountains, by day three he must cross a wide river, day eight will see him on the edge of a desert which will take him two days to cross. In a similar way the organisation will have to predetermine the points it should pass by various key dates.

What form should these corporate landmarks take? The principle is that there should be quantitative targets for every important part of the organisation's operations. There should be as many goals as it is practical to develop. The only constraint is that it must be possible to measure results so that progress can be judged. There is little point in putting a number to something that the organisation either has no intention of measuring (or finds impossible to measure). The preferred targets are those against which results can be measured as a matter of routine from the organisation's information sources, whether these be accounting, marketing research, or personnel records: goals which require a special exercise in order that results can be compared can be worthwhile, if the costs of the exercise are not too high relative to the benefits.

So a goal might be (for a defined date):

- A percentage share of a defined market (or segment of market).
- A ratio such as return on sales.
- An absolute figure for sales.
- A minimum figure for customer complaints.
- A maximum figure for hours lost in industrial disputes.
- An accounting figure such as a liquidity ratio.
- Employment figures.
- A labour turnover rate.
- A value for operational profit improvement.

Another type of goal is a time-table. What so often happens when a plan is written is that there are missing pieces of information: a marketing strategy may have to be evaluated in a test market; a special study may be needed of the benefits of relocating a plant: the list is endless, because strategic thinking forces managers to find these gaps in their knowledge. In this type of problem, the goal would be the date by which the missing data are to be obtained, and the name of the person charged with carrying out the task. It goes without saying that results can be easily measured.

All of these goals can be expressed for different time periods. The time-tables are self-extinguishing: a market share goal might be expressed as a permanent target, or there could be a different target for every year of the plan. And goals can be established at both the total company level and for subsidiaries, departments and divisions.

What emerges is a network of targets of varying degrees of importance which with the profit targets form a model of the company over the time span of the plan.

STANDARDS OF PERFORMANCE

Over a shorter period, say for the first year of the plan and related to the more detailed annual plan and budgetary control system, it is possible to develop a concept of personal standards to measure the performance of the lower management levels, and certain other employees such as sales persons. These will normally form part of a performance management system.

Standards of performance are really a logical development from the concept of goals. They can be used as a method of motivating a wide range of employees who are not directly responsible for the achievement of the goals, but whose personal performance will influence the organisation's success or failure. Not only do they motivate, but they provide a management tool which can be used to judge the success or failure of a person in his or her job. They provide an early warning system for when things are going wrong, and they can spotlight the area in which the failure is occurring. Standards can be set for much shorter intervals of time than goals: there may, for example, be a monthly standard.

They make most sense when they are directly related to the annual plan of a cost centre or profit centre. At this level it is possible to calculate the standards so that the contribution of each to the budget of the centre is taken into account. For example, for a salesperson the following types of standards might be set which, in the judgement of the manager of the profit centre, must be fulfilled if the centre is to achieve its planned results:

- Total sales required.
- Sales standard for particular products.
- Number of new customers to be obtained.
- Customer call frequency.
- Minimum sales level to which small customers are to be upgraded.
- Maximum number of customer complaints.
- An average cost per customer call.

For a warehouse manager it might be possible to set for the operations controlled:

- Maximum number of hours overtime to be worked.
- Man-hour standards for various tasks.
- Standards for maximum amount of wastage or breakage.
- A standard for stock loss.
- Cost standards for various sections of the operation.
- Maximum number of employees on strength at any one time.
- Weight tolerance for re-packing and packing operations.
- Frequency scales are to be checked.

It is important to make standards realistic. If the business has a seasonal pattern, the standards set must follow that pattern. For example, retail jewellers make the bulk of their sales in the run up to Christmas. It would be sensible for sales performance standards to be constructed to this pattern (as indeed the monthly budget should): simple division of annual sales by twelve would produce no worthwhile standards.

TOTAL CONCEPT OF OBJECTIVES

This total concept of vision and objectives is comprehensive and meaningful. It is a little untidy in that some types of objectives are decided very early in the planning process, while others only fall into place as plans are completed. The merit of it is that all the parts do fall into place, and that there is a relationship between the standard of performance established for individuals, and what the organisation is trying to achieve. It is right that this connection should be emphasised, because if the individual does not do his or her job properly then the chances of achieving the vision and objectives may be impaired.

The total concept also has the merit of answering the criticisms of other types of objective which have been raised at various points in this chapter. It is a flexible system. Above all, it gives all levels of management a means of control, which is so important in making sure that all planning does lead to meaningful action.

THE STAKEHOLDER CONCEPT

I should declare my belief that a business should be run for the benefit of its shareholders. This does not mean that other stakeholders (employees, the community, customers and suppliers), all of whom have expectations from the company, should be ignored or treated badly. Part of the success of a modern company is dependent on the way in which the organisation relates to and deals with these groups. The way in which the organisation behaves to these groups is a part of its strategy, and it ignores them at its peril.

There is one school of thought which argues for equal importance of all the stakeholders, so that the shareholder is treated as one among many, and not given a status of pre-eminence. This way of thinking is not new, and was certainly around in the 1960s, although it was not popular, in that most organisations recognised that in situations of adversity it was always the shareholder interests which took first place.

Recently there has been a renewed interest in the stakeholder concept, led by the Royal Society of Arts Inquiry, 1996, and the setting up of the Centre for Tomorrow's Company by the RSA. For those who wish to follow the argument for and against the stakeholder concept I recommend Argenti, 1997 (against), and Wheeler and Sillanpää, 1997 (for).

The effect for those that believe in the concept is a need for the vision, objectives and goals to encompass the plurality of objectives that exist under such a concept. Often the objectives of the different groups are in conflict, and this, and the greater number of equal partners for whom the organisations is believed to exist, will make the methods described in this chapter more complex, although the outline framework can easily be adapted.

REFERENCES

Argenti, J., 1997, "Stakeholders: the case against", *Long Range Planning*, **30**.3, June.

Hussey, D. E., 1998, *Strategic Management: From Theory to Implementation*, 4th edition, Butterworth-Heinemann, Oxford.

RSA Inquiry, 1996, *Tomorrow's Company*, Gower, Aldershot.

Stewart, G. B., 1991, *The Quest for Value*, Harper, New York.

Wheeler, D. and Sillanpää, M., 1997, *The Stakeholder Corporation*, Pitman, London.

3
The Corporate Appraisal

There are at least four parts to the corporate appraisal, three of which will be discussed in this chapter. The internal appraisal is mainly represented by the top arm of the cross in Figure 3.1. However, we cannot separate this entirely from the market, represented by the left arm of the cross, so of necessity this chapter will also discuss some things that are related to market performance. The external appraisal deals mainly with the organisation's position against the background of changing events in the outside world, and some aspects of this will overflow into Chapter 4.

Industry analysis, which deals with the organisation's position within the structure of its industry, also draws on the market situation, and is the subject of the next chapter, *assessing the corporate arena*. It is a critical aspect of the appraisal, but its complexity means that it would be confusing to try to cover it in this chapter. However, the outcome of the industry analysis should flow back to be combined with the outcome of the rest of the appraisal.

Figure 3.1 shows how all four of the elements of the appraisal combine to enable the organisation to determine its strengths and weaknesses, and the opportunities and threats it faces, which in turn allows it to define its distinctive competence.

The main intention of this chapter is to examine how an organisation might assess its capabilities (used in a normal sense: there is also a particular meaning to the word in the strategy literature which we will touch on later), its area of risk and vulnerability, its effectiveness, the degree of flexibility it possesses, and the resources it can command. All this needs to be thought

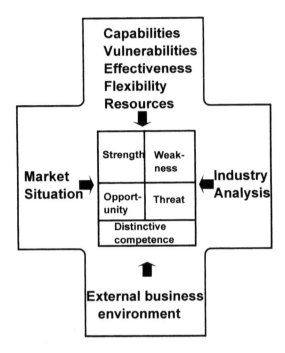

Figure 3.1   The internal and external appraisal.

through in a strategic context, and considered in relation to the trends and events in the broader environment.

Although strategic management is no longer a new subject, there has been a tendency for much of the published material to concentrate on the most exciting aspects of strategic activity. The assessment of company strengths and weaknesses is rarely given any treatment in depth, and this has led to the neglect of this vital step in the planning process by many companies installing their first planning system. In fact many books only suggest the SWOT approach, which is carried out by asking managers, individually or in groups, to list what they see are the strengths and weaknesses of the organisation. There is some value in the approach, but not much if this is all that is done.

Many managers tend to equate strategic planning with the rather more romantic elements of strategy: acquisitions, mergers, and major capital expenditure projects. But before strategy reaches this stage there is a good deal of hard work to be undertaken, at the end of which it may be decided that the company's path to greater profits may lie in improving present operations, rather than embarking on something new. This chapter is about some of that hard work.

Good strategic planning begins with the present, with an objective analysis of an organisation's strengths and weaknesses, and with decisions on the action that should be taken to correct those factors which inhibit the organisation's long-term profit-ability. This stage might well be called establishing the corporate identity, for only by fully defining the factors that make up the company can the planner assist in setting it on the best path.

Perhaps this can be compared with the task of a career counsellor. It is relatively easy to make a list of jobs available to a young man or woman, just as it is simple to produce a superficial list of investment opportunities open to a company. With the career counsellor the real skill comes in taking stock of each applicant, examining qualifications, personality and temperament, defining the areas in which some sort of further development may be required (for example, training), and matching these character-istics and the applicant's aspirations against the various available options. There are well-established techniques that can be used to find out most of what needs to be known about a person. Digging deep into the psyche of an organisation is a more complex opera-tion, but no less important. Failure by the organisation in this area can be as stunting to future development in the corporate sense as can the misplacement of a school-leaver in the personal sense.

But how can an organisation set about establishing its corporate identity? What should it seek to find out about itself?

All senior managers have some idea of what their organisations are best at, and what they are worst at. Unless they have devoted special efforts to this problem, it is likely that they will not know as much as they think they do. The larger the organisation, the harder it becomes to know everything, and even in the smallest, unless a formal analysis has been made of each area, the chances are that some things the organisation does will be the result of history rather than a decision that these things are right. The basic questions that should be asked at various areas and levels of activity are:

1. What are we doing now?
2. What are we achieving by doing this?

3. Why are we doing this?
4. Does what we do fit the customers' requirements?
5. How do we know this?
6. How does what we do compare with competitors, insofar as we are able to deduce this?
7. Are there other ways we could achieve the same benefit?
8. Should we be using these?
9. How does this contribute to our corporate success?
10. How does it help the corporate vision?

The study should lead to action. Immediate benefits can come from profit improvement schemes that may be suggested by the study (improvements frequently yield a higher return on investment than the best of other capital projects), although this is a by-product because our aim is strategic. Identification of weaknesses, which may be serious limiting factors to the organisation's long-range plans, is the first step towards their removal. Obviously not all weaknesses are correctable, and there are some that every organisation has to live with, but knowledge of these means that the organisation can avoid decisions which put strain on areas that cannot withstand it. Some weaknesses can only be removed over a period of time: ways of doing this should be built into the plan.

A corollary is that the company will also identify its strong areas. The object of this is not to flatter management ego, but to show some of the areas on which the company should concentrate its future efforts. Building on corporate strengths may be something of a hackneyed phrase, but it is one which has a lot of truth in it.

As a by-product of the study, opportunities may be identified for future expansion and development that would otherwise not have become apparent.

All this is worthy, but we are also seeking something else. This is an insight into our capabilities and competencies, which will enable us to develop strategies that give us a sustainable competitive position. If we can, we want to re-engineer the industry in which we operate, pushing ourselves so far ahead of competitors that they will be hard pressed to catch up. We cannot all be the architects of change, but we can all use the appraisal to find some means of doing better against competitors.

WAY OF THINKING ABOUT ORGANISATIONS

How should such an evaluation be carried out? Firstly, as far as possible it should be an objective and analytical process. This is why I believe there are severe limitations to the popular SWOT approach, since it can only extract from managers what they already know, and often this is a biased perception. So things that are extremely important may be ignored, and others given an optimistic or pessimistic slant, depending on news that has just come through the door. So the appraisal should be undertaken in a way that its conclusions are drawn from an objective analysis of the organisation. At this point the opinions and insight of managers may be make a valuable contribution to understanding, provided they are not allowed to ignore critical facts that come out of the appraisal.

Secondly it is necessary to think through the purpose of the appraisal:

- The most common purpose is as one of the steps towards developing strategies.
- In an ailing company, the main purpose might be the development of a survival strategy.
- In an organisation which has developed an appropriate strategy, the main need might be to ensure that everything the organisation does is helping it to achieve this strategy.
- In an acquisition situation the appraisal might be what is known as due diligence, where the aims are to ensure that you understand what you are buying, and know how it will fit with your own organisation's strategy.

Figure 3.2 is a reminder that there are different ways of looking at an organisation, and we may need to take more than one viewpoint. Each reveals a little more of the truth that we are struggling to uncover. The top triangle is an essential step, and as it suggests is an objective analysis of the organisation's performance. It rests on a rectangle which represents a functional view of the organisation, for example manufacturing, logistics, information systems, and HRM.

The bars across this box show various cross-organisational ways of thinking. We may want to think about technologies, and where and how they are used across various units of the organisation. We

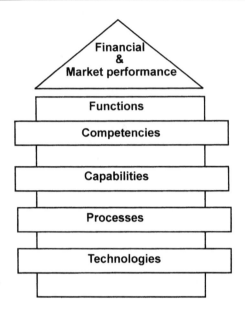

Figure 3.2   Ways of looking at an organisation.

may wish to take a view of the processes, the line of thinking used in Total Quality Management, or business process re-engineering. It may be that capabilities (in this context groupings of processes which give us a clear advantage) may be appropriate. Or we may want to look at competencies, which are groupings of skills and technologies. Although distinguished in the literature, competencies and capabilities are two sides of the same coin, and will be treated together.

It is worth remembering that some of the things uncovered in an appraisal are a form of hygiene factor: failure to do them well may cause the organisation to fail, but doing them right will not make the organisation successful. Others are definitely success factors: without them the organisation may be average or a failure, but with them it has a chance of gaining competitive advantage.

What is relevant to consider in the appraisal will vary with the purpose. For example in an appraisal of your own organisation, existing contracts with suppliers and the service contracts of directors will not normally be of great relevance. In a due diligence situation they may be vital pieces of information, as they may prevent your organisation from implementing the strategy that lay behind the acquisition, may delay implementation, or may increase the costs. Common sense and good business judgement are important in determining relevance, but remember that all humans are affected by the boundaries of their perception, and a real danger is to ignore an area "because it is not important in this business". It is better to err on the side of doing analysis which you later do not use, than to ignore something which is critical.

Relativity is a different but important concept. Obviously you need the basic facts, but even a study of trends may not tell you whether what you have observed is a strength or a weakness. The analysis may be more meaningful if it is looked at relative to something else:

- *Competitors*: you may think, for example, that your costs are low or your manufacturing methods are up to date, but without thinking about your position relative to competitors it may be difficult to evaluate whether you are ahead or behind.
- *Customers*: you may be very pleased with the level of customer service you provide, or the quality of your products, but if you cannot relate this to what the customer expects and requires, you may be in a much weaker position than you believe.
- *External trends*: your competitive position in the home market may appear to be healthy, but your industry is steadily becoming global. Judging a global market by purely domestic criteria may mean that you are missing one of the most vital concerns for your organisation.
- *Vision*: if your organisation has a clear vision and strategy, your findings on support activities such as HR policies should be relative to this. Similarly, if the results of the appraisal and industry analysis lead to the creation of a new vision and strategies, it may be desirable to return to your findings to check that they support the new direction of the organisation.

These questions will not fit every fact that we need to uncover, but they are a good mindset to have, and will help identify other areas in which we should be looking.

Modern organisations are often very large and complex, so the task of appraisal has to match this complexity. Although in a single industry company it might be possible to work through and apply almost every page of the detail in these notes in one single report, a large organisation such as a General Electric or Unilever needs to attune the appraisal to what is relevant at each level. The top management of a company like United Technologies would have a very great interest in the overall financial aspects of the group, where the profits, cash generation and growth are coming from in terms of SBUs and geographical areas, would need a way, such as portfolio analysis, of relating all the SBUs to each other, and might well find it essential to have an overall appraisal of the technological capabilities it possesses. It may well find an analysis by SBU of the extent to which products are national or global very helpful, but there is not much at this level that it could do with a detailed product analysis of every SBU and every country.

At the next level down (the major operating SBU companies like Sikorsky Helicopters and Otis Elevators) more depth and breadth of detail is needed, with a greater detail at its regional headquarters, and the greatest of all at each national company.

In this example there is an interdependency between each of the levels of resolution, which supports the strategic decisions which are taken higher in the organisation, and provides the information that is needed for all levels of strategic decision making.

In practice it is not difficult to plan what should be done at each level of a particular organisation, but it is an essential task if a useful appraisal is to be developed. So one of the first tasks is to think about your organisation, and to approach the task in the way that is most appropriate to its size and complexity.

INTERNAL ELEMENTS

Financial performance and resources

The starting point should be an analysis of the financial per-formance and position of the organisation. There is nothing special about the first part of this, which is to study trends over a reasonable period of time using standard financial ratios, the growth rates, and of course identifying the key figures. This is fairly standard stuff, and is no more than external investment analysts, and the internal accountants do as a matter of course.

We need to dig a little deeper, and look at our financial flexibility and the financial resources which we could muster. The former relates to how the organisation is financed, and how robust this might be to adverse circumstances. It goes deeper than gearing, although this is a part of it. For example when the Ratner retail jewellery group moved into loss in the early 1990s, one of the factors which made life more difficult during the recovery period was that much of the equity was in the form of cumulative preference shares. There was an advantage over loan finance, in that the dividend could be suspended as indeed it was for several years. However the accumulated sum would take preference over ordinary shareholders, and a position was soon reached where the size of this meant that ordinary shareholders had no hope of a dividend in the foreseeable future. Losses and high debt depressed share prices anyway, but the burden of the accumulated preference dividend meant that there was no possibility of raising more share capital. Ultimately there was a financial restructuring, with preference share converted to ordinary shares, reducing the percentage of the company now owned by these ordinary shareholders. The management time that had to be spent dealing with preference share pressure groups, who were demanding the break up of the company, was a diversion from the major task of recovery.

There are many ways of financing an organisation, and it is not possible to consider all of these in the absence of a strategy. It is possible to estimate whether the organisation is at the limit of its financial resources, or whether there is scope to raise more if the strategy demands it.

Sources of profit

A next stage is the identification of the profit contribution of each area. What percentage of profits comes from where? The study should be made first by profit centres and then broken down by product. Of course, many companies will have these data as part of the normal management information system—although the remarks later in this chapter about the basis of cost allocation may be relevant. Having identified the profit strength of each product, it is wise to study past trends, external data, and internal opinions about the future prospects of each product. If, for example, the major contributors show signs of slipping, this should be known. By this stage the company should have an opinion of its present and future "bread-winners". It is worthwhile classifying products, both in relation to their current importance, but also to their position on the product life cycle to give some indication of their future importance to the company.

The next step is very important. This is to examine the allocation of resources between products: not only resources of money and plant, but also the perhaps scarcer resources of management talent and technical skills. What so often happens is that a declining product area is given to the best people to manage "to put it on its feet", when potentially more rewarding areas are not fully exploited because they are left to the second and third grades of management talent. This sort of analysis may show that R & D effort is misplaced. One sometimes sees in an organisation a prestige division which gets all the plums of personnel and finance because of its past glories, while other divisions with far greater potential have to take second place. The sort of decision that should come out of this analysis is where to change the emphasis. The wise investigator will also wish to examine the risks attached to each product.

For instance:

- How much dependence is there on one supplier for each type of raw material?
- How much dependence is there on a few customers for most of sales?
- Is there any vulnerability in any of the types of customers being served (e.g. those who might be moving to a preferred supplier basis)?
- Are the sales being made to the type of customers you thought you were serving?
- What happens to the product if one key person leaves (e.g. a designer in a fashion clothing business)?

Because no company can make profits without customers, the analysis should include the marketplace. Firstly, the company should find out what market position each of its major products holds in the market, or more important, in each segment of the market. With some products, or with smaller companies, the expression of this position as a percentage market share may be difficult, but great precision is rarely needed: what is essential is a fair idea of the standing of each product in the market, compared with the standing of competitive products, together with an appreciation of the potential for growth within the market. The organisation should define why its products hold the position they do: what is special about them that makes people give them preference?

A complete appreciation will require information from marketing research, and in this case should investigate the image of the organisation, as well as the market for its products. The channels of distribution should be included in the study, for it should be remembered that the channels used by the organisation will in all cases be the only ones possible.

Figure 3.3 shows one way in which information such as this might be summarised. Additional columns could be added to suit the needs of different organisations.

Another useful way of presenting information about the sources of profit, for an organisation that does not have too wide a spread of activities is shown in Figure 3.4, a form of expanded ROI chart. This is also useful at subsidiary level, even when a conglomerate is too complex for the approach to be used at corporate level. The main advantage of the ROI chart is that it enables the key issues to be seen immediately, and is a better communications tool than long schedules of figures.

Many companies take pride in their wide product range. The size of this is a fertile field for study since every additional product brings increases to inventories, clerical costs, and frequently to production costs. It is well worthwhile considering the savings that can take place from a reduction in the range. Expressing these potential savings in money terms gives an incentive to take action. In this analysis every pack should be considered as a product. The aim should be to identify all products with inadequate contribution (or potential) to profits, and other products which it might be possible to combine.

Costing conventions

In all the steps outlined so far, the cost added to the product by the business is of vital importance. In many cases the apportionment of costs between products is on some form of allocation basis. It is

Product			Sales		Profit Contribution			Market		
Name	Life cycle	Value	Growth	% Sales	Value	% Sales	% Total	Share	Rel sh	Growth
1										
2										
3										
4										
5										
6										
7										

Product		Financial Assets		Factory		Human resources		Management	
Name	Life cycle	Fixed	Current	Capacity	%	% R & D	% Sales	%	Quality
1									
2									
3									
4									
5									
6									
7									

Figure 3.3   Relating products to resource utilisation.

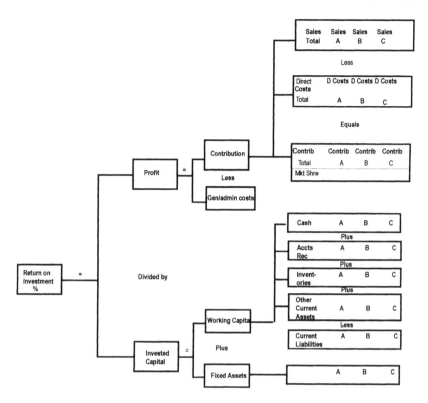

Figure 3.4   ROI chart to show economic structure of the business.

worthwhile studying the basis of apportionment and allocation since although suitable for many purposes it may be inadequate for this study. Many allocations assume that costs fall in a normal distribution; for example, that invoicing costs are a fixed percentage for all products. Inventories may be treated on the same basis. If costs are reallocated on the basis of actual transactions two things may become apparent:

- a skewed distribution between products;
- a skewed distribution between different customers.

An example may make this clearer. A firm offering a lorry sales service is likely to express its sales/delivery costs as a percentage of the sales value, say 5%. The assumption is made that every £1 of sales bears the same percentage of cost: in other words that a normal distribution applies. In fact, everybody really knows that it costs less per unit to sell one customer 100 units than to sell 100 customers one unit each. In addition everybody knows that it takes more time and effort to reach a customer 10 miles away than one who is only 1 mile away. In other words costs do not fall in a normal distribution. Yet not all organisations arrange their cost data so that they can make any decisions on this basis.

Figure 3.5 provides another example of how a cost system which may be good for some purposes can give the wrong signals in others. The example comes from a management consulting firm: the figures are made up for the example but the method of calculation is real, as are the two overhead burden rates. This firm used an absorption costing system, where all overheads are charged to "products", in this case consulting assignments. The example is of the choice facing a project director who has gained an assignment to start immediately, but has the choice of two ways of staffing it. One uses the project director and another employee: the other uses an equally competent external part-timer, who is only paid for work performed. The accountant's schedule shows that more profit is earned if the outsider is used. The main reason why it works out this way is that the 115% overhead is not added to the outsider. There is logic in this, as this burden is partly the cost of the

1. Staff wholly in House				2. Use in house and part time staffing			
Fees	17500			Fees	17500		
Expenses + 10%	1100			Expenses + 10%	1100		
Total Revenue		18600		Total Revenue		18600	
Labour:				Labour:			
10 days at £330	3330			10 days at £330	3330		
10 days at £250	2500						
sub total	5830			sub total	3330		
Overhead: 115%	6704			Overhead: 115%	3830		
Total labour	12534			Total labour	7160		
External consultant				External consultant	4000		£400 per day
Reimbursibles	1000			Reimbursibles	1000		
sub total costs	13534			sub total costs	12160		
Admin burden 10%	1353			Admin burden 10%	1216		
Total costs		14887		Total costs		13376	
Profit		3713		Profit		5224	
Profit %		19.96		Profit %		28.08	

Figure 3.5   Consultancy project costing sheet: two options.

consultant's downtime, and partly a share of space and secretarial costs: the outsider is only paid when employed by a client so no downtime is incurred, and works only on the assignment so uses (in theory) none of the space and support costs. So the accounting conventions tell you to use the staffing of case 2, to make more profit. But a moment's thought tells you that you earn less in this way than in option 1, because you have £4000 additional expense going out of the business. You still have to pay the in-house consultant who would not be used in example 2. So in the circumstances I have described it would be a silly choice.

This example shows the danger of using figures without thought. If the firm had conducted an analysis of its customers calculating the sales to and profit earned from each, and used these conventions, it might also mislead itself. For various reasons the client providing the highest profit, might not be the most valuable client to the firm. Clients giving a lower profit might provide a greater contribution. In fact, in this example, thinking of the project contribution in terms of income less reimbursable expenses is probably more useful for this analysis, although it would need to be supported by an examination of resource utilisation to ensure that the consultancy was not over-staffed, or out of balance in the seniority of its consultants.

Manufacturing

These comments obviously only apply to manufacturing organisations. The appraisal should examine the manufacturing performance as carefully as it studies financial and marketing performance. The facts sought include capacities, capacity utilisation, production costs, quality measures, on time performance measures, labour turnover, absenteeism, and the activities which are outsourced. In particular, it is important to determine whether any of the manufacturing activities which contribute to the core competencies are outsourced. The flexibility of the manufacturing operation should be examined.

People

Money, markets and machines are not the only ingredients of a successful business. Every company depends on people, and no organisation can afford to ignore this. We have already touched on management competence, and to this we should add management succession. This is only one aspect, and the whole question of recruitment and development of people should be studied. If the organisation has difficulty in attracting the right people there must be a reason, and there is little hope of improvement until this reason is identified. A careful stock should be taken of the ability of each key person. There is little point in launching new products if you know your marketing manager is not capable of making them profitable.

List of some of the internal statistics needed for the HR appraisal

1. Total number of employees by:
   —Grades
   —Business areas
   —Locations
   —Meaningful jobs/skills
   —Sex
   —Basis of employment (e.g. permanent, part time, etc.)
2. Age and length of service structure by grades, business areas, locations, meaningful jobs/skills and sex.
3. Labour turnover rates, by grades, etc: by age and by service length.
4. Productivity data by grades, business areas, location, meaningful jobs/skills and sex.
5. Potential of employees in critical jobs (see succession planning), and statistics on promotion.
6. Accidents and other occupational health data, by activity, location, age, etc.
7. Time lost through sickness, by grades, business areas, etc.
8. Industrial relations disputes, by grades, etc.
9. Trade union membership statistics, by union (not relevant for all countries).
10. Recruiting activity and success rates, by grade, etc.: number of unfilled vacancies by grade, etc.
11. Overtime statistics, by grade, etc.
12. Contract and agency employees who are substituting for full-time employees.
13. Number and type of transfers across business units and across functions: across countries.
14. Number of employees by grade, etc. who are on secondment or temporary transfer outside of the planning unit.

There is another valid way of appraising HRM activity. This is to determine whether the various policies and actions contribute to the achievement of the corporate vision and strategy. Hussey, 1996, deals with this in depth, and Hussey, 1998, chapter 21, provides a number of checklists for help in auditing HRM. A useful approach is indicated by Figure 3.6. This assesses which aspects of HRM are helping or hindering the organisation. The items in the left-hand column are examples and should be replaced by what is relevant to the organisation under study. For those who do not see the importance of linking HRM to strategy, let us go back to the consultancy costing system. We saw that the accounting calculation of profit was not the best basis on which to make decisions that were in the economic interests of the firm. But if I tell you that individual consultants were rewarded (salary increments, promotion, and bonuses) based on performance, one measure of which was the total percentage profit they had earned on the projects they managed, you can see that the performance management and reward systems were driving people to do things which were not in the best interests of the firm.

In chapter 12 another model, Figure 12.1, will be introduced which is also of value in the appraisal. Both this and Figure 3.6 are also of value in appraising other support areas.

EXTERNAL ELEMENTS

The consideration of internal evidence is only half of the picture, and will not yield the best results unless attention is given to the world outside the organisation.

Figure 3.7 shows one way of thinking about the environment. It provides a broad check list, although there are many subheadings under each label. In addition to being a reminder of the sort of things that should be considered, the diagram shows that external events are often connected. Economic recession, for example, may bring in its wake political, social and legal changes.

Every company is affected by the economies of the countries in which it operates, but not all companies mirror the ups and downs of the trade cycle. Inflation is a major change agent, because it consists of composite factors which affect social behaviour,

HR Activity	Rating					What could be improved?	What obstacles to be removed?
	Hinders		Neutral		Helps		
	1	2	3	4	5		
Reward system							
Managers							
Sales							
Shop floor							
Culture							
Internal							
Intercultural							
Internal communication							
Briefing groups							
Co. newspaper							
E-mail							
Recruitment							
Managers							
Clerical							
Technicians							
Industrial relations							
Co policy							
Works councils							
Performance Management							
Top management							
Managers							
Clerical							
Technicians							
Management Training							
Senior							
Middle							
Junior							

Figure 3.6 Contribution of HR activity to the business needs. (From Hussey, D. E., 1996, *Business Driven Human Resource Management*, Wiley, Chichester.)

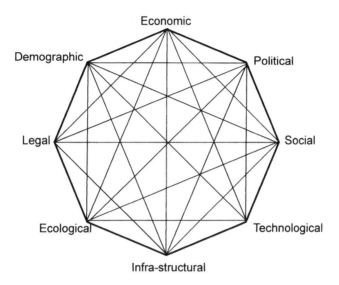

Figure 3.7   The environment.

markets, costs and competitive position, and has a profound effect on cash flow. Exchange fluctuations may be critical.

TECHNOLOGY, PROCESSES, COMPETENCIES, AND CAPABILITIES

Technology

Figure 3.2 made reference to other ways of thinking about the corporate appraisal. Figure 3.8 gives some definitions of each of the terms, from which it can be seen that technology is a building block for competencies, although it also stands alone as a different way of thinking about the organisation, of particular value in an organisation with several different strategic business units, where the interrelationships of the various technologies may be hidden. The appraisal of technology should begin with an audit of what the organisation possesses.

The questions that should be answered include the following, derived from Ford, 1988:

- A process is set of linked activities that take an input and transform it to create an output. (Johansson et al, 1993).
- A capability is a set of business processes strategically understood. (Stalk, Evans & Shulman, 1992).
- A competence is a bundle of skills and technologies that enables a company to provide a particular benefit to customers. (Hamel & Prahalad, 1994).
- Technology: the practice of any or all of the applied sciences that have practical value and/or industrial use: technical methods in a particular field of industry or art. (Chambers 20th Century Dictionary).

Figure 3.8 Some definitions.

- What are the key technologies and "know-how" on which the business depends?
- What sort of record does the organisation have in bringing home-grown technology to market, and what are the reasons behind this record?
- What sort of gap is there between the technological knowledge of the organisation and that of its key customers?
- What is the life cycle position of each of the key technologies?
- What technologies are emerging which could affect our markets?
- Where are the technological strengths and weaknesses: in product or in manufacture?
- Does the organisation fully exploit its technologies?
- Are there any unwanted technologies which could be sold or licensed to other organisations?

A different, and partly similar list of questions may be found in Henry, 1990.

Various ways of charting the results of a technology audit have been suggested, including portfolio methods (see Chapter 8). Figure 3.9 shows another way of gaining a visual impression of the technological links across different activities of the organisation. I originally used this with an engineering organisation, but for reasons of confidentiality have had to illustrate the method with a chart based on a different industry.

Markets	Products	Fats & Oils	Surfactants	Emulsifiers	Skin chemistry	Flavouring
Consumer	Laundry soap	✳	✳			
	Soap flakes	✳	✳	✳		
	Toilet soap	✳	✳		✳	
	Cleaners		✳	✳		
	Fabric softener		✳	✳		
	Shampoo		✳		✳	
	Toothpaste		✳	✳		✳
	Mouth wash		✳			✳
	Deoderant				✳	
	Skin care				✳	
Hotel	Toilet soap	✳	✳		✳	
	Shampoo		✳		✳	
Laundry	Detergent		✳	✳		
	Fabric softener		✳			
Industrial	Detergents	✳	✳	✳		
	Cleaners		✳	✳		
	Toilet soap	✳	✳		✳	

Figure 3.9 Technology appraisal: generalised example. (From Hussey, D. E., 1998, *Strategic Management: from Theory to Implementation*, 4th edition, Butterworth-Heinemann, Oxford).

Processes

As mentioned earlier, in most situations there is little to gain in trying to define every stage in every process. The exception is where a business process re-engineering initiative is intended: although potentially a valuable step, BPR falls outside the scope of the appraisal for strategic planning purposes (those who wish to explore BPR are recommended to consult Johansson et al, 1993). For our purposes processes are part of something else. In addition to the capabilities approach, discussed briefly later in this section, they also form part of the value chain approach (see Porter, 1985), which looks at how the organisation gives value to customers. This method will be described in the next chapter.

Competencies

From the definition in Figure 3.8, we see a competency as a bundle of skills and technologies which can be used for the benefit of the organisation. Identification of these follows the audit of the technologies that the organisation possesses. Hamel and Prahalad, 1994, argue that the key task is to move to a definition of the core competencies. In part this is a task for the corporate appraisal (what are our current core competencies?), but they are also something to revisit in the process of thinking about strategy (how should we add to or build on the competencies in order to create competitive advantage?).

But what is a core competency? In order to qualify, Hamel and Prahalad argue that a core competency must:

- Give access (or potential access) to a wide variety of markets.
- Deliver a clear benefit to the customer (or more accurately, a benefit that the customer perceives).
- Be hard for competitors to copy, so that it provides a clear basis for differentiation.
  A core competence is not, therefore:

- A single skill.
- A competence that all competitors have.
- A product.
- Something possessed by only one small area of the organisation.

Hinterhuber et al, 1996, suggest a number of steps in the identification of core competencies:

- Determining current competencies.
- Assessing the relative strengths of the competencies.
- Identifying those which deliver value to current customers.
- Establishing which are needed for the longer term.
- Examining the portfolio of competencies.

Capabilities

Stalk et al, 1992, argue that competencies are inadequate as a basis on which to build competitive advantage, as the foundation is narrow and technical. What is needed is to add to this the bundles of processes which enable the organisation to be successful at using those technological strengths, such as the way in which the organisation is able to continuously innovate, or the particular approach to customer service which enables them to keep the core competence ahead of competitors. In other words, its not just what you have, but how you use it which makes the difference.

There is no need to try to decide which is the right approach. Combine them, so that they are seen as two elements of the same thing.

Putting it altogether

As listed above, the internal and external appraisals to be examined suggest a chain relationship, with item neatly following item. Of course reality is not like this at all, and the key elements, and there are others which have not been discussed, including industry analysis which will be the subject of the next chapter, have a sort of spider's web relationship, with a tangle of crossed lines but all with a central theme leading to a focal point: the uncovering of the corporate identity.

With the data obtained, it will be possible to write down a series of factual statements about the company, together with the strategic implications. How these statements are formulated depends on the complexity of the company and the personal approach of the investigator. It is important that they be written, since in most companies there are likely to be areas of dispute (in fact it is almost possible to say dogmatically that if everyone agrees with the report, the job has not been done properly), and emotions will be involved. It is much easier to make an objective decision if all the evidence is fully documented.

The reports may not always be pleasant. Few people enjoy trying to convince their chief executive that an area of the company which is dear to his or her heart is not right for the organisation, or of similar unpopular measures. But this sort of study must be approached with integrity, for without a genuine attempt at honest appraisal the whole exercise may become a meaningless gesture.

The final report should show clearly the strong and weak points of the organisation. It should assess the vulnerability of the organisation to likely changes in the environment, and should establish what I like to call the organisation's "risk balance" (which put simply is the number of baskets it has to keep its eggs in!). It is at this point that the organisation is ready to move to the next stage, the analysis of the corporate arena.

Corporate appraisal is complex, but not too difficult to be completed by a competent executive. If the company has a corporate planner he or she should play a major part: indeed, in my opinion, the planner who does not attempt this sort of analysis is not doing the job properly. In most organisations a team approach may be the most effective method, with people from various functions working with the planner. This goes to make for a greater involvement of management, and removes the feeling of imposition that may come from a purely staff investigation.

Some organisations may feel that this sort of study is best tackled by consultants. This can, of course, help to ensure greater objectivity, but I would regard it as an optional method of approach, and by no means essential.

Figure 3.10 is somewhat simpler than a real situation (for many organisations this would be a gross understatement). It also omits things which may be very important in some organisations, such as technology and core competencies/capabilities. The point is to illustrate that only the key findings need appear in the summary, but that each key finding should be based on evidence, and this must be recorded and available if required to justify the statements.

EQUILIBRIUM ANALYSIS

The sort of analytical approach described above is invaluable and should not be skimped. Earlier it was mentioned that there is value in widening management involvement in such an analysis, tapping into insights and knowledge not otherwise easily available. One common approach is to invite managers across a wide

---

Part 1: Weaknesses/Limiting Factors

1. *Management*

	Immediate Strategic Implications
(a) Chief executive aged 65, no obvious successor.	(a) Recruitment, merger, or sale of business.
(b) Weak middle management.	(b) Recruitment, training. (Position can be improved but some weakness will remain for 5 years.)
(c) Marketing manager incapable of handling any expansion.	(c) A serious block. Solve by structure change or replacement.

2. *Marketing*

(a) 80 per cent of profits emanate from product A, market declining at 5% p.a., market share constant.	(a) (i) Reduce dependence. (ii) Change market strategy to improve performance. (iii) Cost reduction to improve position.
(b) 25 products contribute no profit and have no potential.	(b) Cease production, redeploy resources.

Part 2: Strengths

1. *People*
   (a) A high level of technical expertise in production departments.
2. *Marketing*
   (a) Strong image among consumers, particularly for quality, performance and after sales service.
   (b) Five established brand names.
3. *Finance*
   (a) £500 000 available for expansion from own resources. Up to £2m loan capital can be raised without difficulty.

Note. All statements would be supported in the report.

Figure 3.10 Example: one method of summarising the key points from an appraisal.

front to list strengths and weaknesses in a SWOT exercise (many participative planning systems have a requirement for this in the annual planning cycle), or to hold meetings with groups of managers to jointly undertake the SWOT exercise. A typical end product is a shopping list of rather general statements which may be difficult to evaluate. Issues are often exaggerated, and it is rare for the work to lead to any specific actions.

The equilibrium approach is primarily intended for group discussions, and is intended to offer a better solution than the shopping list approach. Its objectives are:

- To achieve a common understanding of strengths and weaknesses.
- To identify strengths as well as weaknesses.
- To decide priorities for corrective action.
- To identify corrective action.

The basic framework of the approach is shown in Figure 3.11. It is a very simple concept which can be taught to any group in a matter of minutes. The horizontal line represents the present state of anything that is to be studied: labour turnover rates, market position, cost structures, profitability, etc. Focus should be given by posing a question such as: "Why is our market share 15%?" The base line then represents the current state—a market share of 15%. It is as high as 15% because certain positive features support it. It is as low as 15% because certain negative features hold it down.

The trick is to get the meeting to identify these two groups of factors, writing them in heading form at the top and bottom of the diagram, across the page. If too many weaknesses are identified attention can be changed to strengths with a remark such as "Now I can't understand why you have any market share at all."

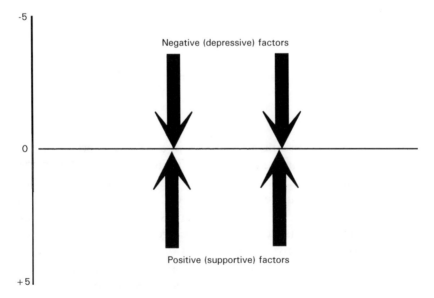

Figure 3.11   Outline of equilibrium approach.

If too many strengths come up one can ask why market share has not risen to 50%.

Criteria for successful use of the approach include a group of people who know the situation, and preparation for the meeting by an analyst who has looked at the factual base available. The analyst should be prepared to challenge (e.g. if the group insists that a plus factor is the firm's reputation, whereas market research shows that it is almost unknown, the factual position should over-ride the impression).

The next step in the use of the technique is to rate the relative significance of the various factors identified. This is the reason for the scaling on the vertical line.

Figure 3.12 illustrates what the completed diagram might look like at the end of the meeting.

Once the information is displayed it is possible to use it:

- Would the position best be improved by strengthening a positive factor or removing a negative one?
- Are there any factors which cannot be altered by the firm, and which should not receive more attention?
- What can be done about the really important factors?

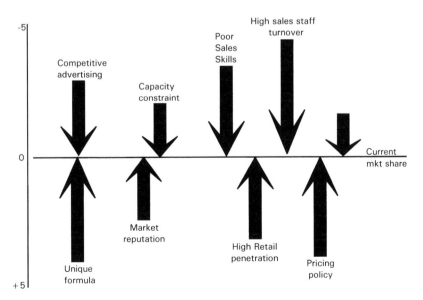

Figure 3.12 Example of equilibrium analysis-market share.

The equilibrium approach could be used again if it was decided to tackle the high sales force turnover, and used to try to identify the factors which attract sales people to the firm, and those that cause them to leave. If the assessments move from the known base of fact, it may be useful to accept them for the time being, but to check them out after the meeting.

What has been discussed in this chapter is nothing more than a function of good management, and many may feel a defensive pride in their own way of running the organisation. Some organisations may indeed already have much of the information available in different parts of the organisation. What is so often lacking is the drawing of all important data together to present the complete picture. The management casebooks are littered with the testimony of organisations that found that they did not have as perfect a knowledge of themselves as they once thought.

Of course, this sort of analysis is not restricted to organisations that are preparing a strategic plan. But the organisation that does it will suddenly realise that it is well on the path towards either validating of questioning its strategy. Either action may lead the way to greater success.

REFERENCES

Ford, D., 1988, "Develop your technology strategy", *Long Range Planning,* **21**.5, October).

Hamel, G. and Prahalad, C. K., 1994, *Competing for the Future*, Harvard Business School Press, Boston, MA.

Henry, J. P., 1990, "Making the technology strategy connection", in Hussey, D. E., editor, *International Review of Strategic Management*, Vol. 1, Wiley, Chichester.

Hinterhuber, H. H., Friedrich, S. A., Handlbauer, G. and Stubec, U., 1996, "The company as a cognitive system of core competences and strategic business units", *Strategic Change*, **5**.4, July–August.

Hussey, D. E, 1996, *Business Driven Human Resource Management*, Wiley, Chichester.

Hussey, D. E., 1998, *Strategic Management: From Theory to Implementation*, 4th edition, Butterworth-Heinemann, Oxford.

Johansson, H. J., McHugh, P., Pendlebury, A. J. and Wheeler, W. A., 1993, *Business Process Reengineering*, Wiley, Chichester.

Stalk, G., Evans, P. and Shulman, L, 1992, "Competing on capabilities", *Harvard Business Review*, March/April.

4
Analysing the Competitive Arena

UNDERSTANDING THE INDUSTRY

The previous chapter stated that the corporate appraisal should provide an understanding of where the company fits in its competitive arena. Techniques of industry structure analysis have been developed which will help the organisation obtain this understanding, and will provide, in addition, a basis for the application of the portfolio analysis techniques described in Chapter 8.

Many of the concepts used in the industry structure analysis approach are not new, and have their roots in classical economic principles of market imperfections. The old established ideas were illuminated, and new ones added, by Porter, 1980, whose thinking has had a considerable influence on management.

The approach described here owes a great deal to Porter's thinking, although it is also based on practical consulting experience and a methodology developed and used in a variety of different industries. Figure 4.1 illustrates the approach. In the outer ring are the analytical steps, beginning with a mapping approach which provides a practical application of the principles of industry analysis. This aids understanding of the competitive arena, and the relative positions of the key competitors. Two further analytical aids are recommended. The first profiles the major competitors, providing a means of compressing vast amounts of data into a form which aids strategic thinking. The second contrasts the segmentation approaches of each significant competitor. Finally,

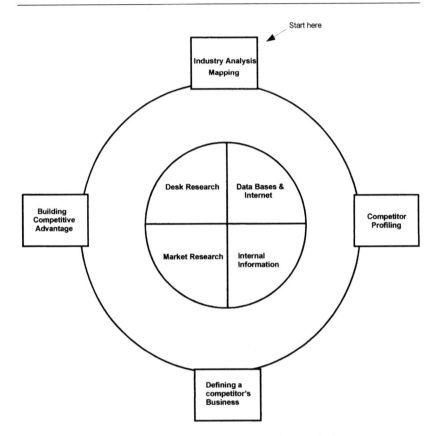

Figure 4.1 Approach to competitor analysis.

the box *building competitive advantage*, is the thinking and decision stage from which strategic actions should emanate.

The inner circle examines the four major sources of information for competitor analysis. These are discussed in broad terms in this chapter, and will reappear in Chapter 7 when the option of acquisition will be discussed.

Individually, each of these steps is a valuable tool of strategic analysis. Together they enable the firm to develop a powerful understanding of the industry and its competitive arena. This is fundamental to the strategy of even the simplest business, and an essential prerequisite of analytical approaches which are designed for the more complex firms.

INDUSTRY STRUCTURE ANALYSIS

The industry analysis approach can be conceived as three linked groups of power relationships, influenced by forces which may lie outside the control of the three groups. The whole model operates within the constraints and opportunities of the business environment.

Environmental factors were discussed in Chapter 3 and, of course, are just as important in industry analysis. Some theorists maintain that the environment affects all firms in the industry equally. This is not usually true and I should not recommend anyone to make this assumption without some careful thought. Our concentration here is on that portion of the model that lies inside the environmental border.

Firms in the industry

It is traditional for analysts to examine such factors as market shares and to pay some attention to the different positioning of each firm in the marketplace. Industry analysis tries to identify all the factors which affect the ferocity of competitive behaviour. The competitiveness of the industry is not revealed by brand shares alone, although these are important. Competitive behaviour is also influenced by many other factors, including:

- *Growth rates of the industry*. Competitive behaviour tends to be less aggressive if industry growth rates are relatively high, because each firm can increase its sales without necessarily increasing its market share. This statement is considerably modified by the position on the life cycle curve. In a new industry high growth rates may bring in new competitors and this will tend to lead to aggressive behaviour. In almost all industries, a fall in the growth rate will tend to intensify competition. Often it is the change which causes new patterns, rather than the growth rate itself. Other things being equal, one would expect to find more aggressive behaviour in an industry whose annual growth rate has fallen suddenly from 10% to 3% than in an industry whose growth has stabilised at 3%.
- *General level of profits*. Lack of profits throughout the industry, or among some significant firms within it, will tend to make

competitive behaviour less predictable. Where profits are high for all, there may be a measure of tolerance of competitors. A change to lower profits may trigger a more aggressive attribute.

- *Level of fixed costs.* Where investment is large and highly specialised, and fixed costs are a relatively high proportion of total costs, competitors tend to "hang on", selling at less than full costs, when the market slumps or there is overcapacity for some other reason. Shipping, oil refining and petrochemicals all provide examples where competitive behaviour may lead to low profits or losses over a very long period of time, because the alternative is plant closure at a time when assets cannot be realised at or above their book value.

- *Economies of scale/experience curve.* Competitive behaviour is likely to be more aggressive when there are clear advantages to being big. This may happen when cost levels are dependent on high volumes, or when the experience curve effect means that progressively higher volumes will lead to progressively lower costs. Lower costs mean prices can be reduced, which in turn means that even higher volumes can be gained. In a growth market, where demand is elastic and mass production normal (for example, motor cycles, calculating machines, electronic components) the experience curve effect can bring dominance to the firm that gets far enough ahead. Competitive behaviour is likely to be very aggressive during this period.

- *Degree of differentiation.* Market imperfections give a degree of protection to individual firms and reduce the impact of competition. Thus it is reasonable to expect the fiercest competition when all firms are offering products of commodity status, and the most peaceful behaviour when each firm offers such a highly differentiated product that it is almost unique.

- *Number of firms and market shares.* A fragmented industry, with no one firm having a significant market share, tends to be more fiercely competitive than one which has a clear market leader who is in a dominant position. To some degree, these tendencies may be modified by the position on the product life cycle. It is unwise to assume that mature markets will all have gone through the shakeout period. Some are highly fragmented because the economic circumstances do not favour large firms (many service industries).

- *New entrant*. In long established industries firms often reach an unspoken form of accommodation with each other, softening the aggressiveness of competition. This will often change with the entry of a new firm who either does not know or chooses to ignore these implicit "rules" (for example, the impact of the low-price airlines like Easyjet). A similar effect may occur if one of the companies appoints a new chief executive from outside the industry.
- *Nature of product*. A perishable product (airline ticket: fresh produce) is likely to be more susceptible to random price cutting than one which can be stored easily and cheaply.

The buyers

There are two reasons for studying the structure of the industry through the chain to the ultimate consumer. The first is to ensure that the whole of the present structure is known, as this may reveal new strategic options, including the all important one of changing the "rules of the game" by finding another way to get the product to the ultimate consumer.

A second reason is to study the relative influence over profits exercised by the various stages in the chain, and the way power is likely to shift in the future. It is not necessarily the industry competitors which determine their own margins and profitability: sometimes the greater power is in the hands of the buyers. Factors which influence the relative location of this power and influence include:

- *Relative size*. If the industry includes firms that are considerably larger than their customers, sheer weight of resources may put them in the dominant position. The converse may apply when the buying organisations are the largest. This is not a universal truth as other factors may outweigh it. For example, the UK grocery products are largely controlled by a few supermarket chains, who not only have most of the retail outlets, but also have developed own label products which they can adjust in volume and price if the branded manufacturers do not toe the line. In this way they may determine the profitability of manufacturers, whose global organisations may be considerably larger than those of the supermarkets.

- *Dependencies.* Bargaining strength may lie with the least dependent of the two parties. This is a composite of the number of industry firms contrasted with the number of buying firms (what flexibility does each have?), and the importance of the product to the profits of each party.
- *Profitability of the buying industry.* The industry firms are likely to be in a healthier position when they are selling to a profitable industry. Where buyers are unprofitable or have low profits, there is likely to be stronger resistance against price increases. This resistance will increase when the buyer is facing an elastic demand curve, and cannot easily pass on the extra costs.
- *Experience of buyers.* Buyers purchasing from a mature industry are likely to have more experience than those dealing with new industry. Thus the more mature the industry, the weaker its bargaining position may become (subject of course to other factors). Where the buying industry is also mature, there may be a tendency for the degree of product differentiation to fall, making it more difficult for the industry to sustain high margins.
- *Threat of integration.* The industry firm that patently has the capability and strength to integrate into its buying industry possesses a key bargaining point. If the buying industry thwarts its profit aims, it has the potential to remove the blockage. The opposite applies when the buying industry can offer a credible threat of backwards integration. In either case the credibility of the threat is enhanced when both parties are aware that such a move would be economically viable.

Supplying firms

It is traditional for organisations to believe that they hold the edge over both their buyers and suppliers, a statement that patently cannot always be true since the organisation itself is a buyer to its supplier. Relations with the supplying industry are rarely studied as a matter of strategic importance. In reality the analysis of suppliers is the converse of the analysis of buyers. The factors to consider can therefore be read off the preceding section.

Entry and exit barriers

The entry and exit barriers will affect the profitability of an industry and the way in which competitors behave. Barriers to entry have been defined as:

> Features of technological or economic conditions of a market which raise the costs of firms wanting to enter the market above those of firms already in the market, or otherwise make new entry difficult. For example, a high degree of product differentiation creates a barrier to entry since a new product might have to spend a great deal on advertising and sales promotion in order to overcome the brand loyalty of consumers to existing brands. Similarly, the existence of marked economies of scale in the industry may require the new firm to enter at a very large scale of output, if it is not to suffer a cost disadvantage. But the need to capture a large part of the market may cause a fall in prices and profits and make entry unprofitable. We would expect the nature of barriers to entry of an industry to be an important determinant of profits earned in the industry. Hence, with very low barriers, we would expect profits in the long run to approach normal profits. On the other hand, high entry barriers will strengthen monopoly power and may permit high profits to be made. Other important sources of entry barriers are patents, exclusive dealing contracts with suppliers or distributors, and vertical integration. On the other hand, entry barriers will be less effective when there is rapid expansion in demand, or technological change. (Bannock, Baxter and Rees, 1978.)

Where entry barriers are very low the industry may become fragmented and competition fierce, with new competitors regularly coming into the market. Industry profitability is to a large extent dependent on market imperfections, and one element of corporate strategy might be to find ways of raising the entry barriers.

There are factors which tie a firm to the industry and make it difficult or impossible for it to leave. Where such exit barriers occur, the firm will hang on, trading as best it can, and depressing profits in the industry.

Exit barriers may be around the need to write off specialised assets for which there is no buyer, particular contracts, or legal requirements which make it costly to meet severance payments to employees. There may also be government pressure on the firm to stay in the business.

Substitutes

The availability of substitutes may have a dramatic effect on the prospects for an industry, and will unleash a further set of competitive relationships. Emergence of a new substitute may bring new firms with different cost structures into the competitive arena. A substitute will often increase the power of the buyer and reduce the power of the seller. The emergence of potential new substitutes is therefore a possibility that should be studied for each industry.

Where the number of existing substitutes is large the possibility that the industry has been ill defined should be considered. It may be that a production view has been taken rather than a marketing view. In any event the substitute industry should be studied as rigorously as the firm's own industry.

In figure 4.2 substitutes appear twice, as they may affect both buyer and supplier power.

Influencers

The influencer box on figure 4.2 does not appear in Porter's concept (1980). A moment's thought will show how important the influencers can be in the competitive arena. I am talking here about a person or organisation who/which has a contractual role in the process, although usually the contract is with the buyer, not the industry firm. One example is the general practitioner who prescribes a medicine to a patient. If it is not prescribed, the chemist cannot sell it. The pharmaceutical industry has another quirk, in that where there is a national health service, all or part of the cost of the medicine may be paid by the government. Other examples are consulting engineers and architects who may specify plant or a building, and thus affect what the industry firms can supply.

THE PROBLEM OF INDUSTRY DEFINITION

Industry analysis may be difficult in that data is rarely perfect, and some pieces of the jigsaw may be hidden. The problems of obtaining and analysing information are nothing compared to the basic problem which is to decide the scope of the industry. This, incidentally, is a problem that also occurs when portfolio analysis is used.

The first point of principle is to stress that it is the market and the competitors which often define the scope. Insular views taken by the individual firm because it happens to make certain products and sell them in certain markets may not necessarily define the scope correctly. Industries are becoming increasingly global in their scope. An electronics firm which insisted that its geo-graphical scope was the UK would probably misdefine the industry. The British motor cycle industry made the mistake of misunderstanding its industry and competitors, which is one reason why Japanese firms were able to beat it virtually to extinction. One element of the decision is to look at competitors and the origin of their products, and to consider whether the business is one where the learning curve effect would make global competition an economic reality.

The product itself requires thought. It may be tempting to a firm that concentrates on only one market segment to insist that this is the industry. In fact this thinking is only valid when such a segment is strategically defensible. That is, when it possesses significant entry barriers. The British motor cycle industry again provides an example of how complacency led to a misunderstanding of the defensibility of its market segments, and it fell to a brilliant segment-by-segment approach from the Japanese.

It is also necessary to decide whether the competitive arena is a product or a concept. Once it may have been appropriate to examine the typewriter industry. Now this industry is caught up in something more complex: information technology. Old distinctions may no longer be appropriate, and one may need to think of complete systems as well as products.

MAPPING THE INDUSTRY

One practical application of the principles of industry structure analysis is to "map" the industry. The method I have used regularly for many industries is to convert the generic model in Figure 4.2 to a specific analysis of a particular industry. As an example Figure 4.3 shows a simplified outline map or chart of the

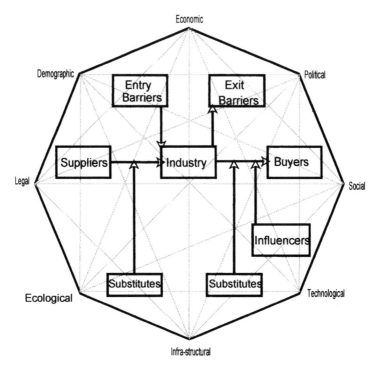

Figure 4.2   The industry and the business environment.

toiletries industry. Even in this simplified example, the buyers have expanded from one box to four, coming closer to the reality of what actually happens between the industry firm and the final consumer. In fact there are more buying groups than I have shown. There are different types of retailer, and our classification should be extended: for example there are supermarkets and other grocery outlets, pharmacists, outlets like Superdrug used to be (a chemist's shop without those products which required the presence of a pharmacist), and departmental stores. There are different types of wholesaler: those dealing with small grocery outlets are not the same as those serving pharmacies. There are other types of buyer such as hotels and airlines. We need to think of customers, the final consumers, and in terms of segments, with some indication of the needs of each.

Figure 4.3 already shows two very different types of industry firm, which behave in very different ways. The branded competitors would include firms such as L'Oreal and various Unilever

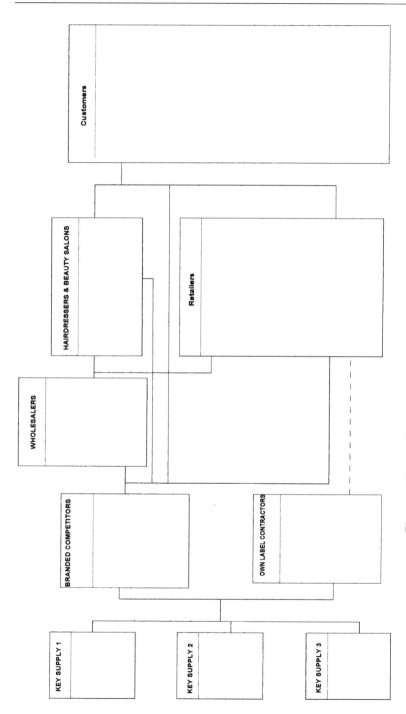

Figure 4.3 Outline chart for toiletry product such as hair care.

companies. Own-label contractors are organisations which exist for one purpose: to supply own-label variants of popular products to retailers. The criteria for success are different for each of these two types of business. But even two groups could be an oversimplification. We would need to determine the boundary to our industry definition. For example, one definition would include hair care products, one of which is shampoo. This is a detergent-based product, which we would certainly want to include if we were studying the detergents industry. Does this mean that we should include household detergents in our map of the toiletries industry? The answer is probably no, but we would have to be aware that some of the competitors might have manufacturing advantages if they were operating in both industries.

Finally, we might see a need to group our industry into products, if the competitors in each group were largely different, even though some firms would appear in more than one group.

The figure provides for three groups of supplier products. This is indicative. We may also want to move further back in the supply chain to examine organisations which supply the raw materials to the various manufacturers of the items we buy. Body Shop is reported to seek out new raw ingredients for its products in the Third World, bypassing the normal processors of perfumes, oils and essences. If all these extra things had been included in the summary figure, the size of the paper would have made it very difficult to read, so part of it has been left to the reader to mentally complete. My normal procedure is to draw the map on A3 paper, using another sheet to record the key implications that can be read from the map, and adding a note on entry and exit barriers, and emerging substitutes. Current substitutes and influencers would be incorporated into the main map.

Once such a model has been drawn, it is possible to decide what aspects are important to the study and to concentrate on these.

The outline map becomes of more value if the key detail of the industry is entered in the appropriate boxes. For our purposes, this means the summary facts which enable us to see the relative significance of different parts of the chain, identify the pressure points, and interpret the competitive arena using the principles shown earlier in this chapter.

Such a map aids more than analysis. It helps the management team to reach a shared understanding of the competitive arena. My experience has been that it often identifies inaccuracies in the information that the organisation has been using, and shows up many areas of ignorance where the organisation should be better informed. It provides a basis for doing more than take a photograph of the situation as it was yesterday. I have found it useful as an aid to creating different scenarios of how the industry might evolve, and where the changes might come from.

CRITICAL SKILLS ANALYSIS

We can now add another concept which is useful in industry analysis, and offers another way of thinking about those strengths and weaknesses which are strategically relevant. It is the concept of critical skills, or key success factors.

It follows a very simple idea. In any business there are a few things that have to be done really well in order to achieve success. There may be no more than six to twelve key items. Get those right and you get the business right.

If the critical skills can be identified for a particular business it becomes possible to see whether the company is deficient in any of those skills. For example, there are obvious differences in the critical success factors that relate to the two groups of industry firms in Figure 4.4.

From this it is possible to see that much of the branded companies' success is related to marketing skills, and that production costs are relative to market positioning. The own-label contractors are dependent on manufacturing and fast product formulation skills, with a knowledge of their relatively few buyers and an ability to negotiate profitable contracts.

Branded toiletries	*Own label contractors*
New product innovation	Ability to copy new products quickly
Market segmentation capability	Understanding the few key buyers
Promotional skills	Flexible manufacturing
Sales force management	Negotiation skills
Costs relative to price	Low cost production

Figure 4.4 Example of critical skills.

Critical skills analysis is useful for finding gaps, or for ensuring that a new business strategy is properly thought out. The concept of six to twelve key skills may be a little theoretical: the question "What do we have to be good at in order to succeed?" is very pertinent.

In practice, I have found it useful to establish the critical skills for each "business area" identified in the industry analysis diagram, and to use a version of this to present the information. Test this idea by jotting down your understanding of the critical skills needed to be successful in each of the following businesses which would appear if we were analysing the fruit and vegetable industry:

1. Manufacturer of glass houses.
2. Large-scale horticulturist.
3. Market wholesaler.
4. Travelling fruit and vegetable wholesaler (selling to retailers from the lorry).
5. Supermarket.

This concept is valuable in giving more insight into the nature of the competitive arena, and it prepares the ground for a more detailed study of competitors.

COMPETITOR ANALYSIS

Industry mapping aids understanding of the forces which determine competitive behaviour in general, and enables identification of those competitors which should be studied at individual level, and those which can be looked at in terms of competitor groups of similarly behaving organisations. The next three stages of competitor analysis are designed to achieve a number of aims, which include:

- Formulation of an appropriate strategy in the reality of the competition. An appropriate strategy might be one which chooses those areas which avoid ferocious competition. Or, for a dominant competitor it may mean ensuring that it retains this position of dominance.
- Finding a superior strategy that gives competitive advantage.

- Being prepared for competitor actions, and expected reactions.
- Identifying ways to influence competitor reactions.

Competitor profiling

Competitor profiling provides a way of looking at competitors, and presenting the results in an easy to read form, on one A3 sheet of paper. Sometimes more pages are needed, particularly when a competitor has to be studied at different levels (product or geographic), but the principle of reducing the analysis to summary statements can be preserved. This process increases understanding of the competitor, focuses attention on the appropriate issues, and provides a format which eases internal communication, and which can be stored in a database.

Figure 4.5 provides an illustration of a profile. In practice this should be modified to suit the types of competitor in the industry, and to include different types of information which may be relevant. Each block of information in the figure is discussed below.

- *Financial results.* The aim is to record a few meaningful figures that give a snapshot of the competitor's recent history. Unfortunately few competitors are single business companies and, even if they are, they may be multinational. The three sub headings across the matrix reflect this. If the competitor were Otis Elevators, "group" would be changed to United Technologies, "division" to Otis' worldwide organisation, and "unit" to the country company we were studying. In fact, in this example, we may find it necessary to insert a sub-heading to cover the geographical region, or we may decide that the Otis organisation is so big that we can miss out the parent company for our purposes. However, this would mean that some of the information suggested would not be appropriate, such as earnings per share (EPS).

  Let us also be clear that some of the information we need for the ideal profile is not available, and cannot be reasonably estimated, and although there is frequently more available than may be believed at first, sometimes nothing can be entered in some of the boxes.

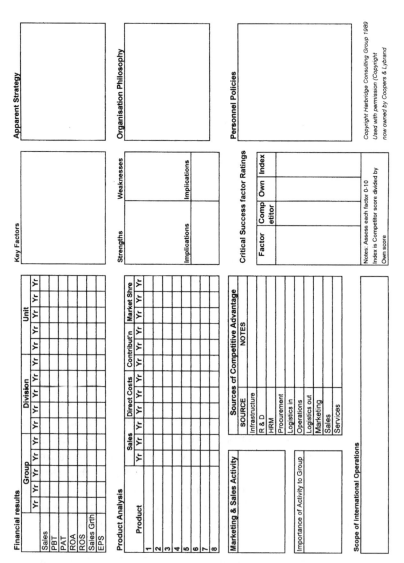

Figure 4.5 Outline competitor profile.

- *Product analysis.* Companies compete at the level of products and services. It is possible to argue that there is competition at the unit level for scarce resources, but for the most part we are concerned with product competition in relation to our industry. Thornton for example is a British manufacturer of chocolates. Among its competitors are Nestlé and Cadbury-Schweppes. The resources that these giants can command, and the synergy between their activities, are of concern to Thornton because they affect how these competitors may behave. However, Thornton only competes with the chocolate confectionery activities, and would have no interest in the wide range of other products the other companies produce. And even within the chocolate confectionery market, Thornton has a niche position and would be more interested in the boxed and speciality chocolate products than chocolate bars.

  As designed, the outline suggests analysis of up to eight products, although this can be extended, and records information under the headings sales, direct costs, contribution, and market share. In many cases what is recorded here will be estimates, based on evidence from sources such as market research and reverse engineering. For some types of product an additional column showing advertising expenditure may be of value, and there is also the option of a column showing growth trends.

- *Marketing and sales activity.* This notes key information about how the competitor influences the market. It may include information about the size and organisation of the sales force, and note promotional activities and their duration. Information about discounting may be of value. Other relevant information might be the number of outlets operated. For example, this would be important if Nestlé were studying Thornton, because a feature of the latter organisation is a network of tied retail outlets trading under the Thornton name. If analysing a professional services firm, it might be relevant to include the number of major organisations they serve, information which often appears in their marketing literature and some journal surveys.

- *Sources of competitive advantage.* The thinking behind this box is derived from the value chain approach (Porter, 1985), which will be discussed later in this chapter. It is an attempt to identify which of the particular activities of the competitor provide value to the customer, and are therefore a source of competitive advantage. The headings here are the generic descriptions used by Porter, and are useful as a reminder to the analysts, but are jargon to most managers. Replace them with a tighter everyday description of the actual source of advantage.

- *Importance of the activity to the whole group.* The argument here is that a competitor is likely to be more aggressive, and to respond more fiercely to attack, if the activity is of importance to its overall results. This means it is of value to try to establish just how important it is. There is no need to be pedantic. It does not need very much analysis to determine that the activities of the training department of a large multinational, which sells its services to other companies, are not particularly important to the overall strategy of the company, and would probably be abandoned if put under severe pressure. A division which has lost money over several years may not receive the same support as if it were a major contributor, and may be vulnerable in that it may not be able to match your modernisation programme, and so will fall further behind. However, a division which contributes most of the profits and cash to a multinational might be considered to carry an invisible sign: "Don't tread on me—I bite".

- *Scope of international operations.* At first sight this may not seem to be important to anyone studying competitors within a particular country. This would probably be a correct assumption if all that was recorded was the number of countries in which the competitor operates. There are two more important aspects.

Firstly there is the competitive advantage given by multi-country operations, which may be economics in production because factories produce on a larger scale, the bigger base of revenue to support R & D, and in certain cases the ability to offer advantages that cannot be matched by all competitors. An example of the last is the business travel agency competitors, where only those that have established a global network can gain the volume business of the increasing number of global customers who want to concentrate their travel purchases on one firm.

Secondly, the way in which a competitor organises its international operations will have a considerable impact on how it takes decisions. Hussey, 1998 states "The competitive reactions to your strategy will be very different if the competitor operates on an individual country basis, what has been termed 'multi-local', than if it manages globally through an integrated strategy. One European-wide grocery products company I studied operated at a disadvantage because each country operation was treated as a separate business, and had to achieve its return on investment targets as its main priority. Its main competitor, who was winning all the battles in every country, treated Europe as one strategic area and would put resources into any country to beat off a competitive threat, regardless of the short-term impact on that subsidiary's bottom line. The virtually uncoordinated country strategies of my client meant that it could rarely win against the superior strategy of the competitor. Knowing how your competitor views global operations is a critical first step to understanding and predicting how it will behave in different circumstances." (page 179).

- *Key factors*. There are always a number of facts about a competitor which help understanding, and which are either a manifestation of its strategy, or suggests that a new strategy may emerge. Under this heading we would record facts such as the location and number of factories, where R & D is undertaken, changes to the top management team, and any recent change in ownership. It is a notepad for whatever is important, and what is worth noting.
- *Apparent strategy*. This is the heart of the profile, and also the most difficult box to complete. The word apparent is used deliberately: it is what can be deduced about what the competitor is trying to do. Although a useful picture can be developed, it should never be forgotten that there is uncertainty, both in whether the deductions are correct, and for how long they will remain correct. Continuous monitoring and analysis of the competitor is the best way of confirming the deductions, spotting inconsistencies, and observing when new strategies appear to be being implemented.
- *Strengths and weaknesses*. This box does not need explanation, but it does require a caution. Although assessments by your own managers may be valid, where possible they should be backed up by an analysis of the hard evidence. There may be a temptation to mix wishful thinking about weaknesses you would like the competitor to have, with an over-estimation of

its strengths and infallibility. One of my American clients had undertaken regular assessments of its competitors, and concluded that a number of them were on the verge of financial collapse: this assessment lost some of its plasibility when it was realised that identical conclusions had been reached every year over the previous five to ten years, and the competitors were still alive and kicking. Customer surveys can be used to reveal some strengths and weaknesses, which might otherwise be seen only from an internal, and biased, perspective.

- *Organisation philosophy*. How an organisation runs itself will have an impact on its strategies, and many operational issues. What role does its head office play in the running of the organisation? Is the competitor a pawn in a much larger strategic game that the head office is playing? How is performance of the competitor judged by its head office? How do its accounting principles affect how it views its costs at the product level? Such questions are not only matters for competitors who are subsidiaries of larger organisations, and even single industry companies are affected by the structure and management style.

- *Personnel policies*. The personnel policies of an organisation have an impact on its strategies and performance. A low reward policy may make it difficult for a competitor to attract and retain staff, affecting operational performance and the longer term success. The quality and qualifications of its employees, the career development opportunities open to them, and the training that is provided are matters which may have strategic importance, and are worth recording.

- *Critical success factor ratings*. The concept and use of critical success factors need no further explanation, and what is suggested here is a development from the previous discussion. The first task is to assess the critical success factors for the industry and to rate your own company against them (a 0–10 rating is suggested). This element would be a constant on the profile of each competitor. Next rate the competitor in the same manner. The index is created by dividing the competitor's score for each factor by your score. Making such judgements about a competitor forces deep consideration, and experience shows that it is best undertaken by a panel of knowledgeable managers rather than by an individual acting alone.

Defining the competitor's business

Not all competitors are in contention with each other. I have found it useful to use matrix diagrams to define both the company and the competitor's businesses. In the simplest form this may be a matrix which shows customer needs against customer groups. Many more combinations are possible, including buying decision process, size of buyer, location, technology and many more. In one recent analysis which I undertook in a life insurance company, a basic matrix showed employment and age. From national statistics in the country and the client's own records we were able to insert on this diagram the percentage of total premium income each cell represented. We then calculated a penetration index, based on number of policies sold and the national population in each cell. Finally we designed a regular market research initiative that would enable market share information for each competitor to be collected for the cells seen as most significant. The focus on significance reduced the market research costs to a reasonable level, and made the whole project manageable.

There are various related display methods which are useful in contrasting competitors. The simple cruciform diagram in Figure 4.6 was one of a number developed for contrasting competitor countries in tourism, against those of a Third World country.

Building competitive advantage

Building competitive advantage requires a painstaking effort to use the various analytical steps. It is where the creative elements of strategy come into play. There are a few ways in which creative thinking may be triggered, and which at the very least will aid understanding of the analysis.

- *Scenario building.* The method used for competitor profiling may also be used to study other key organisations on the industry map, such as major buyers, suppliers, or organisations which influence the buyer. Once this is done it becomes possible to use the map and profiles to deduce the strategic moves that *could* be made by the various "actors": competitors, suppliers, major customers, and end-users. The profiles help assess the probability of such moves, and the likely reactions of the different

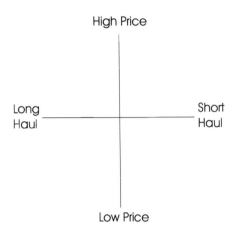

Figure 4.6   Competitive comparisons outline chart.

players in the industry. The next step is to consider what strategic moves might be made by the company itself, and how it might react to other players' moves. A number of different scenarios can be derived and the implications studied.

- *Role playing*. Another useful approach is to role-play competitors. If a small group of managers is assembled, each can take on the role of a different competitor. Within the framework of the industry map, each might first explain the competitor represented, and suggest likely strategic moves, and reactions to moves of other competitors. This should lead to a detailed consideration of competitive strategy. One of the advantages of this and the previous approach is that both explore the dynamic nature of the competitive situation.

- *Changing the rules*. The industry map reveals a certain structure to the industry, but this is not immutable. Industries do change over time, and the balance of power within an industry can be altered. A legitimate strategy might be to gain competitive advantage by changing the structure. One view of the broad options is given in the matrix in Figure 4.7, which argues that it is possible to change the activity or change the structure of the industry. In other words altering the rules of the game.

Cell 1:   *Same activity, same structure.* Here the strategic options are about improving position. This may be by gaining

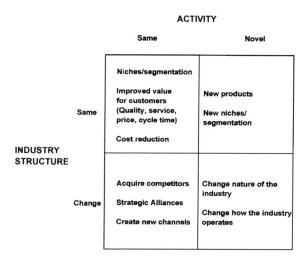

Figure 4.7 Strategic options.

advantage through a changed cost structure, for example the adoption of world-class manufacturing concepts. It may include careful segmentation, or other marketing strategies which beat the competition.

Cell 2: *New activity, same structure.* This is the group of strategies which deals with the introduction of a substitute, better product (not merely an improved version of an old product). For example, in the USA the lightweight, self-propelled booms used on construction sites found a new market and removed a major share from the heavy, cumbersome, truck-mounted telescopic booms that were previously the only product. The company that introduced the self-propelled booms gained a considerable advantage over the companies that had been market leaders in this area.

Cell 3: *Same activity, changed structure.* This is the strategy followed by companies that have tried to achieve leadership in a fragmented industry through the acquisition of competitors.

Cell 4: *New activity, changed structure.* An old example is the supermarkets who began by offering a different approach to grocery retailing, and went on to change the structure of the industry through increasing buying power as they gained dominance in distribution.

A BRIEF NOTE ON INFORMATION SOURCES

Competitor analysis is like completing a jigsaw puzzle. Information rarely comes from a single source, and enlightenment is often gained from relating a number of pieces of information to each other. Sometimes the pattern of the missing pieces can be deduced from what is available. Much of the analysis involves interpretations, assessments and judgements. The skill lies in using as many legitimate sources of information as can be obtained.

This means regular collection of information, supported by periodic drives for extra data. Figure 4.8 shows some of the

Type of initiative	*Examples*	
1. Library research	1.1	Annual reports
	1.2	Press/journal material
	1.3	Investment analysts' reports
	1.4	Government reports
	1.5	Published market intelligence
	1.6	Company literature
	1.7	Company history
	1.8	Academic case studies
	1.9	Computer based information service
	1.10	Competitor advertising
2. Interviews—secondary sources	2.1	Investment analysts
	2.2	Journalists
	2.3	Academics
	2.4	Others with special knowledge
3. Direct contact	3.1	Visits to plants
	3.2	Trade Association Councils
4. Conferences, etc.	4.1	Industry associations
	4.2	Industry conferences and seminars
5. Primary market research	5.1	Consumer surveys
	5.2	Trade (retail/wholesale) surveys
	5.3	Industrial market research
	5.4	Retail audits
	5.5	Diary panels
6. Sales analysis	6.1	Bids loss/gain analysis
7. Engineering	7.1	Product comparison
8. Soft information	8.1	Own managers
	8.2	Own salesmen

Figure 4.8 Sources of competitor information.

sources. Databases can be helpful in that they may pick up journals published in other languages, or not normally scanned by the company. Press-clipping services are useful, but still leave a need for periodic library searches for material that has appeared in books and journals that are not in the clipping service. And there is an ever-increasing amount of information available through the Internet.

Companies publish more than the obvious sales brochures and product literature. Recruitment brochures and company internal magazines are often available, and many give new insights or aid interpretation of another piece of information.

Competitor analysis is an information dependent activity. It also needs analytical tools, such as those described in this chapter, and a measure of strategic flair. Most people involved in strategic management today would see it as one of the most critical stages in effective planning.

THE VALUE CHAIN

In the competitor profile there is a list of headings which aimed to show how the competitor was delivering value to the customers. This was inspired by the value chain concept originated by Porter, 1985. He argued "To diagnose competitive advantage, it is necessary to define a firm's value chain for competing in a particular industry." (page 45). He also maintained that "Competitive advantage cannot be understood by looking at a firm as a whole. It stems from the many discrete activities a firm performs in designing, producing, marketing, delivering, and supporting its product. Each of these activities can contribute to a firm's relative cost position and create a basis for differentiation." (page 33).

Porter envisages an organisation as having five broad operational areas: inbound logistics, operations, outbound logistics, marketing and sales, and service. Each and all of these is potentially capable of delivering unique value to the customer which, provided the economic equation is satisfactory, can create competitive advantage. So the first step is to examine the processes which cluster under these broad headings, to establish where the costs are incurred, and which produce value to the customer.

Supporting these operational activities are procurement, technology, and human resource management departments, and the infrastructure of the firm. These may not be visible to the customer, but nevertheless can create or destroy value. For example, the comprehensive training given by an airline to its cabin staff may create value, not because the customer knows about the training, but through what he or she experiences, the behaviour of the in-flight staff.

The idea is that a chain of value exists inside every organisation, and understanding this and building on it is one way to build a strong competitive position. It follows that understanding a competitor's value chain, to the degree that it is possible to do this from outside, is a useful step in determining an appropriate strategy.

Value is created, according to Johansson et al, 1993, in four broad ways, alone or in combination: improved quality, service, reduced cost to customer and reduced cycle time. The starting point for an assessment of the value chain may be to establish what the *organisation* believes are the processes which deliver value to the customer, but by itself this may be dangerous and inadequate. It is the customer that is the key, and to make any sense of the value chain there is a need to establish what the customer is looking for. However there are limitations to this, when the organisation is considering an innovation that has never been done before, and therefore customers may have no experience or even understanding of it.

So although much of value chain analysis is about self inspection, it may be meaningless unless it has customer inputs. Market surveys may yield some of this information, but greater depth may come from focus groups of current and potential customers. Such marketing research methods can also yield valuable information about the value chains of competitors. A focus on these formal ways of obtaining information should not obscure the important information that is gained when the organisation is always in close contact with its customers, enjoys good relations with them, and discusses there needs with them almost continuously: unfortunately comparatively few organisations have such a close relationship with their customers so that they are really in each others confidence and, in any case, knowing a customer well may not help you understand why their competitors do not buy from you.

Porter's thinking goes beyond the boundaries of the firm, and argues that the industry company is only one series of links in a much larger chain which stretches from the raw materials to the ultimate buyer. Many of the value improvements lie at the interfaces between the organisations which make up this chain. Therefore there is considerable merit in working closely with suppliers, customers and through them the customer's customers, to seek areas of overall improvement. Collaborative work of this kind is, of course, now a feature of modern approaches to quality management, and appears in much of the literature on business process re-engineering, and it is no longer considered stupid to give up an activity which is not performed as well as it could be, and to transfer it to a supplier.

The chapters so far have given a platform from which it is possible to develop strategic thinking. They help an organisation to establish where it is, against the background of some of the things which may change its position in the future. Many strategic possibilities will have been identified as the various approaches are considered. We will move closer to thinking about strategy itself in the next chapter, which covers risk and uncertainty, and which will add another dimension to our thinking.

REFERENCES

Bannock, G., Baxter, R. E. and Rees, R., 1978, *The Penguin Dictionary of Economics*, 2nd Edition, Penguin Books, London.

Hussey, D. E., 1998, *Strategic Management: From Theory to Implementation*, 4th Edition, Butterworth-Heinemann, Oxford.

Johansson, H. J., McHugh, P., Pendlebury, A. J. and Wheeler, W. A., 1993, *Business Process Reengineering*, Wiley, Chichester.

Porter, M. E., 1980, *Competitive Strategy*, Free Press, New York.

Porter, M. E., 1985, *Competitive Advantage*, Free Press, New York.

FURTHER READING

Hussey, D. E. and Jenster, P. V., 1999, *Competitor Information: Analysis and Action*, Wiley, Chichester.

5
Risk and Uncertainty

One of the objectives of strategic planning is the reduction of risk: not the removal of risk, since this is impossible because the future will always be uncertain and will always contain elements of the unknown and the unforeseeable. But any reduction of the odds against an organisation is worthwhile, if achieved at reasonable cost.

Careful analysis may help to remove some degrees of risk, projecting a few rays of light into the darkness of time to come, to show up some of the pitfalls and obstacles and, one hopes, will reflect on some of the opportunities that lie in the organisation's path.

The strategic thinking process includes many ways of progressively defining, measuring and reducing risk, and this chapter is about some of those methods. Much of the chapter is about making assumptions on which to base plans, and using these assumptions to deal with this problem of risk. A brief look will be taken at strategy and its relation to an uncertain future.

A point should be made that an assessment of the risks should form part of any strategic decision process. The prudent organisation does not decide on a strategy, and then assess risks. Instead a consideration of risk and reward precedes the actual decision.

ASSUMPTIONS

Every organisation that sets out to consider a strategy finds that there are numerous items of information missing from its knowledge of things which affect its future. Few people claim to be able to operate a crystal ball, and at first sight the lack of a clairvoyant on the staff may make the task of strategic planning appear impossible. How, for example, can an organisation know what vital profit-reducing action will be taken by government, when even the government may not know? Every year, for which the planning horizon is extended, brings its own increase in uncertainty. The situation need not be as chaotic as it seems, for assumptions can be substituted for the missing elements of knowledge. This means that strategic thinking can be based on a logical structure. But good assumptions can do more than this; they can assist in the assessment of the risks the company faces, and in many cases can lead to actions that would reduce or remove that risk.

An assumption may be defined as a statement of opinion about the occurrence of an event which is outside the control of the organisation. This statement is treated as fact during the development of plans, although the judgement element must never be overlooked.

Assumptions are necessary at all levels of the organisation. Naturally all the relevant assumptions in the overall corporate strategy will be carried over to any detailed functional operating plans that the organisation might require in its planning process, but in addition each of these may have further assumptions of its own. It would not be logical for the overall strategic plan to include the assumption that the marketing department has correctly calculated the financial outcome of its own plans: it would be reasonable for a production division to make such an assumption in its operating plan, where it has to take marketing figures as datum.

The initial reaction of some managers to the making of assumptions is why should they bother, as they haven't a hope of foretelling the future? The stock answer to this is that they are making assumptions even though they do not know it, usually that current events will continue. The tacit assumption is less likely to be correct than an assumption based on a careful evaluation of the facts. Of course, the death knell for a strategic plan is when each manager involved in the planning process operates on his or her own set of assumptions and "hunches". One value of a planning process is that it should co-ordinate the progress of the organisation. To do this effectively it is necessary for the same strategic assumptions to be used by all involved.

This is not to say that opportunity should not be given to managers to discuss the evaluations beforehand, and to play a part in making the necessary judgements. Once issued, the assumptions must be used, even if individual managers disagree and however violent their objections. If risk analysis is carried out correctly no managers need feel aggrieved, since they get their opportunity of evaluating their own bets as well as those imposed on them.

Assumptions should not be used as an escape clause. I have come across operating plans containing statements like:

- "We assume that our forecasts are right."
- "I assume that I will cut staff by 10%."
- "I assume that expenses have been correctly calculated."

These are meaningless, since these are events which are within managers' spheres of influence—for instance, if they do not know if they are going to reduce staff, who else does?

Assumptions should not be blind guesses. In the initial stages of thinking through a strategy the element of guesswork might be fairly high, since the organisation may not have had time to identify the elements that really affect its business. In this case any definition is better than nothing since at least it becomes possible to assess the effect of variance. However, this is not a desirable state of affairs and it is possible to do much better.

Firstly, the organisation should set about defining what outside events and trends really do affect it, work which falls out of the appraisal and assessment of the competitive arena discussed in the previous two chapters. This is where a number of bogies disappear, for many things are not as important as might be imagined. It is too easy to blame poor performance on the economy, the government or the weather, and to let this colour one's opinions about the future: too often these are just scapegoats for a more serious state of affairs. Very often the factor popularly blamed by those inside an organisation for all unfavourable variances has little effect in reality.

Part of the data required for setting planning assumptions will emerge from the external elements of the corporate appraisal. The study of the environment in which the organisation operates is not a once and for all exercise. Instead, it should be a continuous process. There is a need to study the external events which have a bearing on corporate activity. This continuous probing is important regardless of whether the organisation has a formal or informal approach to strategic planning. If something has a high probability of affecting your business, you should try to identify it, understand it, and take appropriate action before it is too late.

It is, of course, impossible to provide a check list of assumptions which will be common to every organisation. Not only will the effect of an event vary between industries, but it will also differ between firms in the same industry. The shaky company may be forced into liquidation by a credit squeeze, leaving more customers to be shared out by those remaining in the industry. A bad English summer might affect the sale of swim-suits (or, more exactly, last year's bad summer may reduce sales of this year's swim-suits) but may not be serious for the firm with a large export trade. So the key assumptions must come out of a study of the expected effect of events on the business of each particular entity.

Obtaining the data on which to base environmental predictions varies from the simple to the difficult.

- Some facts about the future environment are known long before they come into effect. An example at the time of writing is the European common currency. We may only be able to estimate some of the consequences of this, but we know that it has happened. This does not mean that an assessment of the effect on individual organisations is easy, but it does mean that we know that such assessments are important.
- Government and other bodies publish predictions from time to time. Some of these have a high probability of accuracy—for example, population forecasts for the next 5 to 10 years include a large number of people who are already alive: it is in the area of birth rates and immigration that the biggest areas of potential error arise, and the shorter the time span of the forecast, the less important these elements become.
- In some cases a study of past trends from available statistical series may provide the best indicator of future events. The

examination of weather records may, for example, indicate a pattern which may be repeated in future years. If patterns appear to be changing it may be necessary to look at various possible scenarios.

- Often the historic statistical data available are insufficient for a reasoned assessment. Marketing, economic or political research may be required to supplement normal sources of information. For example, in one organisation that used a high volume of powdered milk, the immediate reaction from managers when market prices rose dramatically was that this was just a one-year blip, which sometimes happens with agricultural products. A careful study of the European dairy industry found that, at that time, there had been many structural changes, the European milk mountain had been given out in food aid, and dairy herds had been reduced. There were many assumptions which could be made about future supply and demand, but the one that was certainly wrong was the perceived wisdom that everything would go back to normal the following year.

- Other assessments may have to be built on a study of the background of events. For many organisations the question of world economic development is of considerable importance. Assessment can only be sensibly made after a study of the available political, social and economic facts, a consideration of the opinions of experts in the field and a study of trends in many countries. Fortunately there are many organisations that produce reports about such future trends.

- Futures forecasting is recognised as one means of making predictions that will guide future planning. Predictions of future technological possibilities, often made for time periods well beyond the normal planning horizons, can alter the whole shape of an organisation's strategy. The nature of the organisation's activities will dictate the extent to which it can use such techniques.

Understanding effect of the key environmental trends on the individual business may require the use of particular technique. The assessment may involve the study of past results (Did sales go up or down at the last budget?), marketing research (Do consumers really buy less of product X when it rains?), economic research (Will consumers eat more or less of product Y if their income rises?), and careful judgement (What *would* happen if the company lost most of its business in Southeast Asia?).

At this stage the analyst is ready to set out a concise statement of the planning assumptions. How will the economy change over the next 5 years? What is the likely course of the business cycle? Is there likely to be any change in government legislation in an area vital to the company? Will there be devaluation? How will inflation affect the organisation, and what will the various rates of inflation be?

It will be apparent that someone has to collect and organise the data on which assumptions are to be based. This will involve obtaining the appropriate statistical series, analysing the company's own records and maintaining contact with a network of outside experts whose opinions might be valuable to the interpretation of the environment. Outside agencies may be used to help in their specialist areas: for example, there are many firms which offer an economic forecasting service.

On many occasions the defined assumption will be an opinion, but it will be an opinion on a logical basis, formed after careful study and therefore more likely to be correct than a mere guess.

RISK ANALYSIS

These steps lead naturally to another—a form of risk analysis. If some probability factor can be assigned to assumptions, and if an assessment can be made of the financial results of variance, it becomes possible for top management to judge strategies in a new light. Obviously there is a vast difference in a plan which has a 75% chance of reaching its target compared to one with a 90% chance. If the target is a vital one, it may be necessary to consider additional or different strategies to increase the probability of success.

When assumptions are made, a table of betting odds should be prepared giving the probability of the assumption being correct. When thinking ahead for several years, the analyst should recognise that the probability is unlikely to be the same in each year, and the expected outcome may be set out in the form of Table 5.1. It will not always be worthwhile to predict *which* year an assumption will go wrong.

Table 5.1   Examples of risk analysis assumptions and their probability. (The figures are for illustration only.)

	Probability of being correct in any				
Assumption	1 year	2 years	3 years	4 years	5 years
That no new competitor will enter the market	95%	75%	70%	35%	10%
That there will be no external strikes affecting the company	75%	50%	30%	25%	5%
That inflation will not exceed 5%	90%	85%	50%	50%	33%

The probabilities arise from the exercise that developed the assumption. Frequently they will be based on informed judgement and experience (and, of course, are themselves subject to error). Sometimes they may be calculated from past data (for example, weather records or labour dispute records). The benefit of putting on the betting odds are that the organisation realises that its assumptions may not be correct. This is very important. Of course the organisation should always try to replace subjective with objective data and should never be satisfied with "opinion" probabilities.

Assessment of the results of errors in assumption can provide a cash figure of possible profit variance from the forecast outcome of the strategies. This variance may be favourable or unfavourable, and there may in fact be a scale of variances depending on the intensity of the variance. In my opinion, this assessment should be made by the manager concerned when this form of risk analysis is applied to operational plans. Computer models can be of assistance in improving the scope and validity of these assessments, although it is quite a practical proposition to operate a workable method of analysis without computer assistance. The sort of answer which might result is shown in Table 5.2.

One of the jobs of the analyst will be to draw together all the probabilities of occurrence, and all the risk analyses, into a composite figure, perhaps expressed like this:

- In any one year of the next five we are virtually certain of being within £15 000 of planned profits, and we have a 90% probability of being within £5000, if we follow this strategy.

Table 5.2 Finding profit variance from assumptions.

Assumption that there will be average rainfall during summer	*Profit variance*
Effect on profits of each week of below average rainfall	£5000 favourable
Effect on profits of each week of above average rainfall	£35 000 unfavourable
Total variance unlikely to exceed: favourable	£10 000
unfavourable	£100 000

Similar analyses should be developed for various possible variances in the effect of strategy.

RISK REDUCTION

The use of assumptions does not end here, as they should also be actively used to reduce risk. The "practical" person may feel that the probability exercise is rather academic, but should not have the same feeling about risk reduction.

The first method of risk reduction is the development of contingency plans. These can lead directly from the assumption:

Example 1: The plan is based on the assumption that the major competitor will not change his marketing strategy. What are we going to do if we are wrong? Alternative strategies can be developed for advertising, promotions, etc., so that an immediate response can be made if the competitor does not behave as predicted.

Example 2: An assumption is made that there will be no interruption to distribution through a strike of and blockade by French lorry drivers. A contingency plan can be prepared for the use of alternative methods of transport.

A portfolio of alternative plans can be very valuable as a means of speeding response to changes in conditions (and, of course, can be extended to cover failures in strategy).

The second area of risk reduction is "hedging". An assessment that supplies of an important raw material (on which the company depends) are not at risk, may nevertheless lead to a policy of increasing inventories, or of giving a proportion of business to another supplier, as a hedge in case the assumption is wrong. Often actions such as these cost nothing, and can help the company to safeguard its future profits.

The third area in which risk is reduced is through the operation of an early warning system. If assumptions are clearly defined, and monitored on a regular basis, a change in circumstances will come to light at an early stage. The organisation can then re-examine its strategies and make the necessary adjustments to take it back to its profit targets. If it had not defined assumptions, or if assumptions were not co-ordinated throughout the organisation, the effects of environmental changes might not be realised until the end of the accounting period. One of the benefits of strategic planning is to enable the organisation to react before it suffers from an unkind fate, and the correct use of planning assumptions will help this to come about.

Obviously, no one can foresee every untoward event that may occur. (The unprecedented 1987 storm in Southeast England was unpredictable, but had a major impact on the whole community, and an extreme impact on the profits of builders, electricity supply companies and insurance companies. Builders gained unexpected repair work, electricity companies lost sales through power line problems, and faced large bills to restore supplies, and insurance companies faced very high numbers of claims.) Equally obviously, the organisation that does not try to anticipate any changes will react to some things. Often it will do the right thing for the wrong reason, and it will see those changes in the environment when they are apparent to all. But the organisation which consistently thinks in the way described should consistently have a competitive advantage: in other words, make more correct decisions than it could expect from chance alone.

STRATEGY

In effect, the discussion on contingency plans covered a large part of risk-reducing actions that can be taken during the formation of strategy, but it is worth spending a little time to broaden the line of thought.

Firstly, a sensible approach to strategy will consider various options before a decision is reached. The most favourable option, of course, must be interpreted in terms of the corporate vision and objectives and does not always mean the course which gives the most profit in the short term. This identification of other ways in which the organisation might achieve its objectives, and the same argument applies to the consideration of grand strategies of expansion or acquisition as it does to the various elements that make up a marketing plan, has several advantages. Perhaps the biggest is that the solution first thought of is not always the best one. In addition, as with the deliberate plans made in case of errors in assumption, the organisation has a portfolio of other strategies ready made in case the strategy fails. It must be accepted that even if all the assumptions are correct, a strategy may not be successful because of other factors. To my mind both of these advantages lead to a reduction in risk. There is just one word of warning: the other options must be genuine. The chief executive must be on guard against those managers who make a snap decision of what they intend to do, and then produce a list of "rejected" options as a means of keeping the chief happy. This form of corporate self-delusion helps no one.

There are a number of well-tried techniques which are of value in the consideration of risk in relation to strategy. Each of these can assist in reducing uncertainty.

- Forecasts are more useful as they improve in accuracy. It is not realistic to assume that forecasting will ever become a certain science, but, at the same time, it can be vastly improved in many organisations. A good rule for making a sales forecast is to do it in three stages: the total economy; the total market; the firm's own sales in relation to the market, and the changes to these that different marketing strategies will cause. Statistical trends can be useful (for example, moving averages, semi-averages, "least squares", trend lines) if only so that the forecaster can be sure in his or her own mind of the reasons why the forecasts vary from the extrapolated trend. There is, however, no sound basis for assuming that market trends will follow the growth paths of prior years. Econometric models can bring a greater degree of sophistication to some forecasts, but are complex to build. For some types of forecasts, for example, labour turnover, a statistical extrapolation may provide the basis of the forecast, adjusted by the expected results of action planned by the company (perhaps a high turnover rate may lead to re-evaluation of an element of personnel strategy in order to achieve a lower rate).
- Confidence limits can be placed on forecasts where the company has a back run of forecasts compared with actual results.

Deviations can be measured, and a calculation made to give statistical confidence limits. If, for example, a manager's forecasts have never been more than 90% accurate in the past, is there any reason to expect an improvement in the future? Of course, if circumstances have changed drastically, past data may be no guide.

- Decision trees provide a useful way of setting out complicated alternatives in such a way that management can see the expected results of all the options. For instance, the alternatives facing the founders of the Society for Long Range Planning (now called the Strategic Planning Society) in preparing for its inaugural meeting which could be attended by an unknown number of people might have been summarised in Table 5.3. These are shown in the decision tree in Figure 5.1. It is assumed that there is no possibility of altering this decision once made: if such possibilities did exist they could, of course, be incorporated in the diagram. In this simple example the benefits of the decision-tree approach are minimal the data could easily be perceived in schedule form, and most of us could work out the options in our heads. However, it is not hard to visualise the more normal problem facing management, with all the numerous alternative decisions that can be made, each extending another set of branches. Besides setting down simple options, it is possible to quantify the results (either at current or discounted values) so that the benefits and costs of each decision can be seen, and to show the expected probability of occurrence.

Table 5.3 Viewing the possible options.

Alternative	Outcome	Result
Hire small hall	Less than 100 people attend.	Room just right for audience. Success.
	More than 100 people attend.	Not all will be able to get in. Stigma of bad planning.
Hire large hall	Less than 100 people attend.	Unnecessary expense incurred. Audience appears lost. Meeting a failure.
	More than 100 people attend.	Room just right. Meeting a success.
Hire hall with adjustable partitions	Can cope with whole range of likely attendance.	Room can be made just right. Hire expense as for a large hall.

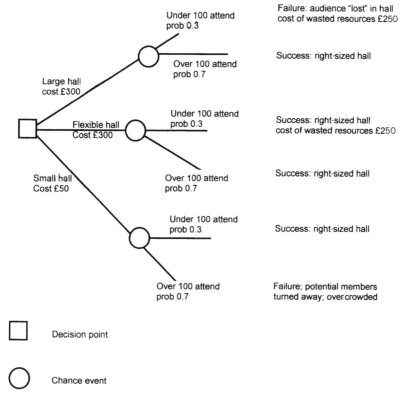

Figure 5.1 Decision tree for the hiring of a hall for the inaugural meeting to found a new society at which an unknown number of people will attend (hypothetical data).

- The various forms of network analysis (critical path, PERT, etc.) are of benefit in identifying all the steps necessary to the implementation of a decision, making sure that all work essential for the next stage has in fact been carried out in time. These methods can shorten the time needed to implement a course of action.
- In an appraisal of a course of action discounted cash flow (d.c.f.), which is explained in greater detail in Chapter 13, may be used. Accepting that forecasts are never absolutely correct, the planner should see that a number of appraisals are made to cover different circumstances: in addition to the expected result, there should be a pessimistic and an optimistic result. This focuses management attention on the fact that there is

not one firm answer, and that the degree of risk, if the pessimistic result applies, may be greater than they are willing to accept. There is, of course, no need to restrict the studies to three: it might be desirable to assess the sensitivity of the d.c.f. rate to various changes in volume, prices, expenses, or capital expenditure values.

• The sensitivity analysis has to be limited if carried out by hand, because of the complexity of the calculations. Using a computer, it is possible to develop a more detailed risk analysis by Monte Carlo techniques. Numerous calculations are made, each of which yields one value for each variable. By random selection one value for each variable is taken from each set of values, and used to produce a d.c.f. analysis. The process is repeated a large number of times so that a frequency distribution of possible d.c.f. rates is built up. From this it is relatively easy to calculate the statistical probability of each rate's occurrence, and to plot these results in diagrammatic form (Figure 5.2). Using this chart, the manager can read off the likelihood of obtaining a return lower than that considered acceptable.

In addition to these specific techniques, there are numerous well-known risk-reducing tools in common operation, such as testing new market concepts before "going national". The process of monitoring and controlling plans means that errors in strategy can be discovered at an early date and, equally important, ensures that managers perform the tasks to which they are committed. In other words, risks due to neglect or non-performance are considerably reduced.

SCENARIO PLANNING AND TURBULENCE

Scenarios have been used over many decades as a way of looking at the future. The argument is that no one is clever enough to make complex accurate forecasts of everything that may happen, so what is really required is to look at a number of possible futures. These are not single event forecasts. They are examinations of complex situations, such as the future of an industry such as telecommunications, or the world political/economic situation in 10 years' time. Within itself, each scenario attempts to be logical: in other words, it does not contain two events which are incompatible with each other, and will include the consequences of one forecast outcome on the other elements of the scenario.

In the 1970s a few organisations developed approaches to strategic thinking based on scenarios, the leading exponent being Shell. Recently there has been a renewed interest in scenarios as a basis for strategic planning, as one way in which organisations can try to find strategies which have the best fit, not just with what the environment is today, but the various ways in which it might develop in the future. The ideal strategy would be one which is robust under all scenarios, and not just the one judged to be most likely. For further information see van der Hejden, 1996 or England, 1998.

The recent work of Ansoff also addresses the issue of environmental risk. His argument is that the way in which an organisation approaches its strategic thinking should be contingent upon the degree of turbulence it is facing. This led him to define five levels or degrees of environmental turbulence, varying from stable to extremely turbulent, against each of which he suggests an appropriate approach to strategic thinking. His hypothesis has been subjected to rigorous research, which proves that organisations which approach strategy in a way which is not appropriate to the level of turbulence do less well than those that get it right. Although much of his approach, and the scenario approach mentioned above, refer to the process of planning, the subject of Chapter 15, they also are part of the whole issue of risk and uncertainty and deserve a mention here.

The application of the methods discussed in this chapter can bring many benefits to an organisation. The benefits are never enough to make strategic decisions easy, but they can make it just that much more certain that there will continue to be an organisation for which to formulate a strategy.

The methods represent only a beginning to the tasks of analysing strategy. The next few chapters will take us deeper into the exploration of strategy.

REFERENCES

Ansoff, H. I. and McDonnell, E., 1990, *Implanting Strategic Management*, 2nd edition, Prentice Hall, Hemel Hempstead.

England, G. R., 1998, *Scenario Planning*, Wiley, Chichester.

Van der Heijden, K., 1996, *Scenarios: the Art of Strategic Conversation*, Wiley, Chichester.

6
Strategic Thinking

THE STRATEGIC TASK

The organisation is now in the position of having identified its strengths and weaknesses: it is aware of the limiting factors which can be removed gradually, as well as those which will act as a constraint on its progress for some considerable time to come. It has defined its objectives—it now knows what the vision of the future organisation it is trying to become and knows the financial results it must achieve over some suitable time-span. The trends in the environment have been assessed, and workable assumptions established on which the strategic thinking can be based.

It is in a position to tackle the strategic task, determining what paths it will take to achieve its objectives. These paths must not only lead it to the profit targets it has set itself, but must ensure that the organisation has the balanced development which is strategically desirable. Even if profits can be met from further investment in current operations, it may be thought that this is too risky a situation and some form of risk-spreading may be required.

Some areas of opportunity will have been revealed by the corporate appraisal and the analysis of the competitive arena, and many major decisions may arise from the factors uncovered by this important step in the thinking process.

But one starting point for the many strategic decisions is the profit target which the organisation has set itself. How it will meet this will be set out in the strategic thinking, whether this results in a written plan, which is the course I favour, or a shared understanding of a strategy expressed less formally. Let us assume that there is a need to put the plan in writing.

As a minimum, a strategic plan should consist of:

- A statement of the corporate vision and objectives.
- The assumptions on which the plan is to be based.
- The strategic issues arising from the corporate appraisal, the environment, and the industry/competitor analysis.
- An assessment of the profit "gap" (see below).
- Strategies arise from the consideration of all these elements, including creative thinking about how opportunities may be exploited, and competitive advantage obtained by changing the industry boundaries.
- A detailed analysis of risk.
- The financial results of the plan.

And, of course, this is really what was indicated in Figure 1.2 in Chapter 1.

The total plan may be underpinned by the operating plans of the established areas of the company.

One of the first tasks is, therefore, the assessment of the profit gap. To assist in this there is a very simple technique called appropriately, "gap analysis", which is shown diagrammatically in Figure 6.1.

The first line on the diagram is the easiest to plot: it represents

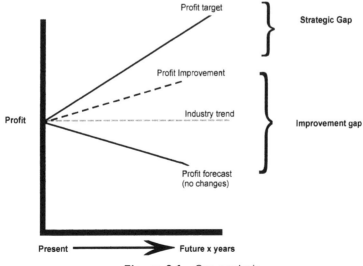

Figure 6.1 Gap analysis.

the organisation's long-range profit targets—the line shown in the diagram is perhaps neater than one is likely to find in practice, but suffices to illustrate what is meant.

Next, and more difficult, comes the profit forecast of the organisation on the assumption that no changes are made to its sphere of operations. Perhaps it is significant that strategic planners usually draw this line so that it plummets downwards at a rapid rate, thus proving a need for strategic planners! In fact the line can move in any direction.

There are three ways of obtaining this line, the forecast of the "present position", but in the final event these will reconcile into one figure. The first line that can be sketched in is the sum of the profit targets which have been set individual operating units: this, of course, assumes that all units will meet, but not exceed, these targets. Profit targets should preferably be agreed in a participative way, and should be discussed in detail with the key managers involved before being firmed up. The second way, which perhaps is a variant of the first, is to make a simple model of the organisation's profits under certain defined assumptions, and to use this forecast in the analysis. Thirdly, it is possible to obtain the operating plans from line management, add these all up, and use this as the relevant data. (It should be stressed that good strategy is rarely arrived at by simply consolidating lower level figures, a theme which will be developed in later pages.)

I find that I usually work by preparing a simple model based on the divisional profit targets, and, in an organisation with a formal planning process, making any necessary adjustments to this after receipt of the operating plans. To me this symbolises the circular relationship of many plans, the numerous "chicken and egg" situations that have to be faced, and a combination of "top-down", "bottom-up" communication.

If corporate targets have been well thought out, there is likely to be a gap between what is required and what is currently expected. This does not follow automatically, of course, and some organisations may find that they can adequately meet their targets (which *might* indicate that a revision of targets should take place). When moving from the gap analysis to strategy, it should not be assumed that existing operations are an immutable element of the strategy. The other factors in the analysis might indicate a need for significant changes.

The next two lines on the figure are perhaps something of a dream, but they are useful as aids to thinking. One is the profit on an equivalent investment which is expected from the rest of the industry in which the organisation operates. This is often difficult to obtain in practice, although the organisation may be able to carry out some useful exercises with what data are available: certainly it should try, for if it is obtaining returns lower than the rest of the industry it may have a lot of problems on its hands. The next line shows the level of improved profits which might come from making alterations to the strategies of the existing sectors of the organisation. Why it is something of a dream is that if all levels of the organisation have been thinking strategically, this will already have been built into the targets and plans of operating management. Where it may be valuable is when the strategy calls for improvement through divestment, or when a corporate improvement plan is required over and above the normal operational actions. In most companies, the "present operations" line and the "improvement" line are likely to merge, within a year or two of the start. There is little point in forecasting a need for improvement, and deferring it for five years.

The difference between the best that can be produced from current operations and the profit target is the important gap for the strategic plan. This is the additional profit that the company must find from the various alternatives open to it: this is what the corporate strategy is all about.

Now, what happens if the strategies devised to fill the gap succeed so handsomely that the target looks as if it will be surpassed, or on the other extreme, if they fail to come within reasonable reach of the target? In the first case the target should be upgraded, since it has obviously been set too low (assuming the forecasts are realistic). In the second case the issue is not so clear cut. If the target is doing its job it should represent the chief executive's interpretation of the profits that have to be earned to satisfy the owners of the business, the shareholders. In these circumstances the chief executive should be prepared to take drastic action: to re-examine all the thinking behind the analyses: to really make sure that no opportunities have been missed, especially those opportunities which another person might spot. I would accept the downgrading of targets as a last resort, but those at the top of the organisation will know that failure to satisfy the shareholders will result ultimately in unpleasant personal consequences. Certainly, failure to devise a means of attaining the corporate objectives must be treated as a very serious matter.

Gap analysis as shown here might be thought to be more suitable for the smaller organisation. However, it is possible to adapt the idea to look at other things besides profit targets, such as the gap between key parts of the vision and current activities. One large global insurance company which I know very well makes this use of gap analysis a key part of every initiative that considers strategy.

FORMATION OF STRATEGY

Every organisation has more than one path along which it may travel. For example, the smallholder growing vegetables can increase sales in a variety of ways:

- Expanding extensively, buying the farm next door.
- Increasing production by intensive methods by applying more resources to the present operations, sowing a better type of seed, applying more fertiliser, irrigating and the like.
- Diversifying, by growing different types of crops from those at present under cultivation, or by adding a goat or a pig.
- Obtaining a higher gross realisation for the produce, by tackling the marketing side of the business in a more sophisticated way.

Our smallholder may follow only one of these paths, or may opt to try all of them. Alternatively, present efforts may be seen as rewarding enough and that the business should carry on doing what it has always done. Probably the smallholder will not even perceive the decision situation as an overall system of choices, and will regard each option as an unrelated decision, without considering any of the others. This may not be serious for a very small business, but it can be very damaging if managers in larger organisations think this way.

Corporate strategy should be seen as an evaluation of the various options open to the company, and a selection of what appears to be the optimum course or courses of action to take. In making this decision the top management should have regard to the organisation's strengths and weaknesses, and the long-range trends that are forecast for the environment.

This evaluation may be extremely complex in, for example, the major multinational company. Ways of approaching this task are the subject of Chapter 8.

Profit should never be the only criteria in deciding a course of action and some account must be taken of risk. Mention has already been made of this (Chapter 5) but it is worth stressing that the strategies eventually decided must be capable of meeting profit targets within a reasonable degree of accuracy. The chief executive cannot afford to be satisfied with a strategy that has only a 50% chance of hitting the required target, although a 90% probability of being within 10% either way might be seen as an acceptable risk. The risk balance of the organisation must also be taken into account. If it is too dependent on one or two products it may feel that its long-term future is being jeopardised, and may slow down on further investment in these areas, preferring to move into another area although the returns may be slightly lower.

The example of the smallholder covered the broad types of choice open to an organisation. Put another way, these are:

- *Finding new markets for existing products.* For example, attacking new segments of the market, selecting new channels of distribution, or expanding geographically.
- *Marketing new products for existing markets.* For example, another style of suit by a clothing company, a new flavour of toothpaste, doing "own-label" branding for others, finding a product that moves through the same channels and can be sold by the usual sales force.
- *Marketing new products for new markets.* Moving into something completely new, such as the tobacco company which diversified into (among other things) potato crisps, and the soft drink firm which moved into tea and other lines. In looking at the tobacco example let us ignore the fact that most tobacco companies which went this route in the 1960s and 1970s have in the 1980s and 1990s divested such operations and gone back to the original core business.
- *Improving the performance of existing products in existing markets.* For example, putting more sales effort behind the products so that turnover is increased, or changing other

marketing strategies (advertising, price, merchandising—or indeed any of the elements of marketing strategy—to the same effect).

These headings come from the famous Ansoff matrix, a version of which appears in Ansoff, 1965, a book which despite its age is still available, although it should be read as a classic, rather than the latest thinking on strategic thinking.

The ways of following these broad courses of action can be thought of under headings such as: research and development, acquisition and merger, expansion, divestment and improvement.

There are perhaps three schools of thought in the selection of options. One, which is hardly relevant to this chapter, is an opportunist strategy. This suggests that expansion and acquisitions should be taken as they arise: each is an *ad hoc* decision stimulated by the opportunities of the moment. In fact an approach which is something akin to this has been given respectability by Mintzberg (see for example Mintzberg and Walters, 1985), who argues that strategies are often not determined by analysis and deliberation, but often emerge from a situation. Now, there is some merit in having an opportunist element in the strategy, and no organisation can afford to turn down a good, relevant opportunity just because it has not been written into a plan. What must be done, though, is to make sure that this opportunity is in line with the visions and objectives, and that the organisation is still moving in the desired direction. The ability to deviate from a planned strategy is a form of the management judgement called for when the strategy was set up: a rigid plan which demands a blind allegiance is not a good plan, and a rigid management is not a good management.

The second school of thought is that the organisation should actively evaluate all foreseeable opportunities open to it, which may mean it entering new industries. Ansoff, 1965 provides a logical and systematic method of evaluating and selecting options. His systems of evaluation take into account the concept of synergy, usually explained by the term "two plus two equals five", and it means that when the new business area is added to the old there should be an interaction which means that the profit generated is greater than it would be if the two parts had been operated separately. So synergy will be related to things like the specialist skills of an organisation, its management talent, its marketing channels, its physical distribution operations, and the products of its research and development effort. This means that the organisation, although it may become a conglomerate through the application of these principles, will not be a glorified unit trust, operating on a risk-spreading plus high profits basis.

For some types of organisations this may be the best way to develop strategy, although modern thinking finds that conglomerate companies do not always add shareholder value to their subsidiaries. Porter, 1987, in an influential article argues that a head office has only very limited ways of adding value to a diversified organisation.

The third, and narrower, school of thought is that organisations should develop along fairly well-defined paths, and that opportunities will only be sought within those paths. The vision of the organisation shows what areas are open to the company in the answer to the question "What business are we in?" This school of thought argues that companies should stay within fields in which they have knowledge. They may move into closely related industries, such as the fruit and vegetable wholesaler, which opened a business merchandising supplies to the growers of the produce they sold, or may integrate backwards or forwards. They may also make seemingly unrelated moves that are part of a larger intention to change the basis of the industry in which they operate. Hamel and Prahalad, for example, would see such moves as one way of adding missing components to the core competencies needed to change the industry and the market it serves.

There is a good deal of merit in this school of thought for certain types of organisation, and where the right sort of growth and returns can be achieved from the defined area. Even within the narrower limits the field of opportunity can be very wide. I think this sort of basic strategic decision appeals to many organisations, and there are a vast number of chief executives who would not allow their businesses to take on the role of a conglomerate. This view is reinforced by the reluctance of financial markets to give wholehearted support to conglomerates.

Modern thinking is that multi-activity companies are only justified when there is added value for the shareholder through being part of a group. Added value can only be obtained if the units within a group can share knowledge, skills, or resources, and a key part of group strategy should be directed at attaining added value. One school of thought argues that if there is no added value, the units should be separated, as the shareholders would be better off this way. Conglomerate companies that can provide no added value have in recent years become targets for stock market raiders, and have frequently been broken up afterwards.

FINDING NEW OPPORTUNITIES

One of the tasks of strategic thinking is to find new areas of opportunity, particularly those which give the organisation a sustainable competitive advantage, and this job should be tackled in an aggressive way. Where should we begin to look?

The marketing-oriented organisation will start at the source of all its profits—the consumer. By studying consumer desires and requirements through a planned programme of marketing research, and through constantly revising market strategies, new opportunities are likely to be uncovered. These have a high probability of being related to the businesses the organisation is currently operating in. This constant probing of markets is vital, whether the organisation is selling products or services, consumer or industrial goods.

The continued studying of the future environment will lead to different ways of doing things, and new areas of business to enter. A trend which is foreseen and which is adverse to the organisation's interests may lead to a strategy which is designed to either take advantage of the new trend, or to do something which will mitigate its effects. This act of trying consciously to foresee the direction of the various factors in the environment is an important one. Not everything can be foreseen, but a surprising number of problem areas and opportunities can result from the constant application of effort to environmental studies.

A third source of new ideas arises from the deliberate evaluation of potential opportunities in new areas. This exercise should, of course, be guided by the vision and objectives of the organisation. The exciting opportunities are those that will change the boundaries of the industry, putting the organisation into a position of advantage because it has changed the rules of the game. Unfortunately this is not something that every organisation can do.

The preliminary data that require to be collected are the extent of the opportunity, the investment required (and several levels will usually be possible) and the expected outcome. So as well as the study of the environmental factors influencing the firm, there is a need for a programme of "desk" research (the study of market data from published sources and informal contacts), comprehensive market surveys where necessary, studies of the records of other companies in the fields of enquiry and the collection of the necessary data from numerous sources.

Desk research may not sound very exciting, but it can yield valuable data about markets and the performance and activities of other companies. It means that some projects can be eliminated at an early stage before great expense is incurred, and that all future steps add to the store of knowledge, rather than duplicating the data available already.

Opportunities may also arise from the corporate appraisal. This can frequently indicate new alternatives and requirements for the firm to consider.

High technology industries in particular should obtain new ideas and products from the research and development effort. The aim should be to *manage* research and development, and to follow a plan, rather than relying on haphazard and chance events. This implies that top management should play a key part in determining R & D projects and priorities, and should not wait until later stages when many of the decisions critical for the future of the organisation have already been taken at a low level in the organisation.

If the internal processes are working well, and all managers are encouraged to give some thought to the future, there is a good chance of stimulating a flow of ideas from managers within the organisation. Each manager will have thoughts about how his or her sphere of responsibility might develop, some of which can provide a very valuable source of opportunity for the organisation.

Finding strategic options for the organisation is not a question of sitting behind a desk waiting for things to happen. There is a great deal of hard work involved, and a requirement for creative thinking. But the deliberate attack on the future is by no means impossible. One object of strategic planning is to remove the chance element from corporate growth, and the more options the organisation finds that are worthy of serious consideration, the more likely it is to be able to select a path that will take it to where it hopes to go.

WHAT SHOULD GO INTO A STRATEGIC PLAN?

There is a lot more to be discussed about strategy, but at this point it is worth pausing to think about how a strategic plan might be written. As mentioned earlier, it is possible to have a soundly thought-out strategy, without writing it down as a formal plan. However, many organisations will need to produce a written plan, so before we go deeper into our exploration of strategic thinking, we should give some thought to what might go into such a document. The outline framework was provided in Figure 1.2, but we should not lose sight of the principles expressed in Figure 1.1.

The approach taken here is to offer a check list of questions which should be considered when preparing a strategic plan. It is not prescriptive, in that I am not suggesting that there is only one way to write such a plan, but if it were my plan I would be worried if it failed the tests set by my check lists.

There are at least two aspects which need consideration. The first is the quality of strategic thinking that goes into the plan: the second is the quality of the planning document, "the plan", as a communication medium and an aid to implementation. Both are important.

If the quality of the strategy is poor, but the plan is superbly written and presented, it will probably help the organisation to do the wrong things effectively, but perhaps with disastrous results. On the other hand when the quality of the strategy is excellent, but the written plan is poor, there is a real danger that it will not be communicated adequately. There may be a failure to implement if there is no clarity about what has to be done.

Attention will be given to both aspects, but before we start I should like to draw attention to a widely observed tendency which I am sure many readers have themselves noticed about plans. Years ago I defined two laws of planning, which all written plans seemed to follow. They are as noticeable in project plans supporting requests for capital expenditure as they are in strategic plans:

1. *In any written plan, everything comes right in the third year.* This does not mean that it will come right, only that the plan says it will. The third year is close enough to appear to have meaning, but far enough away to escape retribution. The underlying psychology is that three years is long enough for things to work out.
2. *The third year never comes.* My second law of planning is that the bounty of the third year is never delivered. Somehow the cornucopia expected three years ago when the plan was made is as empty in the third year as it was in the first two.

Of course things can come to pass as the plan suggests. However, knowing that so many plans show two lean years followed by a time of plenty makes me want to probe very deeply into all plans which follow this pattern. This usually means exploring the information on which the plan was based, as well as studying the strategy itself.

Both of the aspects of the plan which were identified earlier should have a purpose. The most important is the strategic aspect. What objective is the strategy trying to achieve, and is the expected outcome consistent with the aim? This does not mean that the strategy is sound or the plan good, but it indicates whether the writer believes it to be appropriate. If there are no stated objectives, and the expected results are not stated, the plan will be in a vacuum.

The purpose of the written document should also be understood. Clearly it is to describe the strategy that will achieve the objectives. Behind this is another layer of subtlety: for whom is the plan being written? The written document may well take a different form depending on its target readership, and this will affect any critical evaluation of that plan. For example, a business plan written mainly to record the strategy and communicate it within an organisation that is well aware of the background situation may need to contain much less information about the market and company situation than a plan, covering the same strategy, written to gain the support of a remote parent company. In the latter case the decision-makers may have a preferred format for plan presentation, but may lack understanding of the local situation. Part of the rationale for the document may be to persuade and convince upwards, whereas in the first case the purpose was to communicate downwards. A business plan written partly with the intention of gaining support from bankers or major external investors may require a different format again. Before writing a plan, it is worth thinking through what it is to be used for.

Strategies may be good or bad, and even a good strategy may fail through poor implementation, or a poor one succeed because of the skill and flair of individual managers. The following points are designed to help check that there are no basic flaws in the strategy.

Is the strategy identified and clearly stated?

It is impossible to assess a strategy until the strategy is known, a point which is self-evident. Yet surprisingly a very high proportion of the written plans I have seen fail this test. I have ploughed through pages of material on many occasions, and found a history lesson on the organisation, but have had no idea of the strategy it was following. When this happens there is no real plan.

Has it considered competitors and the industry structure?

Competitive positioning is a critical element of strategy. In addition the strategy should be developed with an awareness of competitors, and the moves they are likely to make. The competitive structure of the industry will also affect the possible strategies that might be successful, which implies that the strategy should be considered in the context of the industry structure. If the strategy is to break the rules by changing the power structure of the industry, the method should be clear from the plan. Many of the plans I have examined assume that the desired changes will happen, without there being any reason why they should. Wishful thinking is not the same as a strategy!

Does it match the realities of the market?

All strategies face the test of market realism. New products will only have a chance of succeeding if they meet a requirement of the buyers. Old products will not suddenly increase their sales unless there is a reason. One of the hardest things is to persuade an organisation that has been expanding rapidly on the back of one major consumer durable that there is a saturation point and that product life-cycle theories do in fact apply. Equally hard has been to convince companies to strike a note of realism when taking a successful product into a "new" country. People will not necessarily flock to buy that product just because the corporate plan says they should.

Is the geographical scope appropriate?

In some industries the need for global integration is more important than the need for local responsiveness. The "globality" of the industry must be examined, and strategy tested against this. What appears to be sound on a one-country basis may not be sound when the global nature of the industry is understood—and this is not a static analysis, since global pressures affect more industries each year. In the UK I have often found that managers do not take a world view of their businesses. When I helped in implementing the merger of Vickers and Rolls-Royce Motors in 1980, one of the major achievements was helping to bring about an understanding of the global nature of many of the markets. This led to strategies that were quite different from those previously formulated under the assumption of local businesses (see Stopford, 1989, for a description of this process).

Is it consistent with environmental forces?

The assumptions on which the strategy is based should be stated. No strategy exists in a vacuum, and there are many environmental trends and forces that have an impact on strategy. One test is to examine the extent to which the strategy considers the outside forces.

Are the levels of risk acceptable?

A strategy may look very elegant, but it may also be a disaster if it is a "bet the company" move. In testing a strategy it is important to think of the economic risks the company can take. It may also be valuable to consider whether the chief executive responsible for the strategy is willing to accept the personal risks involved. If not, the strategy may be good but is unlikely to be implemented.

Does it enhance shareholder value?

Some might argue that this test should be number one. I have put it in its present position only because it is not possible to assess the impact on shareholder value until the underlying soundness of the thinking can be gauged. Increasingly, companies are using value-based planning approaches to measure contributions to shareholder value, effectively expressing the outcome of the plans in discounted cash flow terms. There is more to shareholder value than this. A simple example is whether synergy is gained between business units, or whether they are so competitive that they duplicate resources and miss opportunities for joint working or shared resources. Another example is the role of a head office and whether it adds value through how it operates, or merely adds to costs.

Does it match corporate competence and resources?

In other words, can it be done? A common fault is for plans to be too ambitious, to ignore existing factors, or to expect things to happen faster than the organisation can implement them. A related question is: does the plan identify and build on core competencies?

Is the company structure appropriate?

Structure and strategy have to be compatible. Even sound strategies can fail if the structure is designed to fulfil a different strategy to the one chosen. We will return to this and the next point when we consider the management of change in Chapter 14.

Does it match the company culture?

This is a difficult question to answer, but is important. If the strategy calls on the company to act in a manner totally alien to its culture, the strategy has a high chance of failing unless the culture is changed. Scandinavian Airlines offers a good example. In the early 1980s it introduced a strategy, one plank of which was customer responsiveness. The culture at the time was bureaucratic, with all decisions referred upwards. To be responsive meant driving many decisions much lower in the organisation, and to make this happen meant that the company had also to plan for a major change in company culture.

Does it have an appropriate time horizon?

The plan should be developed to cover the time period necessary to fulfil it. A strategy that ended with a major investment, with no outcomes shown for that investment, would clearly be deficient. The plan should not be positioned on the salami system, with just a few slices of investment shown, disguising the fact that the real shape is a semicircular sausage and not a flat circle! There may sometimes be a need to develop the strategy for a longer period than the company's planning process requires. In fact, one of the problems of business units of a larger corporate entity is that often the corporate planning horizon is too long or too short for their situation.

Does the plan have internal consistency?

The final test question on the strategy asks whether the plan is logical and hangs together. It may sound a trivial point to those who plan well themselves, and it is not usually the obvious that goes wrong, such as marketing planning to expand sales without manufacturing being able to produce the increased volume. In my experience the two most common problems are quantification and people. The quantified results of a plan should be related to the strategies in the plan, but sometimes they are put together using ratios and growth factors which do not take account of the costs

and rewards of the actual actions planned. The second co-
ordination area which seems to defy logic is the changes that
have to be made to structure, culture and human resources. This
section of the plan often appears to be put together without any
consideration of the strategies.

THE MISSING QUESTION

The discerning may feel that this list of points to look out for misses
the most important, which is whether the strategy is sound. This is
of course the most critical issue, and one of the most difficult to
reduce to a few sentences. Experience in strategic thinking and
knowledge of those principles that have been defined are the two
most important elements. Yet experience also shows that, because
most of the principles are statements of tendency, rather than rigid
rules, a strategy that defies the accumulated wisdom of the experts is
not necessarily bad. There is also an element of fashion in strategic
thinking. In the 1970s portfolio arguments of having cash cows to
fund stars, and wildcats that may become future stars, would have
figured in the judgements of strategy, whereas today adding shareholder value is seen as of more significance.

The principles and approaches discussed so far, and those we
have yet to discuss should provide a sound basis, for the strategy,
we should borrow also the words of the great economist Alfred
Marshall (1920).

> It is doubtless true that much of this work has less need of elaborate
> scientific methods, than of a shrewd mother-wit, of a sound sense of
> proportion, and of a large experience of life.

He goes on to add a qualification:

> Natural instinct will select rapidly, and combine justly, considerations which
> are relevant to the issue in hand; but it will select chiefly from those which
> are familiar; it will seldom lead a man far below the surface, or far beyond
> the limits of his personal experience.

Although applied to economics, the words are equally relevant
to that branch of economic activity, the formulation of strategy.

THE QUALITY OF THE DOCUMENT

Plans are written for different purposes, and the particular purpose should be considered when the plan is evaluated. There is a wide spectrum of styles and formats that could be applied, and the suggestions below accept that there is no one right way to write up the plan.

Concise but clear

A plan should be as brief as possible, but must communicate the strategy: a verbose plan may be less clear than a concise one, particularly if it is also poorly structured. Sometimes, it is useful to impart information that is relevant to the plan: a good plan would probably separate the information (for example, market evolution) from the strategy section, but would demonstrate that the information has been used through the way the strategy is presented. Experience shows that lengthy narrative information sections that appear in plans often have nothing to do with the decision process in the plan. What is there should be integrated.

Use of diagrams

One of the best ways of relating strategy to complex data is through diagrammatic displays. For example an industry "map" may show the key data about the competitive structure of the industry on one piece of paper. A portfolio diagram allows the strategic situation of various business units to be compared, again on one piece of paper. Matrix displays of any type may add clarity, compress information and relate the strategy to the information.

Structure of the plan

The plan must have a structure, and that structure should aid understanding. Without being dogmatic about order of presentation or content, there should be, as a minimum, sections on the strategic situation, internal strengths and weaknesses, vision and objectives, the chosen strategies, expected results and the action plan. It does not mean that a plan is bad if it lacks these, but it raises a line of questioning.

Too many actions

Corporate strategic plans are fairly broad. Plans at lower levels exchange breadth for depth. In both, a common error is to be over-optimistic about the number of new initiatives that can be implemented in a given period. All strategic actions planned must be considered against the resources of the unit and other claims on time, and should include realistic assessments of the actual time an action will take. A plan should not become a do-it-yourself hangman's kit.

Implementation

The final test is around implementation. Even a sound strategy can fail if attention is not given to implementation. The plan should address this, by establishing goals (milestones) to measure progress, breaking down the strategy into main action plans, and dealing with the issues which arise from this.

Issues may include involvement of those who will be required to implement, training in new skills needed to implement, communication and appropriate control mechanisms.

All of the above points can be compressed into a few sentences. We need to:

- Understand the strategy.
- Be convinced of its soundness in relation to industry structure, competitors, the market and the environment.
- Be convinced that it fits the competence and resources of the organisation.
- Establish that it can be implemented.
- Know the purpose for which the plan is written.

REFERENCES

Ansoff, H. I., 1965, *Corporate Strategy*, McGraw Hill, New York.
Hamel, G. and Prahalad, C. K., 1994, *Competing for the future*, Harvard Business School Press, Boston, MA.

Hayes, R. H., Wheelwright, S. C. and Clark, K. B., 1988, *Dynamic Manufacturing*, Free Press, New York.

Marshall, A. [1920]. *Principles of Economics,* 8th edn. Macmillan, London, 1956.

Mintzberg, H. and Waters, J., 1985, "Of strategies deliberate and emergent", *Strategic Management Journal,* July/Sep.

Porter, M. E., 1987, "From competitive advantage to corporate strategy", *Harvard Business Review,* May/June.

Skinner, W., 1978, *Manufacturing in the Corporate Strategy,* Wiley, New York.

Stern, C. W. and Stalk, G., 1998, *Perspectives on Strategy from The Boston Consulting Group,* Wiley, New York.

Stopford, J. M. (1989). *Vickers Plc A.* London Business School, London.

7
A Closer Look at Strategy

We are now ready to give some consideration to some of the options which may be chosen in order to achieve a particular strategy. However, we should not forget that none of these are undertaken for their own sake: they are possible ways of moving from a strategic intention to its fulfilment. They are all a means to an end.

DIVESTMENT

Sometimes it is necessary to withdraw from an area of the business. This may be because the corporate appraisal reveals that it is unlikely to ever make satisfactory profit levels, that it is seen as having no potential for the future, or that it is a good business, but the organisation does not have the financial resources to invest in it. The trigger may be because of changes in the environment, such as political action in an overseas territory which insists that all employees be indigenous regardless of suitability, or that profits may no longer be repatriated. It may simply be that the company's overall strategy would be better served if management effort were to be concentrated in other directions. Or of course it may just be that the business is poor, and should have been dealt with many years before.

When a divestment decision is taken, any opportunities which may arise in that area are almost certainly bound to be lost to the company for ever, so it is not a decision to be taken lightly. In addition, divestment may cause motivation problems in other areas of the organisation, and may alter the culture of the organisation. So a divestment strategy calls for a fine degree of management judgement and, sometimes, a large amount of management courage.

Of course this sort of decision may be large or small. It may involve the shedding of a product range that requires no change to production facilities, it may mean the closing of a factory or overseas subsidiary, selling those assets no longer required, or it may mean the sale of a section of the business to another organisation as a going concern.

In each case careful planning will be necessary to see that the divestment is handled in the best manner from the organisation's point of view. There may be far-reaching effects on personnel, arising from redundancy and redeployment, and it may be necessary to take steps to use the public relations function to refurbish the corporate image, which may have become a little tarnished during the divestment operation. Steps must be taken to see that the company's assets are disposed of in the most profitable way, and that the divestment is undertaken in a manner which has the least detrimental effect on the company's earnings.

Conflicting interests may have to be reconciled. On the one hand, it may be desirable to give early warning to employees and their trade unions of the action intended: on the other hand, it may be feared that such action would cause the key people to leave too soon, with the inevitable effect on production.

There are a variety of ways of divesting a complete business unit, although the quality of the business being divested will affect what is possible. In addition to offering the activity for sale to another organisation, which has become a common method, it may be made the subject of a management buyout. It may be floated as a public company, with the seller disposing of all or part of the shares, an action which is used particularly when the organisation is trying to return value to the shareholders. It can be broken up, and the assets disposed of in the best way possible. Its assets may be redeployed within the organisation, although this can rarely be achieved without major changes to structure and personnel. Redeployment should not be used unless there is a clear strategic benefit, as it may just be deferring a problem. For example Timex, when it transferred the manufacture of watches from the factory in Dundee, used the plant to move into electronic sub-contracting. There was a massive reduction in the work force, but despite this the new activity was not successful and eventually closed. It appears that the continuation of a plant in Scotland was a matter of an emotional commitment, rather than an essential part of the corporate strategy.

It is also possible to divest an activity by merging it with the business of a much larger competitor, in return for shares in the enlarged activity. This may not realise an immediate return, but it can transfer responsibility of management, and may turn a wholly owned subsidiary into an investment, with a different accounting treatment.

CONSIDERATION OF ALTERNATIVES

All actions that may be considered are to some extent options from which a choice has to be made. If an organisation decides to double the size of a factory, this may be considered a better course than starting up a new factory elsewhere. But within the choice of getting bigger in what you are doing currently, or in some way changing the scope of your activities, there are choices to be made: not only alternative answers to questions like "How big an expansion?", but completely different ways of tackling the problem. These may take the organisation to a crossroads. It can:

- Acquire another company.
- Enter into a strategic alliance with another organisation.
- Obtain a licence for a new product from another organisation.
- Develop a product from its own research, skills, or technologies.
- Outsource more of its own activities.
- In certain types of activity, hire suitable people and begin operations.

For example, it is possible to obtain an increased share of the market by increasing the capacity of production facilities and adjusting marketing strategy, or by buying up a competitor in the same line of business (so long as this does not cause the organisation to fall foul of the monopolies legislation), by adding core competencies to increase technological capability, or by some form of strategic alliance. It may be that the best approach requires higher quality or lower cost, which takes the organisation into another range of options.

A well thought out strategy will evaluate all realistic options as part of the analytical and decision processes. That this is not always done is evidenced by the number of organisations that rush blindly into acquisition, following fashion instead of logic.

ACQUISITION AND MERGER

The acquisition of other businesses is one of the glamour areas of modern management. In theory, acquisition offers a number of advantages where the circumstances are right. These advantages include:

- Opportunity for gain from synergy (although it must be remembered that other strategies could have a higher synergy content).
- The ability to obtain immediate profits, rather than facing a period of loss for several years while business is built on a "green field" approach.
- It may bring valuable patents and licences to the company.
- In some cases it may be less risky than developing a completely new business.
- It may be the best way of obtaining a team of people with the required technical and management skills.
- In some instances it may be the only way to break into a market profitably.
- The reduction of competition (although most countries have legislation to prevent this going too far).
- It may be the only way to weld together a worthwhile business in a fragmented industry (past examples are the textile and machine tools industries): the opportunity may lie in reorganising the industry, rather than decreasing competition.
- There may be financial advantages, such as the ability to acquire a company with large liquid reserves, by an exchange of shares.

Of course, in evaluating the options, it is most important to ensure that the advantages really exist. There have been various studies which suggest that many organisations are disappointed with the results of their acquisition policies, and that the expected additional profits from the synergistic effect have never materialised. In fact, research studies over a period of 30 years have found a high failure rate, most putting it as high as 50%. Failure can occur in a variety of ways, including:

- Lack of strategic fit. During 1998 the Pearson group have been disposing of businesses which no longer fit the strategy: some of these were acquired only a few years ago. Although they may have run those businesses profitably, the opportunity cost of following the wrong strategy can be very high.
- Failure to ensure that what you think you are buying matches reality. Due diligence procedures help, but there are still many situations where the buyer has found major surprises after purchase. For example, Carlson, a US-based leisure company acquired Inspirations, the tour company which owned the charter airline Caledonian, in 1997. Within a few months press reports were discussing the differences between Carlson's understanding of Inspirations and what it actually found after purchase, and hinting at impending litigation. It is clear that the knowledge Carlson had of Inspirations was insufficient, although the reasons for this are unclear. The real issue is whether they could have discovered the key facts before they bought the company, and if the matter goes to litigation we may well find out.
- Poor implementation of the post purchase aspects of the acquisition, resulting in loss of value, confusion, and opportunity cost. Most of the research studies have found this to be one of the causes of acquisition failure.
- The first three causes are all avoidable. It may be that there are others which are beyond anyone's control, such as the Ladbrokes 1998 problem with its purchase of Bass's betting shops. Informal advice from government officials, and past monopoly reports, showed that the purchase would be allowed. However in the event government ruled that Ladbrokes must sell these outlets within six months.

A planned approach does not leave acquisitions to chance. It is deliberate and, one might almost say, cold-blooded. A bid is not made for a company solely because a competitor has recently made an acquisition. It is not an action taken because it is fashionable, but because careful and objective analysis has revealed that this is the best course of action to move along the chosen strategic path to the corporate vision and objectives.

Once the organisation has identified the opportunity area in which it wishes to expand, and has decided that acquisition is the right way to go, it becomes necessary to define with great care what type of company should be bought. At this stage it is too early to try to name companies which might be available, as this will only cloud the vision. Instead an *acquisition profile* should be prepared, stating as finely as possible the characteristics of the desired acquisition. In other words, the corporate identity of the organisation which will meet the strategic requirements should be described as precisely as possible.

The acquisition profile should both identify and quantify those factors which are seen as important attributes of the intended acquisition. Concentration must be on the essential factors, which would cover such items as size, management capability, sphere of operations, technical skills. An example will make this clearer.

Acquisition Profile: Marine Heating & Ventilating Company

1. *Size*:	To cost not more than £20 million at an initial return on capital employed of not less than 10%.
2. *Products*:	Design and manufacture of complete environmental control systems for the shipping industry.
3. *Market position*:	Must have at least 10% of the UK market and must have customers in more than five shipyards. Must have 25% of sales in export markets, including Norway, Holland and Japan. At least 90% of sales must be in original equipment. Turnover—about £30 million per annum.
4. *Technical position*:	Must be accepted in its industry as a leader in technical innovation. Over the past five years an average of at least 5% of annual sales must have been spent on research and development.

5. *Management*:	Competent management at all levels is desirable. Good top management is essential, as is technical management at all levels.
6. *Factories*:	Plant and equipment must be relatively modern (90% of plant must be under five years old). Factory must be located in the north-east of England. The site must have room for expansion, and it must be physically possible to treble output within three years.
7. *Conditions*:	No company will be acquired unless it is possible to obtain all the voting shares.

This example is, of course, a hypothetical one. In practice, some of the characteristics identified may prove to be unimportant, and others which have not been included may be the critical factors. As the object is to mould the acquisition to the requirements of the individual organisation, factors which are vital to one firm may be insignificant to another.

The next stage is the matching of real organisations to the acquisition profile. The way to tackle this is to prepare a list of companies in the field, and to begin to build up a profile of each of them. At an early stage it may be possible to reject some companies which are obviously too large or too small to be suitable. Of course, the shorter the list can be made, the less work there will be in developing the final profiles. There is a danger in being too precipitous. Even a large company may be willing to sell off one sector of its business under some circumstances, or it may be possible to combine two or more small companies to meet the overall requirements of the profile.

A statement that a list of potential candidates is required is one thing: making the list is another, and this is not always easy. Some of the basic sources of data for such a list are discussed below (a more extensive listing of sources and why they arise is in Hussey 1998).

Directories

The many admirable trade directories make an excellent starting place. It will usually be found necessary to extract information from a number of directories, and even then the resulting list may not be complete.

Supplementary sources of data include lists of memberships in Trade Associations, when these can be legitimately obtained. It is often possible to purchase lists of companies in specific product sectors from direct mail firms.

Directories vary in accuracy and in the scope of their content, but will frequently yield information on such items as main products, factory locations, number of employees, turnover, and affiliations to other companies.

Company reports

Information on shareholders and certain statutory financial data can be obtained from a search at Companies' House (the name of the company must be known). In many cases this can be supplemented by the company's published report to shareholders. There are organisations which provide an excellent service in scanning and extracting information from these sources, publishing regular reports on a large number of public companies.

Market intelligence

Publicity statements, newspaper and magazine articles and even trade advertisements can yield a rich harvest of valuable facts. It is easiest to consult these if a market intelligence section is run by the company, which would index and file all potentially valuable data so that it could be retrieved at a later date. Without such a system, the task of scanning back numbers of innumerable publications can be a formidable one, although abstracting services and databases may be of considerable help.

Information from these sources may be varied in nature. Market shares, sales office locations, product range, plant capacity, labour relations records, the size of the company's own lorry fleet, developments in research and development, are a few examples.

Market surveys

Original marketing research provides a good source of data, yielding lists of candidates, market shares, product image and the like. Surveys can also be specially commissioned to investigate, for example, the corporate image of the candidate. Such an action might be desirable to obtain data for the profile above on the degree of acceptance the industry has of the candidate's technical leadership.

Personal knowledge

Within the organisation there are often stores of knowledge of the activities of potential candidates for acquisition. This is not to advocate a policy of industrial espionage, and *definitely* not the "persuasion" of an employee to divulge information about a company for whom he has once worked. But contact with customers or with competitors in the same industry means that it is often possible to build up a dossier of facts from legitimate sources, such as, the extent of sales coverage, methods of sales, competence of management, location of facilities, product strengths and weaknesses, age of top management, employee relations, and, less detailed but potentially useful, further additions to the list of potential candidates.

Databases

There are now many databases which can be readily accessed, and which combine many of the foregoing sources. The two major advantages of databases are that the search can encompass a wide spread of source documents including the most current, and that the search methods allow fast identification of relevant material. The disadvantage is that all sources are not included, and it is easy to miss information which can only be obtained from traditional library search methods. Many databases can be accessed via the Internet.

As new batches of data come to hand, a short list can be compiled of companies which might be acceptable. The final list should be written up in order of desirability. If no companies at all emerge from this process it may be necessary to re-examine either the basic strategy of acquisition, or the profile itself. The ideal partner may not exist, and something less than perfect may have to be accepted.

At this stage there should be some thought given to what should be done if the bid is successful, in order to ensure that the organisation avoids all the failure traps listed earlier

The painstaking work involved in a serious acquisition study is well illustrated by the Guinness and Argyll battle for Distillers. The outcome was that in 1986 Guinness won this bid, although share-rigging actions which were illegal contributed to this victory. Argyll, in preparing their strategy for Distillers, had studied published reports for 15 years, and of the 80 subsidiaries for 10 years. Analysts' reports and press cuttings were examined for more than a 20 year period. Published market research was examined, and original research commissioned to study Distillers' products. An external inspection was made of all Distillers' property and photographs taken for study. From all this Argyll derived a feel for the individual profit centre contributions and an understanding for Distillers which was probably almost as great as that possessed by Distillers' themselves. In this example the stakes were high, but the principle of careful study should be extended to all acquisitions.

The process of opening negotiations with a company, either direct or through an intermediary such as a merchant bank, is outside the scope of this book, as are the many legal implications of takeovers and mergers, and the methods of valuation, although this is not meant to imply that these matters are not important.

At about this point the organisation should draw upon the skills of the appropriate members of the management team to refine the provisional plan for dealing with the company in the event of a successful bid. Responsibility should be assigned to a particular member or members of the team to perform particular duties in connection with the acquisition, and a time-table should be established to ensure that the necessary action takes place. In any integration process, speed is of the utmost importance, and although there will always be areas in which insufficient data are available for sensible decisions, it is vital that any necessary post-acquisition investigations be pursued with alacrity and diligence.

Failure to act within the first few weeks of acquisition can cause difficulties later, particularly if there are redundancies or alterations to management responsibilities in the newly acquired company. Many human problems will be caused if action is unnecessarily staggered over a lengthy period, since each fresh burst of decisions will cause anxiety to those who have not yet been investigated. It goes without saying that appropriate action should be taken to ensure that the services of key staff in the acquired company are secured, which implies that the key staff must be identified at an early stage.

It follows that the speed with which decisions must be made will mean that a broad brush is used, and that some mistakes are possible. This is preferable to the blight of frustration and despair that can settle on a whole company as it desperately awaits the announcement of its fate. Speedy action avoids the paralysis which follows this blight: slow and sporadic outbursts of unpopular decisions may extend it indefinitely.

The third path, to take no action at all to integrate, may mean that the expected synergistic results do not materialise.

So far the discussion has centred on the situation where the organisation is in a position to be very specific on the criteria for the companies it wishes to acquire. In some firms the position may be a little different, in that the choice may have been limited to an organisation of specific characteristics, but there may be broader scope for choice in its operations. It may be of little strategic importance whether the acquisition makes canned meat or frozen peas, although it is likely that some parameters will be set for product and geographical sphere of operations. It is not hard to visualise circumstances when this method would be the most suitable one. A company with a large diversification programme may prefer to operate within the broader frame, on the premise that any four of, for example, ten types of industry would meet its strategic requirements. Another situation where this approach may be preferable is with the conglomerate which is actively seeking investments over a wide range of possibilities. However, this comes with a health warning, that if this is the overall strategy, it should be double checked before any acquisitions are made, as in the developed countries there are many factors which militate against a conglomerate strategy. The same arguments are not always valid in Third World countries, where there may be other circumstances that make conglomerate activity desirable.

AN EXAMPLE OF A BROADER ACQUISITION PROFILE

Business activities

The XZY Company intends to diversify into four new business areas, and to achieve this end will acquire suitable companies in the food industry in Europe, the USA and North Africa.

Acquisition efforts will be concentrated on companies which have a demonstrable record of product development. The companies must have strong franchises in advertised and branded consumer food products, and must hold not less than 10% of the domestic market in their product categories.

Food industry investments will be selected from companies in any of the following areas:

- Coffee and tea.
- Canned foods.
- Pet foods.
- Sweets and chocolates.
- Sauces, pickles and condiments.
- Frozen foods.

Restriction

Not more than two companies will be acquired in any one country, and not more than one will be in North Africa.

Size

The minimum size of any company by turnover will be £30 million per annum, of which at least 75% will be domestic sales.

Profitability criteria

No acquisition will be considered that does not offer the prospect of returning 10% on shareholders' capital, within 3 years and after taxes. The average return on capital employed during those 3 years must not be less than 8%. Profits (after tax) of at least £300 000 per year must be possible.

Any acquisition in North Africa must yield 20% return on capital employed, according to the above definitions.

Ownership and management

No company will be acquired unless at least 80% of equity can be obtained, and 100% is preferred.

The competence of management, proved by past records, and the continued availability of key people is an essential factor in any acquisition.

In either approach to acquisition profiles it is essential to try to establish areas of synergy. The various criteria should, of course, bear this concept in mind, and at the various evaluation stages when the merits of individual acquisition candidates are evaluated, areas of synergy should be very much to the fore.

The acquisition path can bring great rewards, but is also beset with many dangers. It is neither the way for the fainthearted nor the foolhardy.

STRATEGIC ALLIANCES

Joint ventures have always been with us as a strategic option. Perhaps the oil industry offers the longest historical view of the use of this approach, often forced on the companies because of the costs of developing an oilfield, or by the fact that control of production or markets may be divided so that limited collaboration is desirable. During the 1980s, the joint venture option became broadened to a concept of strategic alliances. Today it is probably the airlines that have developed the most complexity and variety in a major commitment to alliances. A strategic alliance may involve investment by two or more companies in a specific venture. It may be broader, and involve forms of collaboration over marketing, technology, manufacture or other factors that are to the benefit of both companies. This second form of strategic alliance is appealing, but much more difficult to manage. In an acquisition or merger the partners become one. In a joint venture it is possible to set up an organisation to fulfil the required purpose, although not always without some clashes of objective between the partners. In the other form of alliance the companies may operate through their existing structures, making it difficult for either party to control what is happening.

The drive for alliances is partly fuelled by the fact that in many industries, for example the defence industries, the number of large players who may be available for acquisition is close to zero. Companies still need to find ways of competing with global competitors who may be operating on a larger scale. Alliances offer one way of doing this, or of obtaining benefits from larger market operations without the risks or requirement for high investment. The avoidance of what may be very high levels of investment may itself be the driving force. In some situations, government controls or protective rules may make alliances the only way of getting into a particular market.

The steps in selecting alliance partners are similar to those in finding acquisition candidates. However, an additional essential step is to ensure that each party is aware of the objectives of the other before any agreement is signed. If the aims of the alliance partners are not compatible, the chances are that the alliance will break up quickly. A second requirement is not to underestimate the amount of management attention needed to make an alliance work. It is worth being realistic about the expected life of an alliance, since once the objectives of the partners changes, the alliance may become unworkable. It follows that alliances that are established for a medium-term purpose have more likelihood of succeeding than an alliance that pretends it is a merger.

EXPANSION

The strategy need not involve acquisition at all, and the concept of synergy may be used in considering the other options which are at the organisation's disposal.

It may, for example, be decided that the best action to take is to expand the areas of activity in which the organisation is already engaged. The decision will have a very high synergy content, but may not improve the balance of risks in the organisation. The strategy would calculate the capital expenditures required for each of the existing areas of the organisation, the time-table of events, and the expected results.

Three ways of diversifying can be conveniently considered under this heading. The first is open to firms wishing to enter industries with a low technological threshold, which is to go ahead and do it. We see this every day in the mushrooming of small businesses, such as specialist retailers, where entry barriers are low. Failure rate may also be high, not because this method of expansion is inherently weak, but because from a zero base, it is difficult to develop a strategy that delivers a long-term, sustainable competitive advantage.

The second method is to hire key personnel with the requisite skills and technical expertise. The disadvantage is, of course, that a good deal of confidence may have to be placed in people who are an unknown quantity. But this strategy would enable diversification into areas of a higher degree of technology than would be possible under the first method.

The third opportunity is to obtain licences for processes, or the rights to patents. Agreements are possible on a royalty basis or, sometimes, outright purchase of the invention, process or formula. In some cases it may be possible to facilitate entry into a new market, by acquiring the licence to a well-known trade mark: in the simplest of situations this may involve little more than a quality-control definition, and the right to apply the brand. Any licensing arrangement may require the hiring of key personnel, although it is frequently possible for the licensor to provide facilities for training. Such agreements may be better as joint ventures, so that a continued flow of data becomes available from the licensor, who is also able to maintain some control over what happens to the licences. Licensing is, of course, very common in industries requiring advanced technology, and for the company selling the licence the method offers a means of gaining income without all the risks of exploiting the opportunity by other means.

Licensing presents a special problem, in that it is not always easy to find organisations with licences on offer. A continued study of technical literature may provide the right leads, but possibly the best way to proceed is, having identified a range of licence requirements, to use the services of one of the agencies which specialises in bringing interested parties together.

RESEARCH AND DEVELOPMENT (R & D)

Growth, diversification and expansion can also be obtained from the firm's own programme of research and development and, of course, this may also be used to help the marketing effort by finding new uses for existing products, or by bringing about continued product improvement.

Research and development is one of the most difficult areas to approach in a strategic manner, yet in many companies it is an area of great expense, on which the future profits depend almost in their entirety. The importance of R & D will vary with the philosophy of the individual company, and the state of technology in its industry.

In my opinion an R & D plan should seek to clearly establish research targets for every product being considered. Why is the research and/or development work needed, and what does it seek to achieve? The setting of this type of target should not be left solely to the manager of the R & D department, who must be guided by marketing needs, and top management strategic requirements. I like the type of research target which not only describes the requirements and physical performance of the product as perceived by marketing department, but also gives guidance on the cost brackets within which the product should ultimately be manufactured. This type of guidance prevents a new product being developed which cannot be sold profitably because its production costs are too high.

Alongside the research and development targets should be set an expression, quantified where possible, of the benefits that success in this area would bring.

Equally important are priorities. The key is to avoid falling into the trap of doing the work which is of most personal interest, rather than work which will contribute most to the organisation's success. Top management should give guidance on the most important strategic areas, and a way will have to be found of reconciling the various claims for attention of the other departments of the organisation.

Another factor required for the plan is the maximum amount the organisation is prepared to invest in research and development on each project. In some cases, as for example pure research, there may be no limit, and the organisation may be willing to invest indefinitely in various lines of research in the hope of gaining a worthwhile discovery. In, for example, development work it may be possible to see that £x research would bring a benefit to the organisation, but that at £3x it might take an overlong period for costs to be recovered. It is, of course, important for the R & D manager to assess whether any worthwhile research is possible within the parameters set.

The strategic plan should also include schedules showing the time required for each project, and the disposition of the resources.

The amount of detailed planning which can be carried out in the R & D area will vary from firm to firm. In some organisations, particularly where the accent is on development work rather than research, it may be possible to plan ahead for a period of only 2 to 3 years, although the organisation as a whole may plan for a longer time span.

The modern tendency is for research thinking to probe deeper and deeper into the future, influencing strategic planning although *detailed* research planning will not necessarily outpace the overall planning system. What enables this longer-term thinking to be effective? It is the careful application of technological forecasting, which can be a very useful and dynamic tool in R & D planning. Its effects will also condition other elements of the overall strategy, for despite its name, technological forecasting can also be used to make forward assessments in fields outside of technology, such as social and economic activity.

A number of "futures" institutes and "think-tanks" now exist to apply the techniques to a wide range of environmental issues, and to improve the methodology.

Unfortunately, many of the supporters of technological forecasting have erected a barrier between themselves and line management. The experts have thrown up such a cloud of jargon, that their ideas and explanations are screened from the view of the executive or manager who is expected to make use of the techniques! It is possible to get behind the smokescreen of jargon.

Technological forecasts seek to provide estimates of developments which are likely to occur in the future (some of the methods used will be explained later). The forecasts provide management with the basis for deciding which technologies are about to be overtaken by new developments, which ones are likely to have a lot of life left in them, and on which areas research should be concentrated (or abandoned) to help bring about the state of affairs which the company sees as both probable and desirable. Unfortunately, the best of the techniques still leaves management with some tough decisions, one of the most difficult being the point at which to switch to a new technology. But in the dark, even the glimmer of a candle can be very welcome, and technological forecasting rates higher than this. It can help decide research direction and priorities, and it introduces a wider range of factors into the decision process. And like all techniques, its usefulness will vary with the size and nature of the company.

A number of tongue-twisting names have been invented for the numerous methods of approach developed by the technological forecasters. Phrases like "normative relevance trees" and "morphological analysis" seem to me to confuse more than they explain and I shall try to avoid all such references in this brief outline of the methodology. It goes without saying that all methods require the participation of people who are experts in their particular field of technology.

One method, which has an obvious link with general economic forecasting, is the examination of trends and their extrapolation into the future. For example, it is possible to plot the development of a particular technology over a span of years, measuring an efficiency function on the vertical axis. Imagine such a chart plotting the development of military weapons: the efficiency index might be the weapons' destructive ability. On our imaginary graph we can plot man's first weapon, "stones", and one of his latest, "H-bombs". In between are spears, bows and arrows, swords, guns, bombs, and the like, each successive development bringing increased destructive ability, and occurring in an ever-decreasing time span. This is the past trend. The next step is to extrapolate this trend in terms of the next likely technological development and its position on the destructive ability index.

A more useful derivation of this method is to plot the capability life-cycle curve of each individual technology, extrapolating the curves so that it becomes possible to estimate the point at which one technology is overtaken by another. The life-cycle curve will have the typical "*S*" shape. Visualise a chart showing bow and arrow and gunpowder technologies. The first example would have a fairly short development time, the bottom of the "*S*" curve, a relatively short climb over a relatively short period as destructive efficiency increases, and a long top of the "*S*" lasting centuries, as

peak technological development was reached. Gunpowder technology would start with a destructive efficiency somewhat below
the other curve, thus for a while both technologies would overlap.
For several hundred years destructive efficiency would increase,
until this technology reached its peak of performance and turned
the top of the "*S*" curve.

This particular application will often reveal the turning point of
a technology's life cycle. It will not always enable management to
predict exactly what will replace a technology, but may act as a
warning that a replacement is probable.

The technological forecaster would be likely to supplement these
extrapolative predictions with forecasts made by other methods.
For example, one approach is to postulate a desirable future
technological state. The forecaster then logically evaluates the
alternative technological developments and routes which would
be necessary in order to achieve this state. From this it becomes
possible to select an R & D path. In effect, the future state is an
objective, and can be seen as similar in principle to the profit
objective which an organisation sets itself, before identifying the
various strategic paths it might take to enable it to achieve the
objective.

Some similarities with this method can be observed in the
scenario approach (which we met in a somewhat different form in
an earlier chapter). This postulates a number of possible future
developments for a particular technology and the intuitive judgement of experts is used to assess what implications each of these
possible futures might have on the technology in question. The
method does not attempt to identify what *will* happen: only the
opportunities and threats that would arise if the "futures" *did*
happen.

One of the most well-known technological forecasting methods is
the Delphi technique. Under this a panel of experts is selected, each
independently making predictions of future developments. The
method relies completely on expert intuition, for none of the
members of the panel has *knowledge* of what will happen. At
best, it provides an informed opinion of various possible break-
throughs and developments and their timing. In the final event it
provides management with a series of alternative futures to which it
might be worth applying research effort in order to achieve them.

It is also possible to proceed in a different way. Experts are given a series of assumptions about new developments in technology, and are asked to evaluate where these would lead if they did come about. Again the results help management to decide whether the assumptions can be treated as valid research objectives, and whether their potential is likely to repay the costs of achieving them.

Yet another method calls for an exhaustive analysis to identify all the technological requirements of a product. By reconstructing these in different ways, and taking note of likely developments, it becomes possible to isolate areas for research.

The various methods all rely on the application of logical thought processes and expert knowledge and judgement to identify worthwhile areas for research and development. Because they are logical and systematic, they are likely to lead to better R & D strategies, helping the company to raise its own level of achievement. In a way, technological forecasting represents a practical way for mankind to gain control over its own technological progress. Because of this alone, it is worthwhile.

IMPROVEMENT

The concept of the manager's duty to continually seek to increase the profitability of operations through improved efficiency is not new. Every government from time to time exhorts industry to achieve a higher level of productivity. Every good manager will from time to time initiate special exercises to try to find better ways of carrying out certain functions. Many organisations possess departments of people dedicated to improvement: value engineers, method study experts and development engineers to name a few. Some organisations operate suggestion schemes in order to widen the scope of the pool from which improvement ideas are drawn.

Through the 1980s and 1990s there was an increasing awareness that organisations needed to look at themselves from a process as well as a functional viewpoint. It also began to be accepted that effectiveness was not an absolute, but relative to the effectiveness of others. So the idea began to develop of benchmarking processes against those of other organisations, and using the findings to develop better ways of doing things. When processes are considered, benchmarking does not have to be undertaken against competitors, as many non competing organisations have certain processes in common. A development of this thinking is to seek success by striving for world class performance, a concept which will be explored further in Chapter 10.

After benchmarking came business process re-engineering (BPR), the idea of seeking better performance by redesigning processes within the organisation. It is a "break it up and rebuild it" type of approach, which has had some outstanding successes and many more failures. At least some of the disappointing results have come from the common management habit of not applying a new method properly, so that many organisations which claim to be applying BPR are not in fact doing so.

The real danger of BPR is that unless a strong grip is kept on the overall vision and strategy, it can become a cost-cutting exercise which will also hamstring the organisation and make it impossible to succeed in some of its chosen strategies. If used, it should be applied in conjunction with the strategy, and not independently of it.

Another popular course of action is to outsource more activity. The reasons for outsourcing may be sound, and include achieving a better result because it is possible to take advantage of the greater expertise in the supplying organisation, and because it may offer more flexibility in times of recession. Outsourcing, in the modern sense, is a form of strategic alliance between supplier and the organisation. Again there is caution. Be very careful about something that has been identified as being a core competence or capability, because it may make it impossible to build on it in the future.

The corporate appraisal will, in many organisations, provide a fund of basic improvement actions which will take some time to implement.

What should a strategic approach do to encourage thinking about productivity improvement, quality, and better overall performance? Firstly, it should force management thinking out of a rut, creating a working environment where the whole organisation accepts that the words "we've always done it this way" have no relevance. Secondly, it should make managers accountable for achieving world-class standards. Thirdly, many of the approaches enable ideas to come from every corner of the organisation and to cut across departmental boundaries.

The point is that although expansion and acquisition are more exciting paths to follow, there is little point going down these routes unless the organisation is already taking every possible action to improving results from everything it currently undertakes term. Improvement may not be as exciting as acquisition, but it may be a lot less risky, and may yield a much greater return on capital. There should be no strategic plan which does not meet a portion, at least of its objectives, by these means.

GLOBALISATION

All the foregoing options need to be considered in the context of the degree of globalisation in the industries in which the organisation operates. Although certain local niche strategies may sometimes be successful in an industry where most players are global, increasingly it is being realised that the rules of the game are changing, and that it is next to impossible to defeat a global player through a country-by-country strategy. One reason behind the demise of the British motor cycle companies was that they had been driven out of their markets before they realised that the new competitors were thinking in world terms. The reason behind the success of the global strategies is partly the lower costs that can be achieved through a mixture of high volumes and standardised products, and partly because the decision base is different.

Prahalad and Doz, 1987 suggest that the key factors in deciding how to operate are the need for integration on a global basis, contrasted with the need for local responsiveness. If these two concerns are seen as two sides of a matrix, it follows that different businesses can be positioned on the matrix and appropriate strategy decided. However, the authors point to a factor which most strategists will have already observed, namely that the number of industries where global integration is the dominant factor increases every year. The pressures are created by customers and competitors, and it is dangerous to assume that an industry which has local responsiveness as the key factor today will remain like this in the future.

Figure 7.1 illustrates how the changes come about. It is derived from points made by Cvar, 1986.

The analysis suggests that there are certain characteristics in

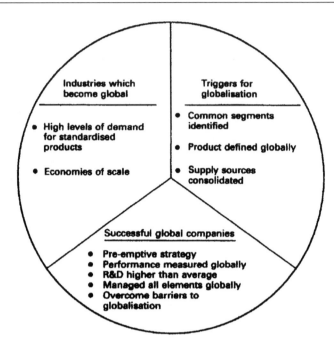

Figure 7.1 Global competition. *(From research findings by Cvar, M. R., 1986. This diagram first appeared in Hussey, D. E., 1990).*

industries that become global, in that there has to be the opportunity for high levels of demand for standardised products which also give rise to economies of scale. Globalisation is not a naturally occurring state but is man made, and the triggers are the identification of common segments in different countries that enable a product to be defined globally. In turn this enables supply sources to be consolidated, so that the competitive cost advantages can be gained. The study also showed that the successful global companies had five factors in common. They had all developed a pre-emptive strategy, effectively becoming the agency that created the global market. All managed their companies on a global concept and measured their performance on this basis. It was also observed that all had higher than average R & D compared to their industry. All had demonstrated a measure of single mindedness in overcoming obstacles to globalisation.

Ohmae, 1985 argues that for long-term success, global businesses have to have a sound position in all of the three geographic centres of the world: USA, Japan and Europe. Those that stay in only one or two of these areas are unlikely to succeed in the long run, because the volumes of production which will fall to those competitors that do penetrate the total triad will give an immense cost advantage. The argument is based on the fact that these areas contain some 600 million people in the largest and most sophisticated markets of the world.

The implication of the global dimension is that for many companies strategic thinking has to stretch beyond the country dimensions that may have been traditional in the industry. Whether the company seeks to create a global business, on the lines suggested by Cvar, or whether it chooses to let a competitor initiate this process, is a matter for the individual company. Once the industry goes global the opportunities for the company with only a local market view will diminish.

REFERENCES

Cvar, M. R., 1986, "Case studies in global competition: Patterns of success and failure", in Porter, M. E., editor, *Competition in Global Industries*, Harvard Business School, Boston, MA.

Hussey, D. E., 1990, "Developments in strategic management", in Hussey, D. E., editor, *International Review of Strategic Management*, Wiley, Chichester.

Hussey, D. E., 1998, "Sources of information for competitor analysis", *Strategic Change*, **7**.6, September/October.

Ohmae, K., 1985, *Triad Power*, Free Press, New York.

Prahalad, C. K. and Doz, Y., 1987, *The Multinational Mission*, Free Press, New York.

FURTHER READING

Acquisitions and Alliances

Bleeke, J. and Ernst, D., editors, 1993, *Collaborating to Compete*, Wiley, New York.

Cartwright, S. and Cooper, C. L., 1996, *Managing Mergers, Acquisitions and Strategic Alliances*, 2nd edition, Butterworth-Heinemann, Oxford.

Mockler, R., 1999, *Multinational Strategic Alliances*, Wiley, Chichester.

Benchmarking & BPR

Johansson, H. J., McHugh, P., Pendlebury, A. J. and Wheeler, W. J., 1993, Wiley, Chichester.

Karlöf, B. and Östblom, S., 1993, *Benchmarking*, Wiley, Chichester.

Watson, G. H., 1993, *Strategic Benchmarking*, Wiley, New York.

Global strategy

Yip, G., 1992, *Total Global Strategy*, Prentice-Hall, Englewood Cliffs, NJ.

8
A Portfolio Approach to Strategy

All of what has been stated about strategic planning has validity for organisations of all types and sizes. Diversified companies also face a further set of strategic problems which are really a need to sort out the business areas into a ranking of attractiveness, so that decisions can be made on which to develop, which to run without growth, and which to get out of.

This need to identify a portfolio strategy, although in this sense the resource applied may be money, people, or technology, occurs in companies of moderate size. It reaches its zenith in the major multinational conglomerates, where the issue of the activity is complicated by the further problem of geographical area. And in all cases there are not only the questions of grow, stay, or divest, but also the dimensions of how big (or small) and at what speed.

Top management of such organisations, after looking at the analysis in the two preceding chapters, might find that they agree in principle but do not see how it helps them solve the problems they are wrestling with. This would be a view with which I have considerable sympathy, since there is a need for a vastly different perspective at top-management level in the really complex companies. Without this it is difficult, or impossible, to develop an overall corporate strategy, or issue sensible strategic guidelines to divisions, or even to judge any plans put up to headquarters by the business units.

It is also clear that such strategic issues cannot always be tackled by examining them solely within the context of the current organisational structure. There may be growth and decline products in every division, there may be overlapping of product market responsibilities (for example, the company may be tackling the same market through more than one subsidiary), or it may be that the geographical areas considered in a strategic sense should be different from the organisational structure established to meet the geographical dispersion of the market. This does not mean that the organisation is wrong in an operational sense: merely that for strategic decisions new combinations might be necessary.

The response to these problems has been the development of a group of techniques of portfolio analysis. At the very simplest level an approach to portfolio analysis might be to rank business activities by size of profits, return on investment or cash flow, on an historic performance basis, adjusted for expected changes, and to classify this list into those which look good, those which are average and those which are poor. Cash flow can be a very good indicator for it is possible that areas with relatively low returns might, with minimum investment, yield funds which can be invested in profit-growth areas.

In many ways this simple analysis may fall short of what is needed. The classification into good, average and poor is easy to suggest, but difficult to do. It is not always a simple task to define the differences, or to overcome the emotive objections that are almost certain to be raised. It also gives little guidance about the size to which the areas should change, or the speed at which the change should be made. Despite these objections, this simple approach can work well and has been used effectively by a number of organisations.

One of the first steps to a more sophisticated analysis is to rethink the company into strategic business areas. This is a market-led exercise which may combine products which respond to different elements of the market (for example, different models of car) and geographical areas, into a relevant base for strategic decisions in relation to characteristics of the market, including competition. In this sense the relevant geographical areas for particular products might be Europe, North America and the rest: or the analysis might suggest only one area, the world.

These classifications require fairly careful considerations about what is a strategic market and what is (for these purposes) an irrelevant segment of that market. Usually they mean that the organisation has to answer questions about its activities which it should be thinking about anyway. The reconsideration of geographical areas is an attempt to think about the products in relation to their market life-cycle characteristics as well as competition. For example, in Third World countries a product may be at the start of its life cycle, and the market might be showing very different characteristics to that in the USA or Europe, where the product may be mature. The consideration of the strategic business areas in relation to marketing considerations brings the need for a parallel study of how the market is supplied: the end result of all the analysis should be a manufacturing strategy to support the investment strategy.

A number of techniques have been developed to help companies examine their strategies from a portfolio viewpoint. The method chosen for illustration was originally developed by Shell Chemicals, 1975. In the first place it was designed for use in the petrochemical industry, but it has been developed, modified and applied to a wide range of industry sectors.

An expansion of the basic technique was made by Hussey, 1978, and used by consultants Harbridge Consulting Group. The original technique, termed the directional policy matrix (DPM), is a two-sided matrix. Hussey put a third dimension to this, called Risk Matrix (RM), which has added a number of exciting possibilities.

The DPM has two axes, which attempt to encompass all the issues which are of critical importance when business prospects are evaluated. The horizontal axis measures prospects for sector profitability: the vertical axis examines the company's competitive capabilities. Thus it is possible to examine whether the market opportunities are good or bad, and the degree of success the company is having in those markets.

Figure 8.1 illustrates the matrix. Each strategic business area is plotted. The position in the matrix is the intersection of a line drawn vertically from the sector prospects axis at the point relevant to the market, and a line drawn horizontally from the competitive capability axis which measures the organisation's relative position. Thus if the organisation had a weak position in a market with unattractive prospects its position would appear in the top left-hand box of the matrix. On the other hand, a strong competitive position in an attractive market would give a plot in the bottom right-hand corner. An organisation with many strategic business areas can, by using this technique, plot the matrix

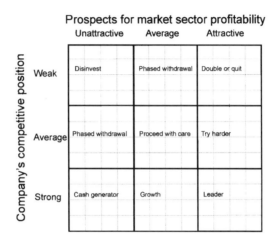

Figure 8.1   Outline directional policy matrix.

position of each. This enables a comparison of the portfolio to be made, and the labels on the matrix provide an indication of the relevant strategy applicable for each, but more of this later.

Each axis represents a complex consideration of many factors. The method of scoring recommended by Shell gives a maximum of 12 points for each axis, but other organisations using the technique have varied this to suit their purposes. The smaller the scale, the more differentiation is possible between strategic business areas. However, the Shell system differentiates sufficiently well.

Figure 8.1 has been scaled in twelfths to make plotting easier. It is also divided into nine equal squares, each indicating a particular strategy. In fact the edges of these squares should be interpreted as flexible lines, since there is a need for judgement to be applied to any strategic business area which is plotted close to or on the borders of any of the nine squares. This is not a problem in practice, since the technique is not meant to be a "black box" which gives exact answers, but a way of gaining a strategic perspective which will aid decisions.

The sector prospects axis consists of three sets of factors: market growth; market profitability and quality; market supply. Each is given an equal weighting (that is each has a top score of 4 points).

Market growth is, of course, a very important determinant of prospects, and there is a lot to be said for seeking opportunities which have good growth prospects: certainly the rate of growth is relevant to investment decisions. All other things being equal it makes more sense to put new investment into areas with high growth than in areas of low growth. But other things are rarely equal, which is why market growth is only one element considered to be important.

Scoring for the market-growth element should be made on the basis of a table, the mid-point of which is the average growth rate for the sectors in which the organisation is interested. An example of such a scale is:

0–4% p.a.	0 points
5–7% p.a.	1 point
8–10% p.a.	2 points
11–14% p.a.	3 points
15% and over	4 points

The second element for consideration is profitability. However, what is important in a business decision is not just whether profits can be made at a high enough level, but whether consistent performance is possible, and whether there is a potential threat to performance because of ease of entry into the market or other factors. The concept may be described as market quality, and a score is reached after consideration of questions such as:

• What is the sector profitability record?
• Are margins maintained in over-capacity situations?
• Are there many customers and few producers (good), or few customers and many producers (bad)?
• How susceptible is the market to substitution by other products?
• How restricted is the technology?
• Does the market develop after-sales business (as, for example, in the spares market caused by the sale of diesel engines)?

These questions will require variation for particular businesses. Some may not be important and there may be other vital factors in some markets which should be included. It is not a difficult task to adjust the list.

The last group of factors consists of a consideration of the industry's ability to supply the market, and to match market growth. This is not only an examination of capacity, but also would embrace raw-material supplies and component availability.

Now for the other axis, the competitive position. Here, too, the axis takes account of three groups of factors of equal weighting: market leadership; supply capability; market support. Each can score a maximum of 4 points.

Market leadership is related to market share but is a little different. It is an attempt to arrive at an estimate of the degree of price leadership the company has. Thus a company in some markets may be the leader with only a 30% share, whereas in another market it may have 50% and not be the leader. Recommended classifications and scoring are:

4 points	Leader	A company whose pre-eminent market position makes it price leader. The market share associated with this state is variable, and does not imply a majority share where there are many competitors.
3 points	Major producer	Where no one company is a leader, but where there may be a number of major producers.
2 points	Viable producer	A strong viable stake, but below the top league.
1 point	Minor	Less than adequate to support R & D in the long run.
0 point	Insignificant	No long-term position.

Production or supply capability covers the organisation's own ability to support its activities in the market-place. For example, in a mechanical engineering market there may be no overall supply problems, but because of size the organisation may face delays and shortages of key bought-in components. Or the organisation may be a more economic producer than its competitors. This element is a composite of questions, such as:

• Economics of production of the company vis à vis the market.
• Capacity availability, and location in relation to the market.
• Raw material and components availability.

Again the questions should be adapted to fit the particular business.

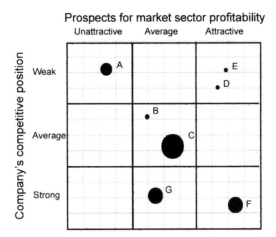

Figure 8.2 Completed DPM (hypothetical company). Circles are proportionate to the net assets used in each business.

The last component of this axis is the company's ability to give market support. This would cover product research and development, distribution, after-sales service and any other elements necessary.

Figure 8.2 shows the matrix with some hypothetical strategic business units filled in. Additional at-a-glance information can be provided by using different colours to indicate the relative importance of each area to corporate profits. The same result can be gained by replacing the dot with a circle, the area of which is proportionate to the importance. An alternative is to use circles which show market size and a "pie slice" representing market share. The hypothetical example is not meant to do anything except demonstrate the use of the method. Companies may find that their plotted positions occur in any distribution.

The meanings, and I must stress that these are indicative only, given to each box are as follows.

Disinvestment

Products falling in this area will probably be losing money, not necessarily every year, but losses in bad years will outweigh the gains in good years. It is unlikely that any activity will surprise management by falling within this area since its poor performance should already be known.

Phased withdrawal

A product with an average to weak position with low unattractive market prospects, or a weak position with average market prospects is unlikely to be earning any significant amounts of cash. The indicated strategy is to realise the value of the assets on a controlled basis to make the resources available for redeployment elsewhere.

Cash generator

A typical situation in this matrix area is when the organisation has a product which is moving towards the end of its life-cycle, and is being replaced in the market by other products. No finance should be allowed for expansion, although the business should have capital to maintain its position and, as long as it is profitable, should be used as a source of cash for other areas. Every effort should be made to maximise profits and cash generation.

Proceed with care

In this position, some investment may be justified but major investments should be made with extreme caution.

Growth

Investment should be made to allow the product to grow with the market. Generally, the product will generate sufficient cash to be self-financing and should not be making demands on other corporate cash resources.

Double or quit

Tomorrow's breadwinners that are among today's R & D projects may come from this area. Putting the strategy simply, those with the best prospects should be selected for full backing and development. The rest should be abandoned.

Try harder

The implication is that the product can be moved towards the leadership box by judicious application of resources. In these circumstances the organisation may wish to make available resources in excess of what the product can generate for itself.

Leader

The strategy should be to maintain this position. At certain stages this may imply a need for resources to expand capacity with a cash need which need not be met entirely from funds generated by the product, although earnings should be above average.

The first use of the matrix is fairly clear. It is to do the strategic sorting-out job discussed earlier. The matrix may also be used to explore gaps in the portfolio. An organisation that has all its interests in the "leader" box is unlikely to generate sufficient cash to exploit all its opportunities: maybe its pressing need is to obtain a cash generator. An organisation with most of its interests in the "proceed with care box" is likely to have a pressing need to seek growth opportunities.

Another use is to evaluate competitors in relation to one's own position in the marketplace. (For this purpose it is possible to use the matrix to compare products instead of strategic business areas. An alternative matrix using life cycle positions is shown in Figure 8.3. Again the positions are of a hypothetical company).

Risk and sensitivity have already been discussed at some length in earlier chapters. The concept of risk can be applied to the DPM in order to provide a different perspective to the portfolio. The RM was developed for this purpose, although it is also a technique which can be used without the DPM. Used together the techniques provide a very powerful tool.

RM is another matrix which is also divided into nine equal squares. The horizontal axis is the same as that of the DPM:

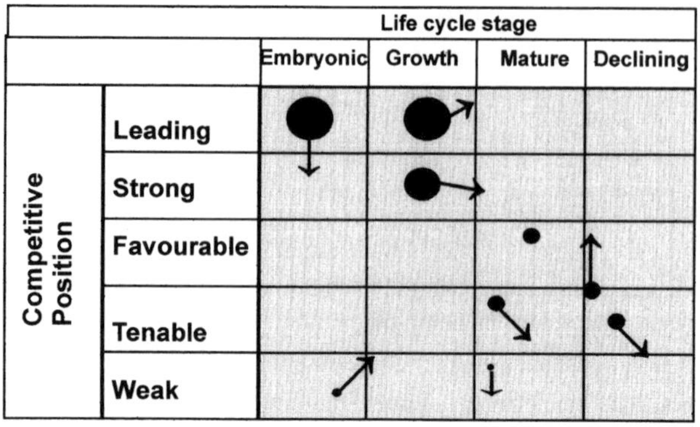

The arrows indicate the way in which the products are expected
to move over the next five years

Figure 8.3   Product portfolio analysis.

prospects for sector profitability. The vertical axis is very different
and measures risks from the business environment.

To rate the company on this axis it is first necessary to draw an
interim working matrix which lists down one side the major environmental risks faced by the company, and across the top, each of
the strategic business areas. This uses a simple score sheet.

	Impact			*Probability*	
Extremely high	6		A certainty	100%	6
	5		Very likely	84%	5
High	4		Quite possible	67%	4
	3		As likely as not	50%	3
Relatively low	2		Probably not	33%	2
	1		Highly unlikely	16%	1
None	0		Impossible	—	0

The major environmental issues may be derived from analysis, as
has been suggested earlier, from brainstorming sessions with groups
in the organisation, or by questionnaires answered by expert
opinion in the organisation about what are the significant threats.
Typically, the result will be 10 to 15 key issues: for example,
inflation, exchange-rate movements, energy policies, nationalisation moves in key countries and similar items.

The next step is to rate each issue for impact and probability:
both being scored on a range of 0–6 as described below.

Once individual ratings have been assessed, the impact score should be multiplied by the probability score giving a maximum score of 36 for each factor and a minimum of 0. Examples are:

Impact	*Probability*	*Score*
Extremely high	A certainty:	$6 \times 6 = 36$
High	Very likely:	$4 \times 5 = 20$
Low	Very likely:	$1 \times 6 = 6$

Enter these scores on the working matrix (the answers will not necessarily be the same for each strategic business area). Add the scores for each strategic business area and calculate an average score (divide total score by the number of relevant environmental factors). This provides an answer for each strategic business area, with a maximum possible average score of 36. The risk axis is therefore graded in the example shown in Figure 8.4 in 36ths.

Using the scores for the two axes it is possible to plot a risk position for each of the strategic business areas.

Now if this is imagined as a third dimension to the matrix (you do not have to try to draw this, as colour coding the DPM enables the results of the RM to be shown) it becomes possible to

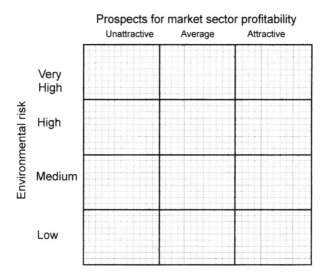

Figure 8.4 The risk matrix.

simultaneously perceive the DPM position and the degree of risk involved. While consideration of RM by itself may lead to strategies to reduce risk or to a realisation that action has to be taken to adjust the organisation's balance of risks, an examination in conjunction with the DPM may lead to other considerations.

For example, a strategic business area which falls in a divest box may have the need for speedy action underlined if the degree of environmental risk is high. Similarly, the organisation ought to be aware of the increased chance of the drying up of a cash generator if this, too, is subject to high risk. A more confident investment in a growth box can be made if the risks involved are low. It may also be easier to make decisions on the "double or quit" areas if the degree of risk is assessed.

The concept of the third dimension to portfolio analysis can be used to explore other factors of significance to the company. It is possible to take a particular issue and to analyse the areas in relation to energy consumption, proneness to inflation or cash requirements.

None of these tools replaces management judgement, but they do help put problems into perspective. The techniques can be applied analytically in an ivory tower way, although this means that they will have a good chance of being rejected in many organisations! A better approach, which leads to acceptance, is to assemble panels of senior and knowledgeable managers to make ratings for the strategic business areas which fall within the boundary of their knowledge. Such facts as can be assembled should be, for this reduces the need for assessments based on judgement and eliminates a great deal of conflict.

In order to pin down the assessments it may be of value to carry out the DPM exercise twice: once based on historic data and the other on forecasts. This helps to define the difference in perception that managers may have, and should avoid the projection of past trends willy-nilly into the future.

Detailed scoring rules for the DPM and the RM, and a worked example can be found in Hussey, 1998. Segev 1995a and b describes several portfolio approaches, and gives detailed rules for them. Segev 1995b includes a disk so that a computer can be used to position the businesses on the matrices.

A final word of caution should be added. Portfolio analysis techniques which lay stress on the competitive position suffer when they come up against a business area where this is unimportant. For example, however profitable horticulture or agriculture might be, the chances are that the company would score badly on the competitive axis (every producer has a minority share). The benefits of farming might be land appreciation and tax advantages which would not show clearly on the matrix.

Similarly a viable policy might be as a small market share operator, providing an alternative for those purchasers who do not like the major market shareholder. This is, of course, more likely to be a small company strategy than a large one, and for small companies DPM is less likely to be useful. For the larger company, the DPM should offer an opportunity to question the strategy, which is not the same as assuming it is wrong.

Portfolio analysis helps the organisation to obtain a view of its business units or products relative to each other. It may also serve as a starting point for assessing whether shareholder value is added or reduced in organisations with a multiplicity of SBUs. Severing the links with an SBU sometimes gives more value to the shareholders than retaining it in a conglomerate organisation. The main ways in which value may be added are:

• if the SBUs gain through shared resources and activities;
• from spill over effects of marketing and research and development;
• through shred knowledge, skills and technologies;
• through a shared image.

Value may be lost if there are none of these benefits, if SBUs are forced to pay for head office services that are either unwanted or more expensive than if bought from outside, or if the management processes either delay decisions, or prevent the SBU from taking investment decisions that are essential for its future growth.

Matrices which plot SBUs or products only allow the start of this analysis. Something else is needed, because SBUs are basically product/market groupings. If businesses were grouped into technology units, or by core competencies, a totally different perspective would emerge, useful for seeing where value was added, and also for developing strategies from a very different perspective.

A number of such portfolio techniques have been developed. Neubauer, 1990 suggests a technology matrix with the axes of technology position and technology relevance. Hinterhuber et al, 1996, suggests that competencies be plotted on a matrix with customer value and relative competitive strength as the two axes.

To be really useful, these portfolio approaches should be supported by another matrix which lists each business unit on one axis, and each technology or core competence on the other, so that it is possible to plot what is common and what is not.

My experience has been that useful portfolio approaches can be designed to examine a number of different factors. Once completed they become excellent tools for sharing information among the management team, and developing a common view of the situation. Gaining a shared commitment to the strategies to change the situation may take a little longer!

Let us end this chapter with a thought that has been stressed several times. Techniques give perspective to management judgement: they do not replace it.

REFERENCES

Anon, 1975, *The Directional Policy Matrix*, Shell Chemicals, London. (A second edition was published in 1979).

Hinterhuber, H. H., Friedrich, S. A., Handlbauer, G., and Stuhec, U., 1996, "The company as a cognitive system of core competences and strategic business units", *Strategic Change*, **5**.4, July/August. It may be more accessible in Hussey, D. E., editor, 1998, *The Strategic Decision Challenge*, Wiley, Chichester.

Hussey, D. E., 1978, "Portfolio analysis: practical experiences with the directional policy matrix", *Long Range Planning*, 11, August.

Hussey, D. E., 1998, *Strategic Management: From Theory to Implementation*, 4th edition, Butterworth-Heinemann, Oxford.

Neubauer, F.-F., 1990, *Portfolio Management*, Kluwer, Deventer, Netherlands.

Segev, E., 1995a, *Corporate Strategy: Portfolio Models*, Thomson, London.

Segev, E., 1995b, *Navigating by Compass*, Thomson, London.

9
Marketing Strategy

If an organisation cannot sell the goods it produces at a realistic price it soon runs into trouble. It is its marketing ability which enables it to translate the needs and desires of its consumers into a formula which makes it possible for a profit to be earned. Failure in the marketing area may prevent the organisation from succeeding, or even lead to its complete downfall.

Marketing therefore should be approached in a strategic way. Somewhere in the organisation, careful attention should be given to marketing strategy. In a modest-sized organisation, the corporate strategy may have a high marketing content. In a large multinational, marketing strategy may not be a matter for the corporate level, but it certainly should be treated as important at the level of each business unit.

Books which explain marketing strategy include many of the concepts already covered, such as portfolio analysis, so there is clearly an overlap in the tools, methods and techniques which may be used (see for example Kotler, 1994 and McNamee, 1998).

Strategic marketing planning should be regarded as an active way of developing the organisation. The long-term survival of the business may depend on the aggressiveness with which the organisation approaches the problem of bringing innovation to its markets. The organisation that does not innovate is likely to be on that desolate path that leads to stagnation: it may travel on quite happily for many years, but unless it is constantly uncovering new ideas, new products, new concepts and new approaches to all areas of marketing strategy, it carries with it the seeds of its own demise. In the modern, fast-changing world, continuous attention must be given to both the needs of customers and the actions of

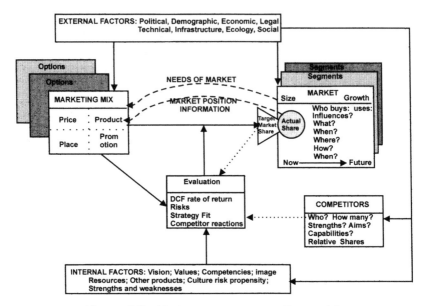

Figure 9.1   Market strategy—an outline model.

competitors. The strategic approach encourages the process of innovation. Flair in marketing, as in all other functions of management, is of the greatest importance, but has to be channelled it into areas which are of the greatest benefit to the organisation.

Figure 9.1 provides one way of looking at marketing strategy. It is compatible with Figure 1.2, but organises the requirements a little differently, and explores the market and the elements of marketing strategy. The heart of the model is the market, and the organisation's interaction with it. The model also makes it clear that there is an evaluation and decision process. Decisions are taken against criteria which reflect the organisation's interests, although the options evaluated will also reflect the requirements of the market.

THE EXTERNAL FACTORS

The importance of the environment has been discussed in detail in several other parts of this book. It was mentioned in connection with corporate strategy (and therefore marketing strategy) when the theme of the corporate appraisal was developed. It appeared in the chapter on assumptions and risk, and has been drawn into the discussion on many other occasions. And, inevitably, it must be raised again in connection with the strategic planning of markets.

There is no necessity to repeat what has been said before about the reasons for studying the environment and it will be noticed that the subheadings in the model are the same as the headings in Figure 3.7. Marketing has, traditionally, more concerned with the effects of external changes than many other functions, and of necessity marketing personnel tend to be outward looking. They have to be, because marketing is particularly concerned with changes in the needs, desires, attitudes and opinions of the buyers and consumers, and these are not independent of what is going on in the environment at large.

THE INTERNAL FACTORS

The model assumes that the vision and values of the organisation are fixed before the marketing strategy is developed, although this is not to suggest that the market is not an influence when vision is formulated. However, the assumption is correct in most situations. The internal factors box also includes the competencies and strengths and weaknesses, which were discussed in Chapter 3. It recognises that the culture of the organisation is important in determining acceptable strategies. It also notes that the marketing strategy of each product range can be affected by other product ranges in the corporate portfolio.

The internal factors box covers factors which provide opportunities, as well as those that constrain what can be done. As we saw in earlier chapters, part of the corporate strategy might be to change some of these factors.

The criteria shown in the evaluation box derive from the internal factors, although the options being evaluated come from the organisation's response to the market and to the competitive environment.

THE MARKET

The first stage in preparing a strategic marketing plan, be it short- or long-term, is the drawing together of the available and relevant market data, as a base on which to assess future patterns of development, and from which forecasts of market size and growth can be made. Information comes from numerous sources, and there can be few organisations who know absolutely nothing about their markets. General demographic data, details of regional differences, and many other basic statistics can be obtained from government publications, and in addition there should be more specific product data from market surveys, retail audits, test market operations, sales analysis and the thousand and one other sources available to an aggressive marketing research department. Strategic thinking is concerned with the way in which present market requirements may change in the future, and in particular, how the organisation may cause them to change through its own actions.

I recommend the discipline of putting these base data into a marketing handbook for each main product or family of products in which the firm deals. Such a step may not be justified for any minor products with limited potential which the organisation may market, but is certainly valuable for any products or services which the organisation approaches in a serious vein. Set formats should be prepared, prescribing the data headings that are considered necessary for the handbook, and these should be used for all the products. (It may, of course, be necessary to have different formats for different types of product: for example, requirements for an industrial market differ from those of the consumer market; the approach to consumer durables will vary from the approach to a fast-moving grocery product.)

Part of the handbook, the strictly factual answers to the various questions raised, can be completed by any competent analyst with access to the appropriate data: in most organisations the marketing research department is an obvious candidate for the task. Inevitably there will always be gaps, where an answer cannot be given to the question raised in the handbook format. Lack of factual data should not prevent completion of the handbook, but assumptions and estimates to fill in these missing parts should be made with the involvement of those with expert knowledge. These answers must be clearly identified as assumptions, so that they are never given a spurious accuracy. The advantage of filling in the gaps in this way is that the basis on which a strategy has been prepared is defined, for there are many situations when a course of action has to be committed before all the facts are known: in reality, it is fair to claim that we never do know *all* the facts. Assumptions and estimates can also provide hypotheses for future marketing research.

Figure 9.2 gives some of the broad information headings which might appear in a handbook of this nature. The important thing is that the format should be designed to meet the specific needs of the firm. If done well, the marketing handbook can be an invaluable aid for strategic thinking. It facilitates the appraisal of current strategies against the real facts of the market: this self-examination, asking the question "why?", is the first step to clear thinking. The handbook shows what information is not really known, and makes clear where decisions are being made on a hunch.

All market facts are really yesterday's news. Marketing strategy is concerned with the world of tomorrow. The handbook is only a stepping-stone to deciding future action, and each fact should be interpreted against the trends in the environment, and the ability of the organisation to initiate changes in the picture revealed by the handbook.

One aspect of the important contribution that marketing research must play in the strategic planning of marketing activity has been revealed in the foregoing discussion. This contribution is the rather passive activity of collecting historical market data. There is also a need for a more dynamic approach than this from the marketing research department. As more thought is given to the future, so the demands on the marketing research facilities change to the provision of a different type of data, to a need for information that will help predict in advance the changing tastes of the consumer. This need was made clear three decades ago by Levitt, 1962 He reviewed the inroads that the small car had made into Detroit's share of the US market.

"How could this unbelievable lag behind consumer wants have been perpetuated so long? Why did not research uncover consumer preferences before consumers buying decisions themselves revealed the facts? Is that not what consumer research is for—to find out before the fact what is going to happen? The answer is that Detroit never properly researched the customer's wants. It only investigated his preferences among the kind of things which it had already decided to offer him. For Detroit was mainly product oriented, not consumer oriented."

The market share lost by the original domestic US car companies

1. GENERAL DATA
   A. Population   age and sex
                                        region households
                                        social class
                                        urban/rural
                                        working/non working
   B. National Income   *per capita*
                                        per household
                                        regional differences
2. PRODUCT PROFILE (by relevant headings as in 1A)
   A. Demography   present users heavy users
                                        non-users
                                        competitive product users
   B. Product Image
   C. Analysis of Uses of Product
   D. Time or Day of Usage Analysis
   E. Frequency of Usage
   F. Frequency of Purchase
   G. Price/Volume Relationships
   H. Brand Shares
3. DISTRIBUTION (by relevant headings as in 1A)
   A. Source of Purchase   all users
                                       heavy users
                                       competitive product users
   B. Brand Shares by Source of Purchase
   C. Retailer Attitudes   to product
                                       to company
                                       to competitors
   D. Wholesaler Attitudes   to product to company to competitors
   E. Profitability of Product to Retailer   compared with all products
                                             compared with competitors
   F. Degree of Customer Service   given for product
                                       given by competitors
   G. Retailer Attitudes to   trade packing
                                       consumer packing
4. MARKET SIZE (by relevant headings as in 1A)
   A. Definition of Market
   B. Size of Total Market   by value
                                       by quantity
   C. Market Forecasts   by value
                                       by quantity
   D. Market Size per Pack Size
   E. Details of Substitute Products
   F. Quantity and Value of Market by Various Channels of Distribution
5. PRICE
   A. Analysis of Consumer Prices
   B. Analysis of Trade Prices
6. PROMOTION
   A. Advertising   by media
                                       by competitor
   B. Merchandising Activity
   C. Special offer, etc., Activity
   D. Response of Retailers to Promotions
7. MARKET SEGMENTATION
8. HISTORICAL DATA
9. PRODUCT COST DATA
                        by standard costs
                        by fixed and variable costs.

These headings are indicative only. A relevant listing can only be made after a study of the organisation's
particular situation. There is no significance in the order in which headings appear.

Figure 9.2 Indicative headings for a market background handbook.

has never been recovered. Similarly Xerox has never recovered the market share lost to Canon and other Japanese firms in the 1970s, allowing them to enter the business in the small copier market to meet needs that Xerox had largely ignored. Despite the excellent work undertaken by Xerox in the 1980s and 1990s in quality control and world-class performance this lost ground has not been recovered. Many dangers await the unwary and the complacent.

A third area where marketing strategy requires support from marketing research is in the field of marketing experimentation and the testing of new concepts. In my experience, the organisation that is really thinking about the future will come up with a stimulating programme of new ideas, and will become rapidly aware of a whole host of things it needs to know to progress these. If an organisation's marketing strategy consists solely of writing down 5-year extrapolations of the past, if it becomes a budgeting exercise that does not stretch the imagination of its marketing management, or if it becomes a repetition of the same dreary old formulae, then it will have surely failed. I have seen "strategic planning" systems that convert everything to numbers on a form, surrounded by so many rules that the spark of individuality is destroyed, and the only result of which is to plough such a deep rut that all hope of innovation is lost forever.

A CONCEPTUAL APPROACH TO MARKETING STRATEGY

The heart of marketing strategy lies in the way the organisation probes its current and potential markets, and works out profitable ways of meeting current market needs, and helps the market to identify needs that it did not know it had. The marketing mix box in Figure 9.1 shows four headings which are useful in thinking through marketing strategies for products and services. It is by no means the only classification available, and Figure 9.3 shows the "four Ps" approach and its mirror image, the "four Cs". The Cs show a customer viewpoint. The Ps stress the actions the organisation can take. Both methods offer a discipline, the adherence to a conceptual approach to strategic thinking.

The format I favour is the "four Ps" approach based on that discussed in great detail in McCarthy 1981, although his

The 4 Ps   The 4 Cs

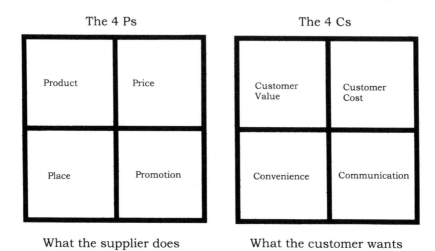

What the supplier does   What the customer wants

Figure 9.3   The marketing mix from two perspectives.

classification was coined many years earlier. It is probably fair to
claim that this is the most widely used classification, and has stood
the test of time. Unfortunately I cannot acknowledge the four Cs, as
I do not know where the idea came from.

The four Ps are:

- Price.
- Product.
- Place.
- Promotion.

Price means what it says. It is concerned with terms of trade,
discounts and price promotions. One important aspect of long-
range price strategies is that some organisations assume that their
strategies should take no account of either cost or price rises, as
these cancel each other out. This, of course, is a gross fallacy, and
those making this assumption have their heads so far buried in
the sand that they will never be able to give their organisation
that quality of vision which was, presumably, the reason they
were put on the payroll. In some countries price strategy is
affected by government policies, and any proposed price increases
must take these into account, as well as the effects on the market
itself. Regardless of government interest in prices, no company will

adjust its prices for every movement in costs: there is a tactical position to be decided for every price rise.

Price may, of course, be an aggressive element of marketing strategy. It may be used to change the pattern of order purchase size, thus reducing unit sales, order processing and physical distribution costs. It may be used to increase the volume of sales: Henry Ford with his cars provided what is probably the most well-known example of this strategy in practice. And of course different price strategies may be applied to different geographical areas, or to the each segment of a particular market. So price must not be neglected in an organisation's market planning, as it is by no means a passive element which automatically compensates for inflationary tendencies.

Product is the next of the four Ps. This element covers the intangible aspects of a product as well as its physical characteristics. The tangible aspects include many different things. Perhaps the most obvious is the shape and composition of the product itself, the way in which it basically sets out to give satisfaction to its consumers. This would cover the design and finish of furniture, the taste and dietary value of a convenience food, the formulation of a toilet preparation, or the curative benefit of a pharmaceutical. Closely allied to the characteristics are the packaging and the size of unit offered for sale. Packaging is, of course, of the utmost importance in the marketing of many items: with an industrial product the main problem might be to package in a way that gives the most convenience to the user: with a grocery product the shape and appeal of the package, which may also be a vehicle to advertise special offer and promotions, may be the deciding element in the attraction of a purchaser. Packaging as a means of preserving goods from damage and storing them until sold is often second in importance to packaging as an active element of selling. There is also a cost aspect attached to each package or size of unit marketed: each additional item brings extra charges for financing inventories and storage, as well as possibly adding to direct production costs. The reduction of variety can often be an important method of planning for improved profits.

From packaging, it is natural to turn one's thoughts to branding. This element covers such items as the marketing of brands to appeal to the various segments of the market, policy for the production of "own label" products for others, and whether the organisation brings out families of brands, or creates a new brand for each product.

The intangible aspects of product strategy cover those items which the organisation offers to purchasers as an inducement to buy. For example, the terms of credit it is prepared to give, any particular guarantees attached to the product, a special delivery service, or free after-sales servicing of appliances. With electrical goods, or motor cars, the widespread availability of service and repair shops might be a highly attractive intangible to the prospective customer.

Place is a term that calls for a little stretching of the imagination, and would be better translated as distribution (except that this word does not begin with P). The heading covers the channel of distribution chosen to get the products from the manufacturer to the consumer. This is an area which is under continual change. An example is the growing importance of telephone services like banking and insurance, the growth in selling through the Internet, and in future selling through digital television. It may be of passing interest to note that two examples of recent distribution changes given in the first edition of the book (1971) were the growth of cash and carry wholesalers, to which we can now add the words "and decline", and selling through vending machines, which still continues. Attention to the distribution aspect of strategy ensures that the organisation takes full advantage of any opportunity to innovate. For example, Direct Line has become a significant force in insurance by being the first organisation to seriously sell car and household insurance over the telephone, giving it major cost savings in overheads, which in turn meant that lower prices could be offered. Its actions have altered the whole structure of the industry.

In planning distribution strategy, the organisation might well set different brand share targets for each of the alternative outlet types: it might aim for different penetration levels for each outlet. It would certainly prescribe very closely the role of wholesalers and other middlemen. And of course, the other elements of strategy, price, promotion and even product can be designed to help give effect to the chosen distribution strategy.

The remaining of our four Ps is Promotion. This covers numerous activities in addition to the mass advertising that immediately springs to mind. Under this heading I would also include merchandising, selling, sales promotion and point of sale activities, sampling and general product public relations. There are numerous variables to choose from, both in relation to the types of promotion used, the weights assigned to each, and the way in which the product image is put across.

Figure 9.4 illustrates some of the factors which might be considered under each of the four Ps. From this, and the forgoing discussion, it is easy to see why Figure 9.1 indicates that there are options in the way the marketing strategies are developed.

None of these elements of strategy exists in isolation, and to some extent each may be considered an alternative to each of the others. The number of possible mixes is infinite. To make real sense, the entire strategy must be designed to increase profits by giving maximum utility to the consumer. It is the organisation which gives most consideration to both these conditions, which is most likely to succeed in the long term. Profits made by supplying something which does not meet customer needs are always at risk to the organisation which reads the market better. Meeting customer needs in a way that does not provide an adequate return, may mean that the organisation cannot survive for very long.

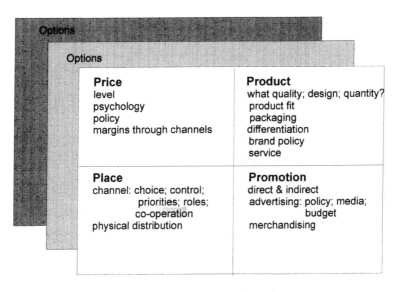

Figure 9.4 The marketing mix.

The conceptual approach outlined above should never be used as a repetitive exercise. Its intention is to free the thinking from the shackles of what is being done today: to stimulate the imagination, not to retard it. In the final event, successful marketing strategy depends not on the way the words are strung together, but on the ability and vision of the people who develop the strategy. Let no one confuse the means with the end.

THE PRODUCT LIFE-CYCLE CONCEPT

The product life-cycle was used in a matrix in the previous chapter without any explanation of what it is, although it is probably something that most readers are familiar with. The life-cycle theory is well known. It holds that every product begins with a period of low sales (and low profits) as it is introduced to the market. This period is followed for successful products by a relatively short spell where sales rapidly escalate, and profits rapidly rise. The growth rate slows down as more competitive products enter the field, and as the market begins to reach saturation point. This period is usually associated with declining profitability as the established brands fight to hold their market share.

Eventually the product reaches maturity. At this point the market at best grows in line with the expansion of population: more likely it will begin to decline. For some products the end may be short and sharp: others may linger on for many years, although each year that passes tends to be associated with declining profitability (although the tendency is also affected by competitive behaviour).

The whole process may be illustrated by the "S"-shaped curve with which many readers will already be familiar. It is illustrated in Figure 9.5.

The product life-cycle has three important uses in market planning. It should be considered when market and sales forecasts are prepared, as skill in predicting the point where the curve begins to bend is an important ingredient in making a realistic forecast. A mathematical extrapolation taken during the period of steep growth would be vastly different from one taken after the product reaches its point of maturity. In making forecasts the

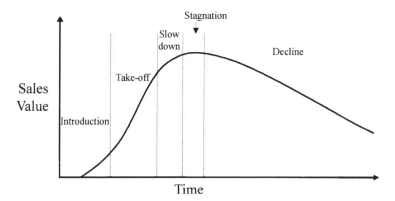

Figure 9.5   Product life cycle curve.

analyst has to apply judgement to determine the likely course of the product.

Having come to this stage, the organisation may find it possible to prepare a plan of action to change the predicted course of events. The market for beds might, for example, be relatively easy to predict, being largely a compound of established replacement rates and the expansion of population. In looking at this forecast, a bed manufacturer may decide that although it cannot do much to affect the birth rate, it can persuade the public to replace their beds more often.

The third use of the concept is even more interesting. This is developing strategies to deliberately expand the uses or distribution of the product, thereby extending the product life-cycle, and postponing the inevitable day when it really does go over the hump. By identifying the points when action must be taken to extend the life-cycle, the organisation puts itself in a position to direct its resources (marketing research, research and development) to finding the means to bring about the desired course of events.

A simple example is the extension of the market by introducing the product to areas where it was not previously available. A more complex and more ingenious solution would be to seek out new uses, or new classes of user, so that the market becomes larger. An example is the introduction of a successful ethical pharmaceutical preparation to the over-the-counter trade, through chemists and grocery outlets. Another example is the efforts of the plastics industry to develop more and more uses for their raw materials.

Every year that passes sees the development of the major resins for an increasing variety of products.

THE PLACE OF FORECASTING

Strategic thinking needs forecasts as a tool, and forecasts of the market under different assumptions are as invaluable. The more accurate a forecast can be made, the greater the potential it has for providing a base for planning.

The expected results of marketing strategies should be expressed in financial terms, and the various options evaluated one against the other.

Forecasting is not the be-all and end-all of planning, and an organisation that is truly innovating will frequently face a situation when forecasting by any scientific means is impossible. If a product is really new, no market for it may currently exist. Test marketing and other tools may be used to evaluate the potential, although in some cases decisions may have to be taken in advance of these results: a successful test marketing operation will be observed by competitors, and if the organisation is slow off the mark in going national, it may find that it loses that lead which may be so important to ultimate success. Even more difficult to evaluate is a change in a marketing concept. Some aspects can be measured experimentally, but others arc almost impossible to tackle in this way.

The strategy for something that is totally new and unpredictable might best be conceived as a series of stages, where the desired direction is set, but the means are re-examined in the light of results. This can work in a number of decisions, but becomes difficult when a massive investment is needed before there is experience of whether the product idea is a good one. For example, in 1998 digital television broadcasting is being launched in the UK, exposing the competitors to large initial capital costs and high risks. As the minimum capital threshold to launch such a service is high, the emergent approach to strategy does not replace the need to undertake extensive marketing research, or for significant attention to forecasting. One might add that this type of strategy should be avoided if the organisation cannot afford the costs of failure, whether an outright flop, or a much slower take off than the strategy anticipated. A "bet the company" strategy may make for good cinema drama, but it is not a sound move for an under-resourced business.

Every company must ensure that it gives the innovative ideas a fair chance. It is very easy to condemn anything new to a Hades of permanent evaluation, seeking a few more facts here, a new financial calculation there, and generally making sure that initiative is stifled, and that only the tried and true ideas, the old ones, are treated seriously.

In all market planning it is important to keep in mind the possibility of the failure of a new product, even if it is not in the same category as digital television. National failure rates for new launches are high. Although careful attention to marketing principles and good marketing research can reduce this risk, they cannot remove it: and the more adventurous an organisation is, the more failures it will be exposed to. Only the senile organisation which has lost all courage and clings miserably to the old and secure, can be sure of avoiding product failures. This inaction carries the danger that senile decay eventually leads to death. As the soldier, crouched behind his barricade and afraid to lift his head to observe the enemy, will inevitably be eventually overrun, so will the firm that has lost the ability to take justifiable risks eventually succumb to the forces of change which surround it.

Those concerned with marketing strategy will need to have more projects under consideration than are needed. If all were successful they would either achieve better results than were expected, or after a pattern of successes the organisation could decide to hold the rest in abeyance. The final course of action will depend on how many successes the organisation can handle at any one time.

INNOVATION

Innovation has been mentioned elsewhere in this chapter. Although innovation is by no means restricted to marketing applications, it is convenient to round off this chapter with some research-based ideas on how to innovate successfully.

Until recently many writers on innovation have concentrated on creativity rather than on the process itself. Management consultants Harbridge House Inc., now owned by Coopers &

Lybrand, researched the common factors identified by successful innovating managers in a number of US organisations. The management practices, or competencies, applied by these managers were listed, from which it could be seen that there was a common core of practices which occurred in all successful situations. Further work was then undertaken to validate the conclusions.

The research led to the development of a model, which is described by Webster, 1990: "...We looked at innovation as having two components, invention and implementation. Within these two components are four segments: creativity, vision, commitment and management".

The definition of innovation by the inventors of this model is: "A better thing to do or a better way to do it that contributes to an organisation's goals. It may be a method, structure, process or product" (Webster 1990).

The model accepts that creativity is important, but argues that there is much to do to change creativity to innovation. The other three segments are a form of transformational leadership: developing a vision of where the innovator wants to go; building commitment to the vision through communication, involvement, reinforcement, support and influence: managing the process by providing direction and control to the project. (A somewhat different leadership model appears in Chapter 14, and could be used in innovation, as it is just a different way of looking at similar ideas.)

The Harbridge House findings recognised that an innovator operates in a broader context, that of the organisation. Thus the innovation has to be compatible with the strategic direction of the firm, the climate and culture must encourage innovation, and the structures and systems must support the innovation process.

My former colleagues, at Harbridge Consulting Group discussed this model with numerous UK organisations. The overwhelming impression was that the majority had recognised the importance of the organisational factors, such as culture, but that little attention was given to the implementation aspects. In management training, a need to improve the innovation of the organisation was generally translated as a need to undertake training in creativity. However, the Harbridge House findings showed that although this was important, it could not succeed because three quarters of a successful innovation related to the ability of the innovator to steer the project through the organisation. In fact a general conclusion is that most organisations had no shortage of creative ideas, but too few of these ever result in an innovation.

Few would deny that innovation is important, and it is clearly an aspect of management which should be encouraged. Perhaps a rebirth of strategic thinking might be the catalyst that enables this to happen.

REFERENCES

Kotler, P., 1994, *Marketing Management: Analysis, Planning, Implementation and Control*, 8th edition, Prentice Hall, Englewood Cliffs, NJ, or a later edition.

Levitt, T., 1962, *Innovation in Marketing*, McGraw-Hill, New York.

McCarthy. E. J., 1981, *Basic Marketing: A Managerial Approach*, 9th edition, Irwin, Homewood, Illinois.

McNamee, P., 1998, *Strategic Market Planning: A Blueprint for Success*, Wiley, Chichester.

Webster, B., 1990, "Innovation: we know we need it but how do we do it", in Hussey, D. E. and Lowe, P., editors, *Key Issues in Management Training*, Kogan Page, London. The original article was published in 1989 in the Management Development Update series issued by Harbridge Consulting Group, London, but is no longer accessible in its original form.

10
Manufacturing Strategy

Historically, manufacturing has often been seen as that rather boring end of the business which frequently fails to deliver the goods sold by the sharp end, and which is full of managers whose focus is short term and whose days are spent on petty detail! Although this might be a fair description of this function in some organisations, it is far from the general truth, and is certainly a million miles from the role the function should be playing. The need is to have a well-defined manufacturing philosophy, and a clearly thought-out manufacturing strategy to support it. Even this does not go far enough as it implies that manufacturing is a reactive activity. In the modern world, manufacturing should not wait until it is told what the corporate strategy is, but should be playing a key part in influencing that strategy. It is fair to say that in many organisations manufacturing is forced into a series of *ad hoc* steps to meet the pressures put on it by the rest of the organisation.

Manufacturing often has to expand to meet expected sales increases by various add-on moves. Too seldom is there a complete rethink of the task of manufacturing. Marketing may be thinking of a global attack on world markets, yet manufacturing may not be conceived in global terms. There are, of course, notable exceptions, and the Japanese in particular seem to have found the ability to integrate global marketing and global manufacturing strategies.

Three major strands of thought have enabled a more effective view to be taken of manufacturing strategy. The first is a contribution from Skinner, 1978, who provided a framework for thinking about these issues and introduced the idea of focus in manufacturing. The second is the concept of world-class performance advocated by Hayes et al, 1988. Thirdly there is the contribution of many people to understanding the learning curve effect and the way this influences costs. Since the learning curve has a fundamental effect on manufacturing strategy this will be considered first.

THE LEARNING CURVE

A phenomenon was first noted in the production of aircraft. Every time cumulative output doubled there was a constant percentage fall of 20% in the unit labour cost. Thus:

4th plane requires 80% of the labour of the 2nd plane.
8th plane requires 80% of the labour of the 4th plane.
100th plane requires 80% of the labour of the 50th plane.

This learning curve effect applies in a variety of industries and in broad terms suggests that unit manufacturing costs fall as volume rises. However, it is somewhat different from a simple application of economy of scale thinking. The phenomenum relates to cumulative production, not simply to output in a given period. Economy of scale implies that unit costs fall as factory capacity increases (assuming that the capacity is utilised). The learning curve effect suggests that regardless of factory size, there will be a fall in costs as workers learn to perform better, and that this learning is the result of their cumulative experience.

A greater level of significance was given to this finding by the Boston Consulting Group who derived the experience curve concept. This demonstrated that in real terms the total costs per unit associated with a product will fall by a constant percentage every time industry volume doubles. When plotted on a logarithmic scale this appears as a linear decline. (For further information see Henderson, 1973, 1974a and 1974b in Stern and Stalk, 1998.) The finding here is that it is not just production costs which fall but the whole costs of the organisation. The factory workers become more proficient, as in the learning curve concept, but so do managers, purchasing, distribution, and marketing and sales activities. In fact the concept has been applied outside manufacturing to service businesses like insurance.

The real value of this thinking comes when demand is sufficiently elastic because here it is possible to gain volume from lower prices, and lower costs from the additional volume. If the equation can be pushed far enough it will mean that new competitors will find it almost impossible to obtain volumes high enough to be able to operate efficiently. Similarly, the laggards among existing competitors will become increasingly uneconomic and be shaken out. It is different when demand is inelastic and there are other competitors, since it is probably not possible to increase output dramatically to gain dramatic reductions of cost. The implication of this is that the conditions for an effective strategy based on experience curve principles, are not independent of the market or the life cycle of the product.

The concept has worked well in many parts of the electronics industry, where the real decline in both prices and costs is easily observable. It is readily visible, for example, in the personal computer market, where many early entrants have been forced out. However, in this industry there is also a change in the structure of the industry, with the pace of development dictated by software manufacturers like Microsoft, and chip providers like Intel.

The implications for manufacturing strategy are clear. An experience curve concept implies relatively few plants supplying global markets, standardised products, and total co-ordination between marketing and manufacturing. When marketing reduces the real price, manufacturing must be ready to supply the increased volume. It implies careful attention to purchasing, outsourcing, and sub-contracting. Above all it implies the maintenance of quality, so that lower prices do not become associated with inferior goods. These are all features of the way in which Japanese electronics, automotive and motor cycle firms operate.

The competitive impact of trying to compete against the machine-like operations of the experience curve by traditional means is best illustrated by the British motor cycle industry. Just before the great collapse in 1974 the best British motor cycle factory produced 18 motor cycles per man year, compared to 350 in the best Japanese factories. The Japanese were, at this stage, unbeatable.

Of course, life is never simple, and there are limitations to the experience curve, the most serious presumably being when it goes into reverse. If demand falls, costs will rise. If this forces price rises, demand may fall further. Each recession brings big problems to organisations dependent on this concept. Henry Ford had never heard of the learning curve, but he used the concept for the Model T Ford, and one day woke up to find that customers no longer wanted this car! It had been overtaken by the products of his competitors, and his solution was to close his factory for a lengthy period while he developed a replacement model.

The lessons from this piece of history are that competitive advantage can be lost when the product is too standardised for market requirements, and the experience curve can bring increased vulnerability if it confines all strategic thinking to standardised lines. Despite these limitations, it is a very powerful phenomenon.

MANUFACTURING STRATEGY

Skinner, 1978 maintains that, traditionally, manufacturing has been managed from the bottom up. This, he says, now fails to meet modern needs and instead a top-down approach should be used, which starts with the competitive strategy of the firm and defines a manufacturing policy to fit it. This definition is essential if those responsible for the day-to-day operations are to do their work effectively. A statement made over 20 years ago is unlikely to be totally accurate today, but more recent contributions suggest that there are still organisations that follow the old thinking. Pendelbury, 1990 stated:

> "Western business has generally been slower than Far Eastern competition in recognising the new realities of competitive life. Corporate strategists and planners, through knowledge, experience and inclination have assumed either that manufacturing was totally compliant to the requirements of marketing or finance, or that its contribution to new thinking would be relatively limited." (page 101)

Under the bottom-up approach, the individual engineers, industrial relations experts, information technology specialists, the production planners and other experts may all have been very efficient. However, efficiency is rarely synonymous with effectiveness, and it needs management input to ensure that the right thing is done. In other words, the need is to give considerably more than passing attention to manufacturing strategy.

The top-down approach relates every aspect of manufacturing to the business strategy, so that it becomes a competitive weapon. Pendlebury, 1990, defines manufacturing strategy as:

> "...a path over a future time period which defines how the manufacturing and related functions such as design, engineering, service, purchasing and supply, distribution, quality, information technology and human resources will be developed, organised, planned and managed to be effective overall in supporting the business strategy and in creating and then sustaining competitive advantage." (page 102).

We will return to some of the specific aspects of manufacturing strategy later in the chapter.

THE FOCUSED FACTORY

One of the practical concepts urged by Skinner is the focused factory, or if this is not possible, creating a number of focused plants within one overall factory. Skinner 1978 argued:

> "A factory that focuses on a narrow product mix for a particular market will outperform the conventional plant, which attempts a broader mission. Because its equipment, supporting systems, and procedures can concentrate on a limited task for one set of customers, its costs and especially its overheads are likely to be lower than those of the conventional plant. But more important, such a plant can become a competitive weapon because the entire apparatus is focused to accomplish the particular manufacturing task demanded by the company's overall strategy and marketing objective." (page 70).

His argument was that manufacturing effectiveness is impossible to achieve if the same plant and workers are producing products that have different objectives. An example is the manufacture of spares on the same machines used to make the original equipment, where the factory sees its main aim as producing a given level of, say motor car engines, and interrupting the work flow to produce spare parts for the after market, often for engines that are no longer in production, can cause inefficiencies in both. Another example is a company making aeronautical components, which uses the highest quality materials, and works to very precise tolerances. The fact that the same machines might be capable of making parts for domestic vacuum cleaners is no reason for using them in this way. It is extremely difficult to train the production workers and managers to work to continually changing standards, depending which contract is going through. Hussey, 1988, page 133 describes how Otis Elevators transformed its Liverpool factory with the focused approach, in this case creating a number of separate mini-plants within the factory.

WORLD-CLASS PRODUCTION

The concept of world-class production moves further away from the traditional view of manufacturing as always following strategic and marketing thinking. Hayes et al, 1988, argue that the organisation should aim to be a world-class performer in manufacturing (we could extend this and argue that the concept should also apply to many other areas of the organisation besides manufacturing). Being at least as good as the best is the only way to achieve sustainable competitive advantage in manufacturing, and of course is only sustainable if the organisation stays in the forefront. Hayes et al, 1988, define world class: "Basically, this means being better than almost every other company in your industry in at least one important aspect of manufacture." (page 21). Being the best in the industry often means that you should look outside the industry to find who is best in the world at a particular process or activity, and then try to emulate this. Learning from other industries is often more effective than trying to learn from a competitor.

I am uneasy about the implication in this definition that world-class performance means being the best in only one aspect of manufacture. In fact the rest of the book does not imply that the job is done when this state is achieved, and the ultimate aim is to be the best in all aspects. Thus world-class performance is a journey, and although the end may never be reached, benefits accrue at every step on the way.

Figure 10.1 summarises a classification used by Hayes et al, and maps the stages an organisation might have reached on its journey to world-class performance, at level four. From this brief summary it is possible to see that there are different philosophies at each stage so becoming world class is more than being excellent: it is also the role that manufacturing plays within the organisation as a whole.

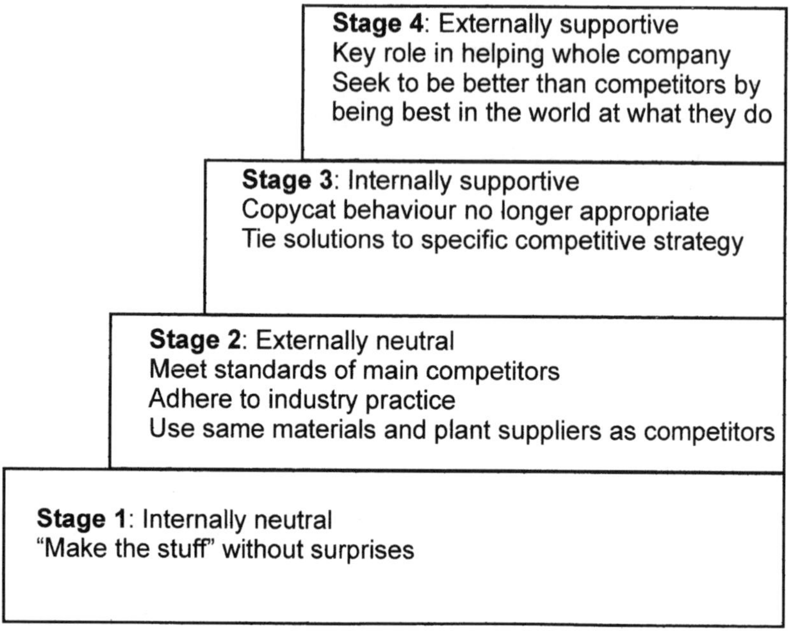

A summary of the stages defined by Hayes et al 1988.

Figure 10.1   Stages in manufacturing philosophy.

So one aspect of manufacturing strategy might be identifying where the organisation is on the stages map, and determining how to take it to being a world-class performer.

MODERN MANUFACTURING CONCEPTS

The tool kit of manufacturing strategy has been steadily enlarging and anyone considering manufacturing strategy should consider among the options some of the modern concepts of manufacture. A brief description of some of them is given here. For more details refer to Hayes et al, 1988.

Flexible manufacturing system (FMS) is a way of handling small batch sizes economically, giving more flexibility of production and reducing throughput times and inventory sizes. The concept is the grouping of parts into families, with manufacture controlled by computer, using machine tools with the ability to change tools automatically. In effect, small batches can be manufactured as efficiently as larger batches, which provides the opportunity to modify standard products to suit individual market needs. FMS can change strategies for global production.

Computer-aided design (CAD) is the use of computers by the designer to design products on screen, and store all the critical information electronically, including all dimensions and tolerances. A library of design elements can be retained in a design database, reducing design time for future products. Not only does CAD speed up the design process, but it makes it easier for designs to be modified and manipulated. Standardisation becomes easier because of the access to the database. It is also much easier to pass design information to others, inside and outside of the same building. Disks are much more manageable than large blueprints.

Computer-aided manufacture (CAM) takes CAD a stage further by using the computer to convert drawings and designs into manufacturing instructions. Information on tools, jigs, routing instructions and the like can be incorporated into the product database. CAM can also produce the instructions needed to drive computer-controlled manufacturing processes.

Just-in-time production (JITP) is a system which ensures that each item is only made at the time it is required, or in the case of purchased items, delivered to the production line when needed. The system reduces inventories throughout the process but requires careful attention to scheduling. Its adherents believe that the system prevents problems from being hidden behind inventories so that they can be dealt with. JITP offers a low-technology approach, based on demand-pulling requirements. However, it requires some stability in demand levels and considerable effort to install and make effective.

Total quality management (TQM) is not a manufacturing method, nor is it restricted to manufacture. Ho, 1998, states:

"TQM provides the overall concept that fosters continuous improvement in an organisation. The TQM philosophy stresses a continuous, integrated, consistent, organisation-wide perspective involving everyone and everything. It focuses primarily on total satisfaction for both internal and external customers, within a management environment that seeks continuous improvement of all systems and processes. TQM emphasises use of all people, usually in multifunctional teams, to bring about improvement from within the organisation. It stresses optimal life cycle costs and uses measurement within a disciplined methodology in achieving improvements.

The key aspects of TQM are the prevention of defects an emphasis on quality in design." (page 8)

TQM moves responsibility for quality away from inspectors, to the people who do the work. It is a learning approach. Above all, it requires a major cultural shift in the organisation, and in my view one reason why it often fails is because there is an attempt to have a different culture on quality than that which exists for everything else in the organisation.

OTHER ISSUES IN MANUFACTURING STRATEGY

One of the results of a piecemeal approach to manufacturing is that incremental investments to boost output tend to be preferred to a fundamental rethink of the entire situation. This incrementalism is reinforced because it will usually result in a relatively high rate of return when discounted cash flow methods of evaluation are used, and in any case requires less management time and less capital than a complete rethink would have required. The result may be that the life of old and near obsolete capacity is continually extended, and that opportunities to reduce unit costs are not taken. What may be overlooked in the evaluation is the actions that competitors may be taking. The danger of the apparently optimum incremental approach is that the firm may lose its competitive position. And by the time this becomes obvious in its effects, it is usually too late to do anything about it.

Historically, the definition of manufacturing strategies and policies has tended to follow from the overall corporate strategy. In reality there is a dynamic relationship between alternative market-related strategies and manufacturing. In many situations price and volume are linked through the marketplace, with different prices giving different volumes. What the company is willing to supply is affected by costs, and, these can be made to vary through different manufacturing strategies. An appropriate manufacturing strategy should, in the formulation phase, con-tribute to total corporate strategy, and thereafter should fulfil certain tasks and duties which derive from that strategy. One of the best examples of this was Swatch, where manufacturing and marketing strategies moved in harmony, so that the new type of watch was designed, engineered and manufactured to the standards and cost required in order to take its innovative place in the market. No incremental approach to manufacturing could have achieved the desired results.

In developing manufacturing strategy there are the obvious matters of capacities, costs, processes, methods, flexibility, quality and speed. Many organisations need to take a global view of manufacturing, as in many industries the old concept of erecting factories in every market is no longer viable. More than any other factor, it is the global nature of competition which is putting pressure on manufacturing.

Manufacturing strategy is too important to be treated haphazardly. Getting it right can make an enormous contribution to the corporate strategy, and the overall corporate results. Getting it wrong can mean depressed profits and lost opportunities.

REFERENCES

Hayes, R. H., Wheelwright, S. C. and Clark, K., 1988, *Dynamic Manufacturing: Creating the Learning Organization*, Free Press, New York.

Henderson, B. D., 1973, "The experience curve reviewed", in Stern, C. W. and Stalk, G., editors, *Perspectives on Strategy*, Wiley, New York.

Henderson, B. D., 1974a, "The experience curve reviewed: why does it work?", in Stern, C. W. and Stalk, G., editors, *Perspectives on Strategy*, Wiley, New York.

Henderson, B. D., 1974b, "The experience curve reviewed: price stability", in Stern, C. W. and Stalk, G., editors, *Perspectives on Strategy*, Wiley, New York.

Ho, S. K. M., 1998, "Change for the better via ISO 9000 and TQM", in Ho, S. K. M., editor, *ISO 9000 and Total Quality Management: Proceedings of the 3rd International Conference*, Hong Kong Baptist University, Hong Kong.

Hussey, D. E., 1988, *Management Training and Corporate Strategy*, Pergamon, Oxford.

Pendelbury, A. J., 1990, "Manufacturing strategy for competitive advantage", in Hussey, D. E., editor, *International Review of Strategic Management*, Vol. 1, Wiley, Chichester.

Skinner, W., 1978, *Manufacturing in the Corporate Strategy*, Wiley, New York.

11

Financial Planning

It would be very easy to begin every chapter in this book with the words "this is a critical area for the success of strategic planning". It would also be true, for every chapter covers an aspect which must be considered important if the strategies are to play an effective part in the management and growth of the company.

Financial strategic planning is a key activity. Everyone knows that the most exciting of development plans will only come about if they can be financed: anyone who has worked on economic development projects in an underdeveloped country will be well aware of that all too familiar taste of bitterness when a carefully developed and patently viable scheme has to be shelved because there is no capital available to implement it.

To remain in business a company has to stay solvent. It must also have sufficient liquid funds to meet its debts and to provide the means of future expansion. Lack of liquidity can bring the collapse of the most aggressive of companies.

So the financial strategy has three main tasks:

- To ensure the company remains solvent.
- To ensure that it has no liquidity problems.
- To provide it with the financial resources for growth.

These are, of course, the aims of good financial management.

I believe that financial strategic planning has two dimensions. The first is the expression of the company's strategic plans so that they positively identify the financial needs, problems and opportunities of the company. The second dimension is in the development of financial strategies, ranging from the selection of a means of financing, to the management of the company's surplus funds, and through to changes in the company's general policies. Somewhere during this second process, financial planning exerts an influence on the company's overall strategies: it may act as a constraint, preventing the company from taking an action that will cause a drop in current profits; it may state that project B simply cannot be financed; or it may act as a goal to stimulate further capital investment so that "cash mountains" are reduced.

THE FIRST DIMENSION OF FINANCIAL PLANNING

Before the more complex aspects of financial strategy can be considered, the company must develop a method of projecting its financial requirements into the future. Financial managers almost invariably work with the future in mind, figuring the needs and resources of the years to come, and the financial director's office in many organisations is the one place where long-range forecasts of performance may be found, and where an attempt has been made to identify future problems.

Strategic planning gives financial management a sharper tool, as it replaces estimates of a purely accounting nature with firm plans and programmes of action based on a clear strategy. It therefore brings to financial management the probability of a higher degree of accuracy, a monitoring and control process that enables revision to take place where appropriate, and a method of identifying financial needs which is future oriented, rather than based on past performance. For the well-run organisation, the strategic approach will not introduce a system of financial planning that is revolutionary, but it will provide a method which is better.

The methods of strategic planning discussed in the appropriate chapters of this book enable the company to prepare an estimate of future profits under a certain defined and detailed strategy, and with a broad picture of the capital investment that would be required to effect this strategy. Sometimes these figures will be expressed as a range, rather than one simple number, but this does not affect the value of the estimate. There should also be an estimate of that other "source" of cash, depreciation, since this can be related to both existing assets, and new investments included in the strategic plan.

Thus from the predetermined intentions of the other segments of the company come detailed estimates of three of the main elements of a simple cash-flow forecast: profits, capital expenditures (or capital inflows from divested assets) and depreciation. The remaining elements of the cash flow fall either within the responsibility of the financial manager or the plans provide the means of estimating changes in position: for example, variations in debtor or creditor relationships, inventory levels, income from non-trading sources (including interest received), interest payable, dividends and taxation.

Two basic documents should be prepared from these data. The first is a statement of fixed and working capital requirements for each year of the strategic plan. This makes more sense if provisional priorities can be assigned to projects. In some cases, as suggested, the resultant figure will in fact be a range: in others more projects may be listed than the company will carry out. For example, the organisation may specify that after further evaluation it intends to undertake project A requiring £500 000 investment or project B requiring £750 000, but has no intention of doing both.

The second document is a cash-flow statement for the same period, giving an estimate of the financial resources that will become available, and showing these against the organisation's needs. In this form the cash-flow statement is a useful tool, but it can be given a still keener edge.

Some form of risk analysis should be applied (see Chapter 5) so that it is possible to see the effect on capital availability that a reduction in profits would have. If the risk analysis suggests that future profits are only 70% secure, it may be desirable to plan on the basis of a reduced cash flow, rather than to rely on a source of funds which may not materialise.

A cash-flow statement on a yearly basis may only be a partial indicator of capital needs and availability. Most businesses have a seasonal variation of one sort or another. To ignore this can be very dangerous, since it could lead the company to under-estimate its capital needs at certain times of the year, thus running into unexpected liquidity problems.

It is necessary for an estimate to be made of constant and variable capital needs. (Constant capital is the fixed capital of the business plus that level of working capital which is needed to maintain operations in the slackest period, say for a month, of the year. Variable capital is that additional element of working capital that may be required over and above the constant level to finance the organisation at other periods in the year.) These will, of course, vary from business to business: the more seasonal the nature of its activities the greater will the gap between constant and variable capital become. A good system of financial planning will include a regularly revised short-term cash-flow forecast based on the annual budget. From this it is possible to calculate constant and variable capital needs for current activities: the longer range plans should provide sufficient data to enable an estimate to be made of constant and variable capital requirements over future years. These will, of course, be related to the longer range cash-flow forecast.

These estimates provide the financial planner with the raw material for the development of financial strategy. Up to this point the planning activity has been rather passive, being simply the analysis of other people's data. The next phase is more dynamic.

THE SECOND DIMENSION OF FINANCIAL PLANNING

In rare and exceptional circumstances it may be that everything adds up conveniently, and that the only financial planning required is to look at the forecasts and decide that cash inflow would equate with cash outflow, so that nothing need be done.

When making this assessment the financial planner should bear the vision and objectives of the organisation in mind. A growth in earnings per share objective may inhibit the raising of capital from new share issues for example. Constraints attached to the objectives may restrict the amount of money which can be borrowed. If the cash flow fits in with the objectives and constraints, and still balances within reasonable limits, there is no apparent problem.

But this is not a likely situation. It may be that the cash flow will show an accumulation of liquid funds that will reveal a strategic problem of its own, or even more probable in an aggressive organisation, pushing growth to the limit, it will reveal a shortfall of resources that has to be made up through borrowing or equity injections of one sort or another.

This picture in itself will be an over-simplification, since the cash flows will be based on certain policies which themselves may be changed to give a different outcome. Additionally, the picture revealed by the forecasts may not suit the overall strategy of the organisation, and certain changes may have to be made: for example, it may be argued that the acquisition planned for 18 months hence would be more readily financed by an exchange of shares than a cash offer. This may make it desirable to defer another strategy, to ensure that the organisation's own shares are in a stronger position on the Stock Exchange, and therefore more attractive to the vendor of the potential acquisition.

Many elements of the cash flow require a defined financial policy. That policy is part of the financial strategy and may be varied to enable the organisation to achieve its overall objectives. It is worthwhile examining some of the areas that respond to financial strategic planning and some of the policy changes which may result.

WORKING CAPITAL

The organisation that has a surplus of funds may become wasteful in its use of working capital. When it gets to the stage of having to borrow (particularly in times of credit squeeze, or when interest rates are high) it tends to look inwards to see how it can be more sparing in its use of money. If economies can be made, they will also have the effect of increasing the percentage return on capital, and may thus assist in meeting the organisation's goals in another way. Working capital may be reduced by decreasing the amount of trade credit given, increasing the amount taken, or applying more stringent control to raw material and finished product inventories. Naturally these areas are not the sole responsibility of financial management. Every manager has a duty to consider this aspect of the organisation's policy, and the questioning aspects of strategic planning, such as the corporate appraisal, may be expected to create an interest in the problem. But it is frequently the financial side of the business which focuses full attention on these policies. It is likely to be the financial manager who is aware that the cost of money has risen and that where last year it was economic to buy raw materials in extra large quantities to secure better terms, under current conditions the cost of financing the extra inventories may exceed the discount gained. Similarly, it is the financial manager who is best fitted to see when trade debtors are too high, and what action should be taken to reduce the amount of credit given.

DIVIDENDS

An organisation is run for its shareholders (although many would argue that it is not run for their sole benefit: there are other "stakeholders" also), and the dividend policy will have an important effect on the cash-flow position. If capital is needed for growth it may be possible in the case of a private company managed by its owners to reduce dividend payments. In this case the owners are in a position to assess the chance of future earnings against present cash receipts and are qualified to take the appropriate decision. With a public company it will almost certainly be undesirable to reduce dividend levels (unless, of course, the company expects to earn a reduced level of profits). Such an action would almost certainly have an effect on the company's share price on the stock exchange. This could mean that existing shareholders would lose capital, as well as taking a reduced income. It could result in protests from shareholders, and incidentally make the company a potentially more attractive take-over fish for another company's net. The effect will vary with the size of the decrease in dividend, and what this represents as an earnings percentage of current share price.

A decision to increase dividends may be taken when the earnings position is so good that the board feels that it would be in the best interests of both the company and shareholders. Alternatively, such a move may be made to strengthen the company's position on the stock exchange. Generally the market is happiest with a constant dividend policy, rather than one that fluctuates from year to year, and will also scrutinise the dividend cover, so that increases that appear to the market to be imprudent, thus threatening future earnings, will lead to an adverse reaction from the stock market.

TAXATION

Taxation planning is a specialist subject all to itself, and one which has its own experts. (The cash-flow statement should show tax in the year of payment, not the year in which it is incurred.) The complications of tax legislation will vary in its effect from business to business, and may be particularly complex for the multinational company which deals with the tax laws of many different countries. Fiscal incentives may affect the expansion or diversification policies, and must be taken into account when detailed evaluation is made of projects.

The objective of taxation planning should be to ensure that the organisation pays only that minimum amount of tax which it is legally bound to, and no more. It is about tax avoidance, which is legal, rather than tax evasion, which is not.

In the forward cash-flow forecasts, assumptions have to be made about levels of taxation likely to apply in the future. This can be a difficult operation, and especially hard for a multinational business, and the assessments made are unlikely to always be correct. As with some of the other factors, it may be advisable to apply some form of risk or sensitivity analysis to the figures, so that the effect of an erroneous forecast can be considered.

FIXED CAPITAL

The estimates of fixed capital requirements will be rather broad, and in thinking about these the financial manager is beginning to move in the direction of the next problem, how to use the cash flow to ensure the future of the organisation. Nevertheless, at this early stage, it may be necessary to explore some of the options attached to the estimates. If the provisional figures suggest a tight capital position, it may be worthwhile re-examining policies about renting or buying business premises, or hiring rather than purchasing assets. In this way it may be possible to reduce the capital requirement without having to cut out investment essential to the success of the plan.

DEPRECIATION

Depreciation is part of the matching principle of accounting, and its aim is to relate a portion of the cost of each asset to its expected useful life. Within limits a company may make its own depreciation policies, and depreciation is an item of the greatest importance in the cash flow of many organisations. In fact depreciation rates and calculation methods do vary from one firm to another, and an extra high or extra low rate of depreciation will have a matching effect on the level of declared profits.

Although a cautious depreciation policy may appeal to the prudent, it is dangerous if it results in the organisation's assets being under-valued. Again this policy could make the organisation become a candidate for a take-over bid, and could result in shareholders receiving less for their shares than is really their due. Over-cautious financial management is rarely good management. Depreciation, of course, is a non-cash expense. Cash flowed out when the asset was purchased, and does not therefore leave the business again when the accountants "charge" depreciation.

THE PROBLEM OF EXCESS LIQUID FUNDS

It may be that the cash-flow forecasts will show a surplus of liquid funds over requirements, even after the adjustments made under a careful sensitivity analysis. The use of surplus capital presents a planning problem for the financial management of the organisation: if the surpluses are embarrassingly large, they may represent a strategic problem. There have been cases where a company has been a subject of a take-over bid, largely because of its liquid funds position. In any event, a very high ratio of non-operating to operating capital may make it difficult or impossible for the company to earn an acceptable return on investment.

Where cash surpluses exist, whether they are moderate or excessive, it is the duty of the financial management to earn the maximum from them. The cash-flow forecasts, and the estimates of the variable capital element, provide financial management with a tool to assess the length of term that can be offered when investing surplus funds.

The existence of surplus cash should not prevent the organisation from applying good financial management practice, and it should be as stringent in its examination of working capital requirements as it would be in a time of financial shortage.

One thing that should not be overlooked in long-term financial planning is the possibility that an acquisition may be financed by means other than a cash purchase, or by a mix of cash and other means. This is discussed later.

Analysis of the environment is of great importance to financial planning, whether in conditions of excess or shortage of liquid funds. Financial management must be interested in the general trends of interest rates, and in the expected position of the money market. From forecasts of general economic health, it is but a step to assessments of the probability of the degree of credit squeeze the country might be expected to be labouring under. The financial manager should also be interested in prospects of devaluation in the countries within which the organisation has a financial relationship. Fluctuations in foreign exchange rates are close to impossible to predict with accuracy, so good financial management might include hedging actions to lay off some of the risks. Financial management may also have an input when decisions are made about which countries to do business with, and which currencies to use in any bids.

In its need to consider external factors, the financial sector of the organisation is no different from the other parts of the organisation, although the type of risks and effects to which it is subject may not be the same.

THE PROBLEM OF FINANCING PROJECTS FROM OTHER SOURCES

For many organisations the luxury of surplus money in the bank is a state they may dream of but will never experience. And for many it is an undesirable state, for there is a good deal to be said for gaining a larger return on shareholders' equity from the use of borrowed capital. This presumes that the organisation can earn more on its projects than the interest it pays. (It is a very thought-provoking situation when an organisation earns less for its owners than if they had put their money on deposit in a building society.)

Certain elements of financial policy have to be considered before the organisation can plan its sources of funds. Perhaps the first is the extent of gearing which will be considered acceptable. In other words, a policy for debt/equity ratio should be laid down (unless such a policy forms one of the constraints under which the organisation operates, such as the family-owned company that will not consider borrowing under any circumstance).

A second area of the policy is the way in which the organisation will use short-, medium- or long-term financing. If the management holds the traditional view that short-term borrowing must never be used to finance the purchase of fixed assets, this should be defined. Clarification of policy at this stage can save considerable wasted time at the development of strategies.

The strategic financial plan should try to show where the funds that the organisation requires will come from. In normal circumstances the organisation has a choice between raising further equity, or obtaining a short-, medium- or long-term loan of one type or another. In every organisation there is an upper limit, beyond which it is unlikely it will be able to obtain any additional finance.

In making its decisions the organisation will have to consider a number of factors, varying from the state of the money market to control and yield, as well as bearing in mind the ever-present need to maintain both liquidity and solvency.

The main factors to consider before extending the equity base of the operation are:

- The possibility of loss of control through the issue of further shares (assuming here that there are no unpaid balances on existing shares that can be called up).
- The effect on stock exchange prices which an additional share issue might have: again, through a weakening in price, this could lead to a loss of control.
- The particular state of the money market and the relative costs of borrowing and the market price of the company's shares.
- The need to maintain as much flexibility as possible. Some options close the door to others, or leave the organisation with little room to manoeuvre if it moves into a time of difficulty.

Of course this is an over-simplification of the situation. A private company in a very strong and healthy position might find it advantageous to go public, and in these circumstances might so arrange things that the original owners still retain effective control. However, not all entrepreneurs have been happy with the results of stock market pressures on their activities. Alan Sugar tried to buy back Amstrad after it had gone public, and Richard Branson succeeded in his bid to take Virgin back into private ownership.

If the plans show that major acquisitions are being sought, the organisation may have to be prepared to change its capital structure in order to be able to make an offer based on exchange of shares. This might be very desirable from the point of view of the vendor organisation, even if less attractive to the buyer. Taxation conditions mean cash is not always an acceptable alternative for shareholders, and an exchange of shares becomes necessary even when the would-be buyer has sufficient liquid resources, and would prefer not to dilute the equity base. If the acquisition strategy is really serious, the company must be willing to shape its financial strategy to suit.

There are alternatives to cash or shares as purchase consideration, varying from straight debt to convertible loan stock. The final solution can, of course, only be found in the light of the particular acquisition. What is important for the long-range financial plan is an awareness of the alternatives, the selection of priorities, and the clearing away of the difficulties that might prevent the company from implementing its preferred solution. However, the need to consider flexibility should also be considered when determining the strategy. The Ratner jewellery chain made many acquisitions in the 1980s, many of which were financed by cumulative preference shares and bank loans. When it suddenly crashed into loss in the early 1990s, the level of debt became a pressing problem, and dividends were suspended. Preference shares have an advantage in that, unlike a loan, the organisation does not guarantee to pay a dividend. For Ratner (which changed its name to Signet) it also meant that after several years of non-payment, the amount that would have to be paid to preference shareholders meant that ordinary shareholders could see little possibility of being paid a dividend in the future. Apart for any other problems, this meant that even if the company had wanted to raise more equity, the share price was so low, and the prospects of a return so doubtful, that this option was not possible. Meanwhile, the preference shareholders were demanding the break up of the organisation so that they could recover something from their investments, which would have left the ordinary shareholders with nothing. In 1997, all the shareholders of both classes agreed to a restructure, the preference shareholders, being given ordinary shares in exchange for there preference shares and accumulated dividend claims. The annual report for 1997/8 shows that no dividend had yet been declared. Apart from the loss of flexibility of the method of financing and, as analysts were saying before the downturn, a greater level of loan finance than was prudent, the financial strategy of the company caused a major diversion of top management time to the preference shareholders, at a time when the business need was for all effort to be spent on turning the organisation around.

One maxim of greater importance to all funding operations is that it pays to be right in the assessment of funds needed. Often it is a much simpler matter to raise one large loan than two smaller ones: for example, in many situations the obtaining of £5 250 000 may be an easier operation than that of raising one loan of £5 200 000 and another, later, of £50 000. Raising too much money, on the other hand, may lead to additional expense. But on the whole it makes more sense to be optimistic rather than pessimistic in assessing the amounts needed. The lack of that last few thousand pounds can endanger not only the particular project but the whole organisation.

Sources for raising loan funds are well known. Under normal circumstances bank overdraft may be the simplest and cheapest method of obtaining working capital, particularly for a business with a seasonal rise in working capital requirements. In times of credit squeeze this source may not be so readily available, and worse, the existing facilities may be withdrawn at short notice. If the strategic plan shows a situation arising in the future that can be solved with a bank overdraft, there may be little for the financial director to do to prepare the ground, apart from making sure that the organisation and its likely need are known to the various banks with whom it deals. It may be advantageous to obtain promises of support before the need arises, while the organisation has the weapon of being able to transfer the account to another bank that might promise to be more obliging. Similarly, it may be advantageous to divide current business between two or more banks, in order to be more flexible in the future: much depends on the size of the account. In some circumstances it may be better tactics to be a medium-sized customer of one bank than a relatively small customer of three. The organisation is not restricted to domestic banks, and may have the option of raising money outside its main country of operations. The multinational company may have a complex network of loan finance from all the countries in which it operates, particularly as borrowing in the currency of a subsidiary company, for activities in the country of borrowing, can minimise the risk from changing exchange rates when the loan is repaid.

Debentures are a traditional source of long-term debt, and tend to carry a relatively low interest rate to match the risks. There are different types of debentures that can be issued, but the success of an issue is likely to be dependent on both the standing of the company and the state of the money market. If the general rates of interest are high, debentures may be an unwise approach for the company, since to be attractive the rates of interest offered will also be high, and the company will have to continue to pay this rate over the whole period of the debenture, even though the general rates in some of these years may be lower. More recently large organisations have issued bonds of various types, which do not require the pledging of particular assets as security.

Industrial medium- and long-term loans are often available from specialist undertakings.

For the organisation which cannot, or does not wish to, use these sources of funds there are others available. It may be desirable to sell and lease back industrial property, thus freeing capital hitherto locked up in land and buildings. No interest is incurred on this transaction, although a rent will have to be paid which will have its effect on the costs of production of the company's current range of output.

Some form of lease-hire may be used for certain other assets. The principle most usually applies to motor vehicles, but can be extended to items such as office furniture and equipment such as computers. A firm with a large lorry fleet could release a considerable amount of capital by turning to lease hire, and some companies believe that lease hire is in any case the cheapest method of operating for them.

It is also possible for a strategy to be devised that achieves the desired result, but avoids the need for new capital investment. Examples are outsourcing and strategic alliances, both of which have been discussed elsewhere.

Additional working capital can be obtained from factoring debtors. For many this may be an expensive solution, but may be a possibility which cannot be ignored.

An organisation with multinational operations should think internationally when it comes to raising money. It may operate on an overdraft in Australia, and have a credit balance in South Africa. Here there is a need not only to compare interest rates against each other, but to consider legislation, government policies, and the economic possibilities of each country and its currency. It may also be easier to raise a loan in one country than in another, and some countries may have specialist industrial loan bodies which others do not possess.

The legal environment must be considered in all decisions. It is of no use to plan to obtain all your Zimbabwe subsidiaries' requirements locally, if they fall outside the borrowing restrictions which may be imposed by the government on companies whose ownership is vested outside the country. Some countries have legislation preventing the free flow of funds between international boundaries. No financial planner can afford to plead ignorance of restrictions when devising the firm's financial strategy. In the worst cases this could be a criminal offence, although it is more likely the sources of funds which were planned will just not be available when the time comes, and the organisation may have to curtail its expansion plans or even be put in a position of poor liquidity.

The organisation's emerging financial strategy should also take the tool of public relations into account. It may be that from an awareness of the future financial position will come a realisation of the need to set particular PR objectives for the financial function. The company which is well known to the investing public has a better chance of success when it goes to that public for funds. Similarly the explanation for an off-trend drop in profits may be accepted by the stock market if the organisation has the right sort of image, but rejected totally if it has no positive image at all.

Just as the cash-flow forecast assists in deciding the term for which surplus funds can be invested, so it determines the length of time for which surplus funds may be required. Again judgement should be made after a careful sensitivity analysis. If the cash flow shows that the company will require capital to meet a one-off peak next year, it makes sense to seek some form of short-term loan. To raise additional equity capital, or obtain debenture funds, would be wasteful, as in subsequent years the company would be over-capitalised. In the first case its earnings would have to be distributed over a wider base of share ownership: in the second there would be a fixed interest burden over the life of the debenture. One should not, of course, overlook in these calculations the fact that provision has to be made for interest, and for the loans themselves to be repaid!

The final result of the financial strategy should be a clear picture for management of the organisation's long-term capital requirements, and a detailed strategy for obtaining them. Actions that require immediate attention should be identified, and the necessary aspects of financial policy defined. This document should become a part of the normal management processes of the company, and be subject to continued monitoring and revision. And on this document may depend the future success or failure of the undertaking. For unless it secures its future capital requirements the probability of a company's reaching its objectives and carrying out its strategies may be very slim indeed.

12
Planning for Human Resources

THE NEED

The achievement of any set of corporate objectives requires the deployment of the two basic resources of money and people. Deficiency in either of these areas can reduce the best-laid strategy to a valueless pipe-dream.

Organisations seem to find it more difficult to develop human resource strategies which are linked to the business strategy, despite a widespread recognition that this is important. Where the limiting effects of a capital shortage are fairly easy to foresee, the constraint caused by a deficiency of human resources is not so obvious, neither is the possibility that some of the well-established personnel policies may be making the implementation of the business strategy more difficult. The quality of all money is the same, but the requirement of people has both a quality and a quantity parameter. While lack of capital may be an insurmountable obstacle, the right number of bodies can often be obtained by emergency measures, such as paying above-average salaries, whatever effects this might have on corporate profitability. The task of strategic planning in the human resources field is more complex than that of providing company capital needs.

Worthwhile strategic human resource planning can only take place if the human resource function is regarded as a genuine partner in the management team, or in small organisations where there is no HR function, where the managers themselves actively consider the HR aspects of every decision they make. HRM, as a minimum, must be kept fully informed of business plans, since these can radically change the perception of personnel issues. An HR department that is regarded solely as a records office, and which plays no part in management decision-making, is unlikely to be able to make a worthwhile contribution to the achievement of corporate objectives. To play an effective part in a company's future, HRM must, of right, have a place at the management table, to dine on the full menu of information and free discussion: it should not be regarded as the child, fed on a restricted diet of what is good for it, or, worse, as the dog under the table, pouncing hungrily on the scraps and titbits of data which are thrown down to it by its masters.

All managers have some responsibility for HR matters, and these should be considered in conjunction with the other relevant factors in any decision process. In addition, HRM has a particular duty to ensure that HR issues are woven into the fabric of each strategic decision, and that every aspect of HR policy works to make the strategy effective.

THE INTEGRATED ORGANISATION

One of the basic tasks of any manager is to organise, and all enterprises establish a system of relationships between people. In the smallest of businesses there may be no formal definition of these relationships. The chief executive knows everybody, participates in virtually every decision, and may well perform a range of functions personally. As organisations increase in size and diversity of operations, the complexity of relationships increases, and it becomes more important to formalise the organisation structure. There are few organisations of any size which do not possess an organisation chart, yet this snapshot of structure (which is what most of us think of when the word organisation is mentioned) is really the wrong place to start.

The fundamental problem in the design of structure is the need to differentiate tasks into work packages, or jobs, to link these into units of managerial control. However, increasing differentiation brings an increasing requirement for co-ordination, and the layers of complexity which are added to the structure, until the ultimate form of the global matrix is reached, are efforts to grasp this issue.

In the mid-1960s Harvard Business School began a series of research studies into the relationship of strategy and structure. At the simplest level the relationship is self-evident. If a new business venture is to be entered into, it has to be organised, and may add a new stream of managerial activity. The establishment of new companies in other countries also brings the need for staff and co-ordination departments. The Harvard research programme went wider than this, and established overall relationships between structure and strategy.

By the 1970s many of the leading companies had reorganised on strategic business unit lines, a more advanced form of divisionalisation which brings a greater strategic focus. There has also been a trend, by no means universal, to organise on a global strategic business unit basis, leading to the demise of the "international division" and replacing it with a matrix organisation.

Towards the end of the 1980s, and through the 1990s the fashion has been for flatter organisations, with more power being devolved from the corporate centre to the operating units, as organisations struggled with the two strategic drivers of customer needs and cost effectiveness.

It would be surprising if strategy and structure were unrelated, as this would defy common sense. However, there is no one appropriate organisational structure for business, although clearly some structures are more appropriate than others. This led to the contingency theory of organisation, developed by Lawrence and Lorsch, 1967, another Harvard team. The theory was developed from a study of poor and good performing organisations in a variety of different environmental circumstances. Some of the broad findings were that the right choice of structure is dependent on the growth strategy of the firm, the diversity of products and markets, the rate of new product innovation, the degree of competition and the rate of change in the environment.

The research has consistently found that, where the environment is unstable, high performance is associated with decentralised structures, and low performance with centralised, presumably because the centralised structures slow down the reaction and decision making time. The converse applies when firms operate in a stable environment.

There was also a difference in the optimum organisation of routine and non-routine tasks. High performance was associated with mechanistic organisations when the task was routine, and loose, more ambiguous structures when the task was non-routine. Again the converse applies. The reason seems to lie in the repetitive nature of routine work, allowing standard policies to be formulated. Re-inventing the wheel wastes time in this situation. When tasks are not routine, decisions require individual attention and do not fit a predetermined pattern. The situation may thus be ambiguous and not amenable to mechanistic solutions.

Competitive situations create a form of environmental instability. Here the high performers tend to be decentralised organisations with formal control procedures. Choice of the appropriate control instruments is an important part of organisational design.

An organisation is rarely the same throughout. Even when the overall environment is unstable, sub-environments (such as accounting) may be stable and the tasks routine. Thus the appropriate organisational form will vary with the sub-environments within the organisation. Successful firms appear to be those which have recognised this, have differentiated their functions so that they adapt to the sub-environments, and have found ways to integrate this differentiation.

An organisation is more than strategy and structure, and if these two elements are related then others should be also. Other elements, such as control, have begun to be mentioned. This is taken further in Figure 12.1, which owes much to the work of a number of writers and researchers, but is leavened by my own experience. The elements of organisation shown in this figure are self-evident, but will repay some thought. They are all inter-related, in that a change in one factor may cause (or be caused by) a change in another. For example, a new definition of tasks may either be caused by problems with people to fulfil the jobs, as changing the nature of tasks may bring a requirement for people of different skills, experience or other abilities. This in turn may require changes to the reward structure. It does not stop there, as a new specification of tasks may also cause changes to the information required in order for the tasks to be performed. We could move right round the model, but as a detailed example will be given later, this can be postponed. However, we can turn things round and argue that a change in any one of the elements may be frustrated

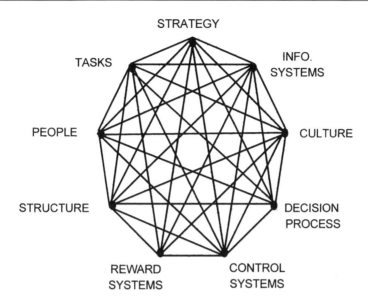

Figure 12.1 An integrated view of organisation.

if the other elements are not compatible with it. It may also be argued that the only element that should be allowed to drive the others should be the strategy.

The integrated concept is important for an understanding of organisation, and stresses that good organisational design is a complex activity, which cannot be undertaken effectively without taking into account the dynamic relationship of all the elements. It also clearly shows another problem caused by strategy, that tasks will change as an organisation progresses, and people who are an ideal fit at one stage in the organisation's development may become inappropriate at a subsequent stage.

There are two strands to follow here. The first is that the progression of a business through its life cycle will bring new requirements to tasks, jobs and the type of people required. The manager who is a superb start-up operator may be incapable of managing a large organisation. The second strand extends this thinking to portfolio organisations.

Strand one has a research basis, but fits a hypotheses which many of us would have drawn up from our own experience. The change as a business moves through various stages of development on its journey through its life cycle. Every aspect of Figure 12.1 is liable to require change at each stage in the life cycle, as the organisation changes from the acorn, so to speak, to the mature oak tree, and this of course may take many years. The exact point of transition from one stage to another is not always clear, which is one reason why elements of the integrated organisation may continue beyond their sell-by date.

If the first strand is accepted, it requires no great leap of logic to argue that an organisation that has a portfolio of businesses (remember Chapter 8) in different positions on the portfolio matrix should accept that the skills required from the various management teams are not identical. For example, it takes a different talent to manage a cash generator business than a new venture expected to travel on a high growth path. The mature business is likely to operate in conditions of moderate stability, with known competitors, experienced buyers and established market patterns. For a new business in a new market, uncertainty is the most predictable problem. Some people can tolerate uncertainty and ambiguity more than others. In addition managing a business to squeeze out cash without damaging its long-term prospects calls for different skills from those needed to cope with a rapidly expanding firm.

BUSINESS-DRIVEN HRM STRATEGY

The foregoing should have begun to show why HRM strategies and policies should be driven by the strategies of the business, and also why HRM managers should have an active part in the formulation of strategy. To make the need even clearer, Figure 12.2 takes the integrated organisation model, and shows some of the HRM implications of a "rightsizing" decision. The inverted commas are there because the word is a politically correct euphemism for making the organisation smaller, removing layers of management and functions, resulting in a large-scale redundancy. Let us assume that some 10% of total employees will lose their jobs, with a disproportionate number of casualties among middle managers.

Harbridge Consulting Group's research studies, which I managed when rightsizing was at its peak, showed that many of the HR implications which appear in Figure 12.2 were not considered

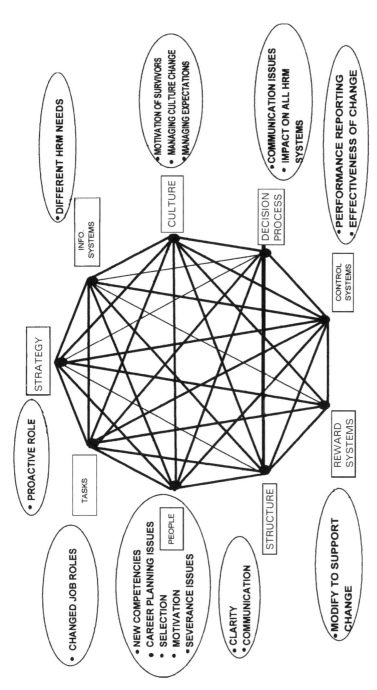

Figure 12.2 Impact of "rightsizing": some HRM issues.

at the time the rightsizing decision was made, the only universal exception being the severance issues (see Tovey 1991 and Mason 1993). Although the flatter organisation meant that managers at all levels had to manage and be managed in a different way, the research found that few organisations in the survey had provided any management training or coaching to help make the change effective. The point is that the strategy of cost reduction is not secured when 10% of the employees walk through the door for the last time with their redundancy cheques: it is only effective when the new organisation is functioning effectively to enable the overall intentions of the organisation to be made effective.

Strategies come in all shapes and sizes and their effects on HRM will vary. However, it should not be assumed that all current HRM strategies are business driven, because if no one has ever looked at them in relation to corporate strategy, the chances are that many would fail the business driven test. So how do we develop HRM strategy? Figure 12.3, taken from Hussey 1996, helps to point the way.

The figure offers a simple guide to thinking about every aspect of HRM. Hussey, 1996, offers some modified versions for different aspects of HRM, but they all follow the same pattern. HRM strategy should consider the strategic needs of the organisation, and any trends in the external environment which impact on HR. It should audit what strategies and policies the organisation is following, and assess the gap between what is being done and what is needed. Some things may already have been started to close the gap and these should be brought into the assessment. At this point revised strategies and policies should be determined, and converted to actions, which should be monitored.

Figure 12.4 looks at the same issue in a slightly different way. The white triangles are policies and strategies for various aspects of HRM (the headings are a sample only), which should be driven by the strategy, and therefore the answers are not a universal "good practice" that can be transferred without change to another organisation with a different strategy. The grey border outside the triangles are purely administrative aspects of HRM, where "good practice" may be similar between organisations. In too many organisations the strategic and administrative elements are confused, and there is a lack of differentiation in those aspects which should be specially designed for the organisation.

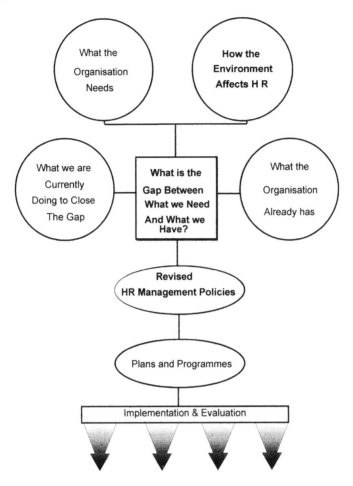

Figure 12.3 A framework for planning HRM. (From Hussey, D. E., 1996, *Business Driven Human Resource Management*), Wiley, Chichester.

The final tool offered (Figure 12.5) before we look at some specifics is a simple way of beginning a consideration of the impact of strategy on people. It takes key points from the vision, values, objectives and strategies, and assess some of the management competencies needed for success. The next step is to highlight areas where there may be a deficiency. Simple tools like this are not perfect, but they enable a quick feel to be obtained of a situation, as a precursor to more detailed study.

Just as in financial planning it is useful to look forward at the sources of and requirements for funds, so it is of value to do

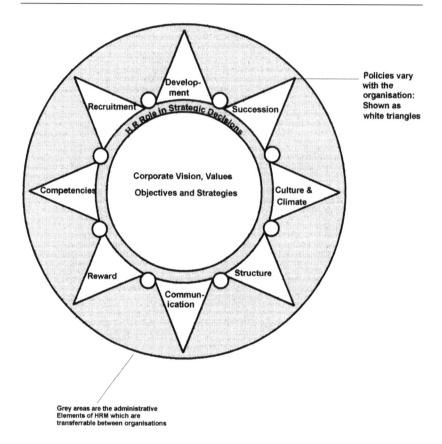

Figure 12.4 Relationship of HRM and corporate strategy. (From Hussey, D. E., 1996, *Business Driven Human Resource Management*), Wiley, Chichester.

something similar for the human resource needs. This activity used to be called manpower planning. The steps involved are set out in Figure 12.6. The issues are discussed under the headings managerial and non-managerial planning but the model is relevant to both.

MANAGERIAL PLANNING

Once the organisation's business strategy has been developed, it becomes possible to look at the way in which it will ensure that it has the right types of people in management jobs in the future. The need for adequate top management succession planning was

(ILLUSTRATIVE ONLY)

STRATEGIC SOURCES		BROAD AREAS OF COMPETENCY						
TYPE	NEED	MARKET PLANNING	CULTURAL DIFFERENCES	NEGOTIATION SKILLS	ALLIANCE MANAGEMENT	PERFORMANCE MANAGEMENT	PROJECT MANAGEMENT
VISION	GLOBAL	X	X				X
	CUSTOMER RESPONSIVE						
STRATEGIES	EUROPEAN EXPANSION	X	X	X			X
	DELAYERING		X			X	X
	STRATEGIC ALLIANCE			X	X		
VALUES	PEOPLE CENTRED					X	
	INTEGRITY					X	
	EMPOWERED PEOPLE					X	
OBJECTIVES	DOUBLE MKT SHARE	X					
	25% P.A REVENUE GROWTH	X					
	25% RETURN ON CAPITAL EMPLOYED	X					

Figure 12.5 Part of a matrix analysis of competencies needed. (From Hussey, D. E., 1996, *Business Driven Human Resource Management*, Wiley, Chichester).

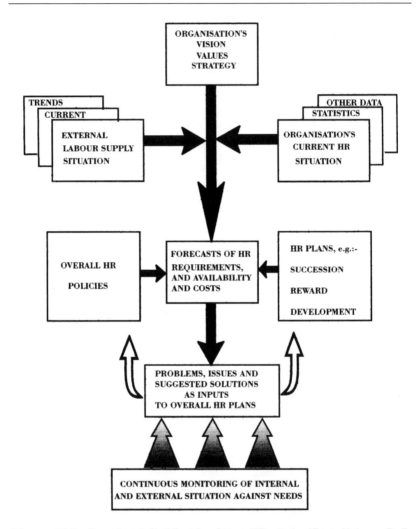

Figure 12.6 Framework for planning future HR needs. (From Hussey, D. E., 1996, Business Driven Human Resource Management. Wiley, Chichester).

instanced in Chapter 3, *The Corporate Appraisal*, and, of course, there is also a requirement to fill the other ranks of management with the right number of people of adequate quality.

A good way to look at this problem is for a management succession chart to be compiled for a number of years into the future. This records the retiring date or probable promotion date of each manager, names one or two potential successors, and shows the ultimate level each person is likely to achieve. Where a person has no further potential for promotion, either on account of personal attributes, or age, this should be clearly stated. The ability to make such assessments requires a workable and fair means of rating personal performance. Get suspicious if you find statements like "ready for promotion in two years" against a name. I remember well one insurance company where we looked back over several years of succession planning assessments to find that identical statements of this kind had been made for the same people every time. It was always "ready in two years", even though five had passed since the first occasion.

It must, of course, be accepted that a succession chart which shows too much good material ready to be promoted, with too low a probability of movement into higher management positions, may point to a problem area. Good, ambitious managers may become restless and leave if opportunities for promotion are low. While it may be comforting to have every key position covered three or four times, it may be completely unrealistic and the company can easily find that all its best prospects have departed by the time they are needed.

The chart will also reveal gaps in succession planning. An assessment then has to be made of those gaps which must be filled with a potential successor, and those where the cost of so doing would exceed the benefits gained. Much will depend on the type of management position, the length of time the company would be likely to have to recruit an outsider, and the probability that the present incumbent will leave. The perfect state of having every position covered is simply not attainable; the organisation just has to decide its level of acceptable risks.

These charts should be confidential to the HRM and senior management, and should not be circulated widely. This does not mean that individuals whose careers look as if they are coming to a dead end should not receive counselling: some, of course may have no wish to progress further. What the exercise is really about is to assess the key problems that the charts show that the organisation will face over the next few years, and the ways in which solutions can be found. The interest is in the total problem, not the assessments of individuals that enabled the problem to be defined. In looking at these problems allowances should be made for resignations and vacancies caused by death or serious illness. The larger organisation has an advantage over the smaller in this type of exercise, since it is likely to have a requirement for a fair number of managers of similar skills, and since it becomes easier to apply statistical techniques in the assessment of natural wastage.

The various management succession strategies open to an organisation involve recruitment, inter-departmental transfers, and training and the personal development of key people.

One aspect of management planning which would not be fully revealed from the organisation plans, is the changing characteristics required for management. The manager of the early 1980s had to have much more mathematical ability than the manager of 15 years before, while today's manager in addition must have a greater expertise in information systems and computers than those 1980 managers, and must be competent to cope with new techniques and concepts. A quality of management for the future is flexibility of outlook, and the ability to retrain where necessary. This is a function of mental processes, rather than chronological age, and inevitably there will always be some casualties. To make sure that the management plan is complete, attempts should be made to forecast the different types of skills that are expected to be needed in the future, and to ensure that new recruits possess the basic attributes.

NON-MANAGERIAL PLANNING

Managerial planning only covers one aspect of the organisation's human resources. Non managerial planning is equally important to the company's future well-being, because failure to provide an adequate workforce may result in failure to achieve corporate objectives.

A good base of statistics is required. Non-managerial planning can usually be assisted by statistical techniques as, in most organisations, it deals with much larger numbers than is the case with management planning.

The basic statistics required include an analysis of employee numbers by job categories and, where valid, location. The system of job classification may be a purely internal one, or it may be based on published government classifications to facilitate comparisons with national statistics. Within each category there should be breakdowns by sex and age. For each of these sub-categories there should be an analysis of employees leaving the company, preferably classified by reason for leaving. Significant conclusions can be drawn from this type of data. An organisation may find that it has an ageing labour force, and may be able to forecast potential shortages of labour which will arise from impending retirements. Similarly, there may be groups of workers with a higher than normal resignation rate, which indicate a possible failure of the organisation to match up to standards and conditions of employment for this type of person.

Besides the series giving numbers of employee, there should also be a series with similar sub-headings, giving the average and range of wage rates paid. Some attempt should also be made to assess productivity increases: this is never as easy as it sounds, and often has to be based on carefully defined assumptions. The trends for the number of hours worked per unit of output, and the labour costs per unit of output, are of great importance in forecasting.

All these statistics will have more meaning if they can be compared with appropriate national and regional statistics. In many cases deviations from the external series will highlight areas of current or potential problems. It then becomes important to analyse the reasons for deviations.

Armed with these data, the analyst should turn to the organisation's strategies, to assess how the nature of operations is intended to alter over the next few years. New ventures, business expansion, and any areas which are to be closed down will have an obvious effect on future personnel requirements, and these effects should be calculated in terms of numbers of people, by job category.

The expected increases in productivity should be forecast, partly from trends and partly from deliberate actions that will be an outcome of the strategies. In addition, there should be con- sideration of any intended changes from permanent to temporary employees, and the impact of any outsourcing decisions should be studied. All this makes it possible to develop soundly based forecasts of the numbers of people needed.

So far it has been assumed that the number of employees is reasonably constant throughout the year. In practice, there may be seasonal factors to be taken into account, and the timing of increased personnel requirements as a result of new or expanded activities may become important. In some cases monthly forecasts may be required for each of the years for which the plan is being developed: in others it may be possible to quote an annual figure, merely indicating the extent of seasonal requirements as an adjustment.

This forecast will provide the company with an estimate of how many people must be available in various job categories at certain time periods. To be useful, a further forecast must be made, taking into account retirements, death and resignation/dismissal rates, so that the company can see how many people it will have to obtain in each job category.

A further step in the planning stage is to assess how employee requirements will be met. The forecasts may indicate an area where a change in training methods would enable employees to move from one category to another. The analyst must estimate how many vacancies can be filled from promotion (not forgetting to allow for the gaps caused by those promoted). By comparison with national figures it should become possible to indicate areas where recruitment will be fairly easy, and those where it may be difficult. If supplies of certain categories of labour are foreseen as becoming very tight in future, this could indicate that management action may be required to find ways of reducing demand for people of this type: for example, a tight labour situation could well lead the company to devote some of its financial resources to a search for less labour-intensive methods of production. Such a course of action could well arise as a by-product of the manpower plan.

The manpower requirements projected may indicate a change in the types of people recruited, the decision being to obtain persons with the potential to fill positions foreseen 3 to 4 years ahead, rather than to fulfil immediate needs.

Where the plan shows a vast turnover of certain types of employee, it must also enquire why this is so, and produce a strategy to alleviate the position. For example, a department with an establishment of 50 people which had 150 different people passing through it every year would point to a very serious position. Recruiting and initial training costs would obviously be very high, and because people are always coming and going the establishment is probably set higher than needed. The plan should lead to corrective action, and this may require a very careful study before remedies can be devised. If correction is planned, the effects of this should be reflected in the number of people shown in the recruitment plan for future years. The study leading to the corrective strategy may concern itself with very deep issues. In some cases high labour turnover may be a function of the particular labour market, or may reflect inadequate salary scales or conditions of employment, compared with those offered by competitors. Often reasons are more complex, and require investigation of morale, employee attitudes, promotion opportunities, the company's image, and opportunities for self development.

The recruitment strategy will be derived from the estimates of requirements and should consider how the numbers required may be obtained. It may indicate that no specific action is required, and that there will be no difficulties in filling vacancies from the normal sources. On the other hand, it may suggest the need for specific action. Perhaps it may be necessary to use the tool of public relations to improve the image of the organisation in its labour-recruiting area. The organisation may have to begin a programme of visits to schools or universities, in order to ensure its fair share of the right type of people. Changes may be necessary in conditions of employment, in salary scales or in training methods. A decision may have to be taken to widen the catchment area for recruitment.

MANAGEMENT DEVELOPMENT, TRAINING AND EDUCATION

It is not possible to cover every aspect of HRM strategy in a short chapter, so I have chosen only one area as an example: management development, training and education. An extension to other areas can be found in brief in Hussey, 1998, and Hussey, 1996, offers a comprehensive discussion of the subject. There is a reason for this choice, in that management training is a much-neglected tool to aid the implementation of strategic decisions, so in addition to providing and extension of our thinking about HRM strategy, it may also lead to some useful ideas on implementation.

Figure 12.7 is a development from Figure 12.3. The "what the organisation already has" component requires some explanation, because it relates to the skills and capabilities of the managers in the

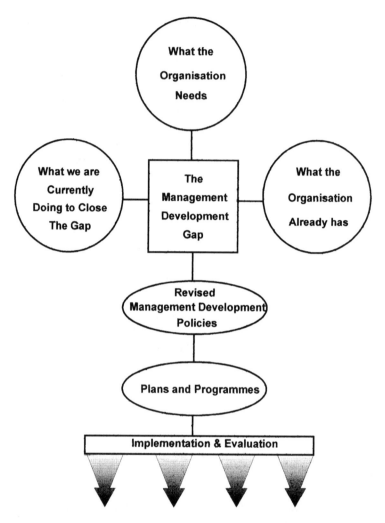

Figure 12.7 Business driven management development. (From Hussey, D. E., 1996, Business Driven Human Resource Management, Wiley, Chichester).

organisation. To find out what the organisation has requires some or all of performance management systems, assessment centres, and various diagnostic tools. The weakness of many of the traditional methods is that they are based on the perceptions of the managers and his or her subordinates, and if neither see a need for development, it will not be recognised. Frequently, when new business strategies are being made, there are new needs which neither are aware of. This is the reason for the "what the organisation needs" element of the model. It is possible, in some situations to link this directly to the methods used to assess "what the organisation has", for example through the design of assessment centres. The reality is that in most organisations the only method of assessment in wide use is an annual training needs assessment, usually linked to the performance management system.

The "what we are currently doing" part of the model requires an audit of the development, training and educational initiatives the organisation already has. This goes deeper than, for example, just listing training courses, but relates to the objectives of each course, the content, the target population, and the percentage of the target actually receiving the training. Not all organisations can easily provide this information, which itself indicates a weak link with the vision and objectives of the organisation.

New policies for management development might well arise from an understanding of the management development gap. For example Figure 12.8 suggests that there is value in looking at management development needs under three classifications. To simplify things let us see how this classification might help us think of a policy for training courses. The most important priority is for training programmes which have a direct relationship with a corporate objective, for example, to help implement a major strategy, to make an acquisition effective, or to enable managers to understand and cope with a significant change in their jobs (the rightsizing example mentioned earlier, perhaps). Not only should this area of need have a priority when funds are allocated, but the policy may be that the whole target population might be compelled to attend.

The second classification still covers initiatives which are seen for the good of the organisation, but they are longer term and more developmental. Here there is likely to be a careful matching of those invited to attend to the initiative, and the organisation might decide not to compel people to attend if they do not wish to. The priority budget level would be influenced by the strength of the first priority need, although there would be commitments to some longer term initiatives, like an in-house MBA programme. The third area contains needs which may be important for individuals but have little obvious value to the organisation, apart from encouraging an attitude of learning. An appropriate policy here might be to be a

The size of each element shows a possible proportion of the spend on management development: the priority order of allocating available funds would be

1. direct impact
2. longer term impact
3. personal needs

The actual proportion of spend would reflect these priorities.

Figure 12.8   Three policy areas which help drive management development.

facilitator rather than a provider, with the expectation that individuals would pay some or all of the costs, and give up some of their own time to the initiative. I am not arguing that these should be universal policies, but am only suggesting how the strategic approach can lead to a different perception of needs and how to fill them. The rest of the strategy then consists of the detailed plans and programmes developed to meet each of the priority areas.

The results of the strategic approach can be far reaching. Because things like the training activities of organisations tend to have grown up from a series of well intentioned, but often wrongly directed, initiatives, many would fall away, to be replaced with results oriented initiatives. The role of different training mechanisms can be more clearly determined and related to the aims of the initiative. For example, it may be desirable to use highly tailored courses and workshops for corporate needs, and to use more standardised courses and distance learning for the purely individual needs.

In the underlying philosophy the switch should be from a purely cost based decision on available options, to one of cost benefit analysis. It is common practice for training managers to take an out-of-pocket expenses view of training initiatives. The cost of participants' time in attending training initiatives is rarely considered, and almost nobody considers the real economic factor, the opportunity cost of this time. As a result many current decisions on training matters are aimed at reducing the cost of the initiative, rather than increasing its benefits. This has led to many decisions which are wrong for the companies concerned.

The strategic view postulated here would improve the total approach to management development, allowing this function to add more value to the organisation, without necessarily spending more. At the same time it would provide a permanent mechanism for aiding the implementation of strategies, and remove many of the problems that currently occur when the organisation finds, far too late, that it has an implementation problem.

Developing a business-driven HRM strategy is not easy, as apart from problems of information collection, there may be many vested interests in the way, and the whole exercise can easily become tangled in internal politics. But so too can the development of strategies for any other area of an organisation, and the difficulty is no excuse for muddling on in the same old manner. The rewards for business-driven human resource strategies are potentially very great. For the organisation there is the certainty that everything is helping to drive the organisation where it is trying to go, as well as the opportunity to use HRM as an active tool of implementation. For HRM there is the opportunity to begin to make a measurable contribution to corporate results, which would shift many actions from an act of faith into a reasoned business decision.

REFERENCES

Hussey, D. E., 1996, *Business Driven Human Resource Management,* Wiley, Chichester.

Hussey, D. E., 1998, *Strategic Management: From Theory to Implementation,* Butterworth-Heinemann, Oxford.

Lawrence, P. R. and Lorsch, J. W., 1967, Organisation and Environment, Harvard, Boston, MA.

Mason, A., 1993, *Management Training in Medium-sized UK Business Organisations,* Harbridge Consulting Group, London.

Tovey, L., 1991, *Management Training and Development in Large UK Business Organisations,* Harbridge Consulting Group, London.

13
Project Plans—Capital Investment Appraisal

Every undertaking has a duty to endeavour to use all its factors of production to best advantage. This means that it should develop the habit of carefully scrutinising and evaluating every capital expenditure, for it is only by so doing that it can be certain that its resource of finance is being used wisely. Major projects will involve the use of the organisation's resources of people, and a commitment of capital to an unsound activity will also squander some of these all-important human resources. It must be a principle of good management that all resources are used carefully, and this applies whether the organisation is lean or fat, whether it has a small bank balance or a large one.

No approach to strategy can be considered complete unless it includes ways for treating capital expenditure decisions with the seriousness they deserve. Of course, it is quite possible for an organisation to apply sophisticated measures to these decisions, without attempting any formal approach to formulating strategy. Benefits will certainly arise from such a course, but in this case they will be limited to the knowledge that the organisation has done all that is humanly possible to ensure that any project it undertakes is viable. The organisation that practises a strategic approach shares this benefit, and has the added advantage of ensuring that the project is in the organisation's best interests. In other words, every capital expenditure should do something to help the company along its chosen strategic path towards its objectives.

The formal planning approach means that additional criteria, unique to the individual company, will be developed in the evaluation process. Capital should not be allocated according to emotion, the relative strengths of individual departmental managers, or to the most successful division in terms of last years' profits.

Every business is called upon to undertake various different types of capital expenditure. Apart from normal increases in working capital arising from business expansion, the following types of expenditure can be identified:

- minor;
- replacement of existing assets;
- investment/development;
- profit improvement.

MINOR EXPENDITURES

There can be no business which does not face a host of minor capital expenditure decisions every year. In many of these the division between capital and expense may be very hazy, and the final treatment in the books may be a secret known only to the accountants. This is not important for the present analysis.

Few of these minor expenditures respond to any complicated methods of analysis. To my mind it is pedantic to consider a complex study leading to a decision such as buying a new desk, an additional PC, or a projector for the training room.

What is needed for this type of expenditure is a simple system which ensures that a responsible person approves and authorises each proposal, and that a justification is given in writing in each case. Authority for approving the proposals may vest in different people: for example, a departmental manager may be given authority to approve expenditures up to £5 000, a divisional manager may have a limit of £30 000, and all other proposals may have to be referred to the board. These limits are indicative only, and must be related to the requirements of the organisation.

REPLACEMENT OF EXISTING ASSETS

All fixed assets of the organisation are liable to depreciation, and sooner or later many of them will have to be replaced. Replacement need not coincide with the life given to an asset for book depreciation, and the asset will seldom be replaced by an identical item, and in any case as we saw in the chapter on financial strategy, book depreciation is provided under the matching principle of accounting, and is not an attempt to create a fund for the replacement of an asset. The organisation may find it of benefit to use OR techniques to choose the optimum replacement times: it is more sensible to renew a piece of machinery before it begins to cause production bottle-necks, rather than attempting to close the stable door after the horse has bolted (particularly as it is not always possible to obtain immediate delivery of many items of equipment).

In all replacement situations the opportunity should be taken to evaluate the various options that may be available. Firstly, the expenditure must be considered against the long-term future of the particular activity to which it refers: there is no point in spending further in an area of business which is soon to be abandoned. Secondly, it is necessary to look at the decision in the light of technological developments. This may widen the decision area, since, for example, the need to replace one particular piece of machinery may accelerate a decision to refurbish a complete section of the plant.

In some cases it may be difficult to differentiate between a replacement and another type of decision. For example, a mixture of expansion needs and technological obsolescence may lead to the building of a complete new plant and the closing down of an old one.

Replacement decisions should feature in the financial business and strategies. It should be possible to identify the approximate amounts of capital which will be required for these purposes for at least a few years into the future, an essential component of sound financial planning.

Even more important is the opportunity to identify problem areas before they occur. For example, the possibility of changing from buying to hiring sales person's vehicles, or of altering an entire packing line because of the need to replace the filler units, should be considered well in advance of their occurrence. The planned approach should enable the organisation to avoid many panic situations.

In many cases evaluation methods may be very much simpler for replacement decisions, although complex situations may call for

more sophisticated techniques. It is not desirable to be too dogmatic over the method to be used, since a decision must be made
on the merits of each individual situation. Even the simplest of
replacement capital expenditure proposals should be supported
by a written justification, and should follow the approval
methods laid down for minor projects. The complex situations
may require a detailed report, using the principles outlined later
in this chapter.

INVESTMENT/DEVELOPMENT EXPENDITURE

Capital spent on development or new investments is perhaps the
major force which enables the organisation to expand. In general,
the two types of capital discussed above are necessary to allow the
organisation to carry on with its current activities. It is the variety
and number of new development projects which determines an
organisation's ability to close the expansion gap revealed by the
strategic analysis, or to make a breakthrough change in its
production methods.

Each of the development projects should have its place in either
the strategy. In many cases the project will be identified only in
broad terms, or indeed it may be shown as one of a number of
options, the final choice of which still has to be made.

This, of course, is the ideal position, but in a real, live organisation there may be situations when an unanticipated opportunity
arises. The method of treatment here is for the organisation in
effect to amend its overall strategies so that priorities are re-
assigned and the effect of the new opportunity on the overall
strategic plan can be clearly seen.

Where a project is derived from the strategic plan, it becomes
relatively easy to confirm that it is in accord with the vision and
objectives, and each project can be given some sort of priority
rating, quite apart from its own financial evaluation criteria. The
"maverick" projects are not so easily placed, and greater care has to
be put into their evaluation. It is not that the techniques to judge
economic viability or financial success will vary: it is simply that,
particularly in a situation of scarce resources, management must be
certain that the project in question does not displace another
project of greater strategic importance to the organisation.

Every organisation should have more ideas, more projects in the queue than it can possibly fulfil. The organisation that is devoid of ideas, that has lost the power of innovatory thought, is unlikely to have ambitious objectives (or if they are ambitious, is unlikely to achieve them). I am always suspicious of the business whose *only* hope for expansion lies in acquisition: this may bring immediate growth, but is unlikely to give long-term development, for in the ultimate the organisation will stumble again over its own inability to get out of its rut.

The selection of each project becomes, in a virile company, very much a question of the choice between options. More will be said on this subject later.

PROFIT IMPROVEMENT EXPENDITURE

Many improvement projects may be carried out with no capital expenditure. In other cases the improvement can only come if an injection of capital is applied to the affected area. Return on investment on this sort of project is usually very high, often in excess of 100%.

Some improvement projects can be identified in advance, and their capital costs written into the long-range plan. By their very nature, many of these projects are not so obvious at an early stage. For financial planning purposes it may be necessary to estimate a sum of capital to be allocated to this type of project.

OPTIONS

The word "options" has cropped up time and time again in this book, and a recurring theme is that one perspective of strategic planning is the identification of and choice between "options". In project analysis there are two phases in this selection process. The first is the choice of project, a concept which was explained in detail in the chapters on strategy. Secondly, there are what might be termed the internal options attached to each project.

For example, the organisation may decide to evaluate in depth a project to expand output of a particular product. Some of the options that should be considered are:

- How large an expansion to undertake.
- Whether to expand an established factory or open a new one: if a new factory is to be opened, where should it be sited?
- Whether it would be to the organisation's better interests to have the product outsourced.
- The different types of plant or variety of building that could be provided.
- Whether to buy or lease the particular items of plant and machinery required.

This list is not exhaustive. The important point is that in every situation there is *always* more than one possible course of action. The aim in project analysis is to ensure that all realistic options are considered, and the methods of analysis used should be capable of producing a quantitative comparison.

Quantitative analysis will never reveal all the answers, and should always be accompanied by a qualitative study, which would cover points such as the effect on employee morale of a particular course of action, what it will do to the corporate PR image, or indeed, whether it is a good or bad strategic move for the organisation. This qualitative analysis is a most important step in the decision process, and should not be neglected. It is always very tempting to be hypnotised by the numbers thrown up by quantitative techniques: but these never represent the ultimate solution. Business judgement is always the most important criterion in deciding what to do. No matter how good the mathematics, judgement has to be applied both in the selection of data for analysis, and in making the final entrepreneurial decisions.

Mathematical techniques are invaluable in helping the manager to come to a decision, and they also provide a standard against which performance in the future can be measured. This question of monitoring and controlling is a theme which was mentioned in chapter 1, and will receive more attention in the next chapter.

I consider it important for all major capital expenditure of this type to be supported by a comprehensive written report. Methods of quantitative analysis used should be the same for all projects, with the exception that only as much analysis as makes sense should be carried out, and that if the project does not respond to the methods chosen, the analysis procedures should be shortened. If the same method of analysis is used, it becomes easier to compare one project against another: easier, but not easy. However much the reports and analysis are standardised, there will still be variations in the quality of the assessments and judgements used in the analysis. Risk analysis can help to identify these differences, but will never entirely remove them.

PROJECT ANALYSIS

The best insurance an organisation can have that its sophisticated analysis techniques are based on well-founded data is for it to ensure that project appraisal is always approached with care. This means that objective evaluation must be made of the sources of data, and that all managers in the organisation must understand the quantitative methods of analysis used. This does not suggest that all managers must be capable of actually carrying out all the calculations personally (one can drive a car without being a mechanic), but they must be able to interpret results. I have been involved in situations where a manager has quite cheerfully manipulated a sales forecast in order to produce the "right" discounted cash flow (d.c.f.) rate: having done this became convinced that the magic of d.c.f. would ensure the right results when the project was implemented.

There is always a very real danger that managers, because of personal or emotional reasons, or a firm and genuine conviction that the project is right, will not approach project analysis in an objective fashion. Bias is something that can easily creep into any investigation. Yet, in my view, managers must play a part in investigating a project for which they will ultimately be responsible. Four steps are necessary to try to overcome this problem:

- Acceptance by all management of the principles behind the planned approach.
- Enforcing the principle of ultimate management responsibility for the recommendations made.
- Ensuring that all projects are examined by an independent assessor.

- Enforcing a post-project audit procedure, so that everyone knows that a failed project cannot be swept under the carpet.

Not all projects will become the eventual operating responsibility of a current manager, although a large number of them will. Where it is possible to identify management responsibility in advance, the manager concerned should form part of the team investigating the project, and should also be made clearly aware that he or she is being held accountable for results. Failure of the project to come within reasonable limits of its targets will be held as a personal failure. In this way, managers will tend to temper natural optimism with caution, and will also do best to implement the project in the way originally intended. Where managers are not involved, they can claim that failure is due to bad planning, rather than errors on their part, and a gulf can widen between the project report and performance.

In many cases, a project may be for something new, and at the time of investigation the organisation may not know who is to eventually run it. The same principle of accountability from the first stages cannot be applied here. It is well worthwhile assigning one or more experienced line managers to the project investigating team, using their capabilities as a balancing factor against a purely staff evaluation.

Every organisation should submit each project to an independent internal assessor, who may be an accountant performing this analysis as part of his or her regular duties, the corporate planner, or a specialist project analyst. The assessor's duty is to work on the project from a fairly early stage, to question the assumptions on which the study is based, to try to ensure that all data produced are logical and that all loose ends are tidied up, to make certain that all sensible alternatives are considered and, finally, to undertake the mathematical analysis. In one organisation where I was consulting, the assessor was called the project preventer by all the other managers, although this was not his job title! In fairness I should add that the nickname did not match his attitude.

Project evaluation has a greater chance of success when it is a team effort of both staff and line managers. Like strategic planning itself, it carries an unbearable burden of disadvantages if it becomes regarded as a staff ivory-tower exercise. Both staff and line have a major part to play in the study.

Each completed report, with the recommended course of action, should go forward to the board for final decision, or to a committee where the board has delegated responsibility.

The analysis has to look into the future. The length of time for which projections are compiled will vary with the needs of the organisation, and sometimes from one type of investigation to another although attempts should be made to standardise within each organisation. The 5-year period used in so many corporate plans will be too short for many purposes: one should always remember that the lead time for a major project will rarely be less than 12 months, and will often exceed 3 years. In the latter cases, a 5-year forecast will give very little data for analysis.

As a generalisation, I should recommend that a time-span of 10 years from the first capital expenditure be taken as the basis of mathematical analysis: this means that all forecasts must be for this period plus the lead time before the first capital expenditure. This is a recommendation which I should be prepared to change to meet special circumstances. It is something which top management should decide.

Each project will throw up special factors for investigation which are unique to its own circumstances: similarly not all projects will require the same breadth of analysis. The following should, therefore, be interpreted only as being indicative of the scope of a project investigation.

Objective

The objective of each project should be defined and written down before the investigation begins. This should also describe the project in a few words, so that the board can swiftly grasp its scope if it becomes a firm recommendation at a later stage. There should also be a statement showing how the project fits into the strategy.

Marketing

The market must never be overlooked. Marketing research should form an essential part of most major capital expenditure studies, although it is an area which is still neglected by many organisations. There can be only one excuse for failure to study the market in advance of decisions to invest in it: when the top management of the company considers that the costs of the research are more excessive than the likely costs of failure. In other words, each project has a limit to the investigatory expenditure it can bear, but this limit should be the result of a deliberate decision, rather than something which just happens by default.

In my view the final project report should carry a summary of market background data, but should be cross-referenced to the various survey reports for detailed facts. To attempt to show all relevant market research data in the project report would lead to a document of enormous size. Market studies should be carried out in a way which enable market forecasts to be made.

The natural step from consideration of the market is the preparation of a marketing plan for the project. Again, if the plan is detailed it may be better to give only a short summary of the approach to marketing, keeping the main plan in a separate document. The marketing plan is an essential for any project investigation because, until it has been considered, it is difficult to produce realistic sales forecasts, or to prepare assessments of marketing and selling costs. Advertising, selling and physical distribution expenses, in particular, frequently represent a very high proportion of total costs. Care must be taken when estimating these, if the resultant figures are to mean anything. Most people with experience of project analysis will, I think, accept that the calculations of sales volumes and costs in the marketing and selling areas are more difficult to estimate accurately than the technically based production costs (although these are usually dependent on sound estimates of volume).

It may be necessary to re-examine the marketing plan at a later date. A project with a long lead time may be so far away that it is prudent to accept that many elements of the plan will change.

Physical distribution must be given particularly intense consideration, since not only does it play a vital part in the success or failure of a project, but it may also involve considerable capital investment if an in-house activity. The importance of physical distribution will vary with the nature of the project: it needs no explanation to support the statement that the distribution of mail order computer software by post is a vastly different proposition from the distribution of frozen foods by specialist road transport and requiring the support of a chain of refrigerated warehouses.

Production

From the marketing consideration it is possible to move to the technical problems. The study should cover the way in which the product is to be made, and should include specifications of the plant and machinery and of the buildings. In many cases this is an over-simplification, and there may be a number of discussions between marketing, research and development, and production before final solutions are reached. These solutions may frequently involve modification of the original marketing requirements. For example, predicted sales volumes affect both the method of manufacture and the costs of production: the costs of production may in turn cause changes to be made in the original forecasts. This is but another instance of the circular series of relationships which is a feature of much business activity.

It is at this point that much of the detailed data necessary for the detailed financial analysis is obtained. Raw-material costs, packaging material costs, and all the elements of direct and indirect production cost can be prepared. This requires an intimate knowledge of the processes recommended, the capital costs of the plant and buildings, the personnel levels required, and the costs of the various types of labour required. Production costs should be calculated both on a total annual basis for financial analysis, and on a product unit basis (by fixed and variable costs) so that exercises may be carried out on the effects of increases or decreases in volume.

The complexity of analysis will vary from project to project. Technical calculations may be moderately simple where the proposal is for the expansion of an existing plant, or very, very complicated when they involve the construction of an entirely new plant, using a process of manufacture which is foreign to the organisation. The preparation of these estimates may involve detailed discussions with raw-material suppliers, plant and machinery manufacturers and architects. The use of engineering and management consultants should be considered when this suits the circumstances of the organisation.

These studies are likely to result in a very large volume of reports, diagrams, charts and calculations. It is necessary that this data is clearly annotated, and considered part of the project proposal, although the actual project report should contain only a brief summary of the recommendations.

Location

Closely allied to both marketing and production factors is the siting of the project. This is not a problem when the investigation is covering a simple expansion to an existing plant. It may be very complicated when a new factory is considered, since the decision may be not only between towns but between countries as well.

The aim should be to choose a site which enables the organisation to operate at the highest net profit. The effects of the pull of the market, compared with the pull of the raw material sources, are described in most elementary economic textbooks, along with the other factors for consideration, such as cost and availability of land, power, water, waste-disposal facilities, labour and supporting services, and the existence of fiscal barriers or incentives. These need not concern us here.

There is a vast difference between identifying the factors in principle, and actually taking them into account in a practical study: the difficulties of breaking sales forecasts down into a regional basis are immense of themselves. In location studies it is usually good sense to make use of the appropriate OR techniques, and to use mathematical models for the analysis of options. Where the organisation does not possess the necessary skills it may have to engage outside help. Carefully defined assumptions and the elimination of the obviously unsuitable will, in any event, reduce the problem to a manageable size, but will still leave a tremendous volume of work if the job is to be carried out well.

There is no need to stress that the penalty for failure to obtain the best location for a factory may be a permanent additional annual expense, a sort of perpetual fine for not doing the job properly in the first place.

People

No project study can be considered complete if it ignores the human factor. There are a number of problems for consideration all of which are simplified if the organisation has already developed a sound HRM strategy: if only for the reason that some of the difficulties will have been anticipated and prepared for.

The project report should show clearly how the new proposal is to be manned. Particular attention should be paid to the key posts, but at the same time the investigators must be certain that the general personnel requirements of the project can be met.

Any effects on existing personnel, for example, if the project requires the expansion, relocation or divestment of a particular sphere of activity, must be studied and planned in detail. Additionally, any organisational changes that will be necessary must be carefully planned.

Commercial risks

Every project involves risk of one type or another. As far as possible, the commercial risks should be analysed and studied, so that top management can assess whether the rewards compensate for the dangers. An assessment of the degree of risk is important. Some of the areas which typify this sort of risk are shown below:

- Change in competitors' strategy.
- Product obsolescence.
- Loss of major export market through changes in currency values.
- Political events.
- Nationalisation.
- Increased government control (for example, on profit margins, or on product standards, or prohibitions on certain raw materials).
- Worsening labour relations in the industry.

Assumptions

At each stage in the study it will be found necessary to make assumptions to cover the unknown elements of fact. These should be recorded, and it goes without saying that they should be consistent for all aspects of the study.

Capital

One of the most important elements of any capital expenditure appraisal is the amount of capital required. This, of course, is stating the obvious. The studies described above will enable requirements to be identified, although the particular way in which these data should be presented may require a little clarification.

Estimates must be made of the two types of capital, fixed and working, required for every project. Fixed capital needs can be assessed from the studies made, and usually the majority of these needs will derive from the production elements. What may be more difficult is to identify the time when this capital has to become available. In a large project, capital expenditures may be spread over a period of several years. The project analysts need to know fairly accurately when capital is needed, as this will affect the mathematical analyses of the project, and the way in which the project will be financed.

Working capital needs will, as a general rule, tend to increase as the business expands, and can be estimated from the sales and production figures, when these are related to planned raw material and finished goods inventory levels, and to accounts receivable and payable.

One important principle is that care must be taken to identify all consequential investments arising because of management commitment to this particular project. It is grossly wrong for top management to be led to making more and more investments in order to "protect" the first one. A simple example is where the creation of a new activity may lead to an expansion in the numbers of head office staff, and a need to buy or rent additional office accommodation. One sees the same thing happening with acquisitions. To protect the new business venture, additional means are required within a year or two to modernise buildings and equipment. Or another example is the purchase of a warehouse for £x, when the manager has an intention to come back next year for another £x in order to modify the building to suit the real requirements. I have heard this described as the salami principle: top management is served up a slice at a time, and never is put in a position of being able to appreciate the true shape of the sausage.

Methods of analysis

This is not a book about financial techniques and consequently the methods of mathematical analysis will be given only very general treatment. Sense can only be made of a project if it is assessed on a marginal basis. No attempt should be made in the project report to allocate overheads or other charges that the organisation would incur, even if it did not make the capital expenditure under appraisal. This is not to say that *after* the investment decision is made, normal accounting practice for that organisation should not be followed. Similarly any additional overheads that will arise because of the new project must be charged to it.

Having said this, I should like to make the point that a project should never be looked at in isolation. An activity that is in a loss position may still be in a loss position, despite an injection of capital into an expansion project which *by itself* has a very high return on investment. If projects are always considered only from a marginal point of view, it is very easy to overlook circumstances like this, and to end up expanding an area that should be closed, or throwing good money after bad.

Whatever methods of evaluation are used, it is essential for the organisation to set standards against which they can be judged. For example, an expression of a return on investment rate as, say, 15% only has real meaning if one knows within the organisation whether this is good or bad. The standards adopted should be the minimum that the organisation will find acceptable. This does not mean that all projects above this are automatically accepted, but it will ensure that in all but the most unusual circumstances projects falling below this rate are rejected without being put to the board. The standard set may naturally vary with both the type of project and the geographical area of the proposed investment. Thus it is quite sensible to apply a standard of, say, 15% ROI for UK projects and 25% for African projects, where the degree of risk may be considered higher. These rates are given as examples only, and are not intended to be recommendations. The organisation must set the standard itself.

There are a number of ways of analysing the figures produced during the investigation, although none of these are perfect. Some are better than others, but even these have faults. The most prudent way is to use more than one method, and, as mentioned earlier, to season the results with a modicum of management judgement.

The most effective methods of analysis are those using the discounted cash-flow principles. These methods enable weight to be given to the present value of money, on the basis that £1 today is worth more to the organisation than £1 next year, because it can earn interest on the £1 if it has it today. All the cash inflows and outflows are therefore discounted on a time basis. The rate of discounting is fixed internally by the company, but should represent the sort of return the company should be earning.

The principle can be illustrated by the following figures. At a 10% interest rate £1 will grow to £1.61 over a period of 5 years:

Year	
0	£1.00
1	£1.10
2	£1.21
3	£1.33
4	£1.46
5	£1.61

It is possible, by using the reciprocal of the compound interest factor, to plot the present value of a future £1. This shows the declining present value of future money as its expenditure is postponed.

Year	
0	£1.000
1	£0.909
2	£0.826
3	£0.751
4	£0.683
5	£0.621

If the chosen rate had been 15%, the table of present values of £1 would have been:

Year 0	£1.000
1	£0.870
2	*£0.756*
3	£0.658
4	£0.572
5	£0.497

Two of the methods of analysis using d.c.f. are net present value (NPV) and the d.c.f. rate of return. The former seeks to measure the net present value in the last year of the time span chosen at the selected rate of return. If a 10% rate were chosen, NPV would be nil if the project equated with the standard, negative if it were below 10%, and positive if it were above it. The higher the NPV the "better" the project (in purely mathematical terms).

A second criteria emerges from NPV analysis, and this is the number of years before the project pays back at the discounted values. This will usually be later than year of payback, at un-discounted values. The length of analysis affects the final answer, although the figures in the later years have less weight than those in the earlier years. For example, at 10% the discounting factor would only be 0.149 at the 20th year. This, of course, means that the larger margins of error which tend to creep in during the last years of a forecast, have less weight than the more accurate figures that might be expected in the first years.

The NPV can be expressed as a d.c.f. rate of return. This is, the rate of discount that would apply to reduce the NPV to nil by the last year of the analysis. Calculation of the d.c.f. rate was originally done by trial and error, by manual methods, and normally could be worked out within the limits of accuracy needed after only two or three sets of calculations at different discounting rates. Today spread sheet programmes and even calculators do the job for us in a matter of seconds.

D.c.f. is important because it enables taxation and fiscal incentives to be taken into account, and because it recognises that depreciation does not represent an actual outflow of cash from the firm. The method can be used in conjunction with decision trees, and also provides a basis for the quantification of risk.

When calculating d.c.f. it is quite simple to work out an average return on investment (ROI) rate for the project, and this should be done as a matter of course. ROI is an old friend, and one that still has a great deal of value in project analysis. ROI and d.c.f. will frequently give different answers. A project with the same annual figure for capital employed for each year of its life might have an average ROI of 10% if:

1. ROI was 10% for each year, or
2. Earnings were greater in the later than earlier years, but when averaged come to 10%, or
3. Earnings were greater in earlier than later years.

D.c.f. analysis would indicate that situation 3 was the best project, because greater weight would be given to money earned in the present. Situation 2 would come out clearly as the worst of the three.

For internal comparison of projects it is also worthwhile using return on sales and turnover ratios. Apart from their use in comparisons between one proposal and another they also help to ensure that each project is realistic.

FINANCING

The last act in project analysis is to recommend the way in which the proposal will be financed. This, of course, is a direct link with the financial strategy, and in most cases a decision on method will have already been made. The project report provides an opportunity of checking the financial strategy for the particular project in question, and revising it where necessary.

No one should obtain the impression that a system of project analysis and appraisal, as outlined in this chapter, will automatically solve all their problems. What it will do, is to give them the chance of being right more often than they are wrong. It gives management a realistic and workable way of making a decision out of the many options that confront them. And the organisation that chooses more wisely than its competitors is the one that is most likely to succeed in the long run.

14
Implementing Strategic Change

Strategic planning without action is a useless activity. It may provide a certain amount of mental stimulation, but it will not add one iota to the organisation's prosperity. An essential part of any strategic planning must be a means of making the plans actually happen, and preventing them from becoming a sterile exercise by forcing them to be used in the day-to-day running of the organisation. It is fair to say that one reason why strategies fail in some organisation's is simply that too little thought is given to this aspect. This of course takes us back to points made in the first chapter, and particularly to Figure 1.1. Implementation is one of the five factors which are critical to strategic success.

This is not to argue a slavish attention to the letter of the strategy, regardless of whether the action is still appropriate. The best strategies are flexible rather than rigid. The strategy that becomes part of day-to-day management is more likely to be flexible by decision, since it may be deliberately adapted to changes in circumstances: throughout, the vision and objectives should remain constant, and any changes should be carefully considered and evaluated. Altering a strategy is often desirable, but must never be carried out lightly and without thought. This is very different form the strategy that is not taken into the management process, and just shifts its emphasis and changes its shape because no one is trying to implement it.

RESEARCH INTO IMPLEMENTATION

Much of the research into effective strategic management has been directed at the planning process or the strategic decisions, almost as if the desired end products were plans instead of actions. There is much that is useful in these studies, but they do not address the issue of implementation of strategy. One of the few research-based considerations of this subject appears in Alexander, 1991. He undertook surveys in public and private sector organisations, and identified the major problems which were found in the implementation of strategy are summarised from Alexander's research, but the comments are my own interpretation. There were some differences between the sectors, just as there were differences between individual organisations within each sector. The list below is summarised from his findings and gives a perception of the 10 most common problems found in practice. The comments are my own.

1. *It took longer than expected.* This could be due to several causes, varying from failure to identify all the key actions to failure to build commitment.
2. *There were major unidentified problems during implementation.* On the surface this appears an analytical issue, or possibly in some cases a realisation that we are not always able to anticipate everything. It may also be an involvement issue, in that wide involvement can often identify problems and actions that would otherwise be missed.
3. *Implementation activities were not co-ordinated effectively enough.* This is most likely to be a failure in management.
4. *Management were distracted by other activities and crises and did not implement.* This may have been appropriate if priorities changed. Just as likely is the possibility that management was not committed to the plan, which is a behavioural issue.
5. *The capabilities of managers involved in implementation actions were inadequate.* This may be a recruitment or training issue. Those who make plans should not assume that everyone is competent to fulfil all necessary actions or to work in a different way.
6. *Inadequate training and instruction were given to lower level employees.* It is easy to assume that the factory workers can

operate new plant without help, that clerks will easily change to a new procedure, or that sales people will change priorities. Such assumptions may be damaging.

7. *Events in the outside world impacted on the plan.* This could be failure to take proper account of the external environment, or the fact that there will always be some unpredictable changes.

8. *Departmental managers did not provide enough leadership.* This again is a behavioural problem, which could have been caused by ignorance or poor management.

9. *Key implementation tasks and activities were not adequately defined.* It is critical to break a broad strategy down to the tasks that have to be undertaken to implement it.

10. *The information systems were inadequate to monitor perfor-mance.* Clearly if you do not know whether or not an action has been implemented it is difficult to manage the process.

Kaplan, 1995, found that many organisations have a "...funda-mental disconnect between the development and formulation of their strategy and the implementation of that strategy into useful action". Four major barriers to effective implementation were identified.

- Vision that could not be actioned, because it was not translated into operational terms.
- Strategy is not linked to departmental and individual gaols (incentives are tied to annual financial performance instead of to long range strategy: only 21% of executive management and 6% of middle management have objectives that are tied to the strategy).
- Resource allocation is based on short-term budgets and not the strategy (only just over a third of organisations have a direct link between the strategy and the budgeting process.
- Control is directed at short-term performance and rarely eval-uates progress on long-term objectives.

What these two sets of findings suggest is that the strategy can fail because it is inadequate, or because it is not properly implemented. It is the second of these points which is the subject of this chapter. Before moving on, refer back to Figure 12.1, for this is a very useful model to use when thinking about implementation. Some of the

Kaplan findings reinforce the relevance of the figure; for example, reward systems that encouraged the wrong performance.

Although Figure 12.1, and much of the earlier discussion on human resource strategy, is partly about implementation, I should like in this chapter to provide a framework for thinking about the whole issue.

"EASIER" MODEL OF CHANGE LEADERSHIP

Figure 14.1 is a change leadership model. It is used here to help us think about strategy, but it is applicable in any change situation of any complexity. The only rider that should be added is that the way it is applied is to some degree situational. It is possible to use the model is a participative way, and this is the ideal. However, although the actions under each heading would be applied differently, it may also be used in a dictatorial way.

Generally the text books advise against driving change, which is the dictatorial approach, and recommend leading it, the participative model. However sometimes it is necessary to drive. When the need for the change is extremely urgent, and resistance is very high, sometimes change can only be driven. For example the change to modern technology in the UK newspaper industry, with the strikes and lockouts that went with it, was probably the only

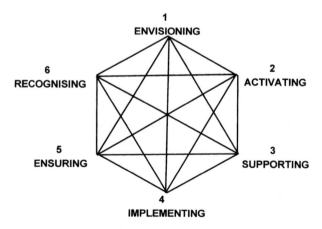

Figure 14.1   An approach to strategy implementation.

way in which the change could have been implemented. Resistance was so high that there was no realistic chance of a reasonable solution by agreement, and the matter was urgent, in that the companies in the industry were not very profitable. There was another factor, in that the consequences of not carrying the print workers along were not very high, as with the new technology it did not really matter whether they were retrained or new people hired.

In describing the EASIER model I assume that the extreme dictatorial approach is not called for, but neither is the totally democratic situation when every single person has a vote on the outcome. The situation is one where the strategy decision process has involved a number of key people, management takes the decisions, and sets out to lead the organisation into the new situation. There may be resistance, but it is not so fierce as to make any form of participation unworkable, and there may be urgency, but things are not so urgent that no attention can be given to the human issues of change.

The mnemonic is just to remember the labels on the model. The first three EAS labels refer to issues which are largely behavioural. The IER labels tend to be the system and process aspects. Each affects the other, which is why they are connected by lines: for example every control system, which falls under the ensuring label, has behavioural as well as system issues.

No part of the model can be ignored. For example, there is not the option of concentrating on the IER labels, while giving little or no attention to the rest. Another point of emphasis is that the implementation process has to be planned. How complex and fundamental it is will affect the ease or difficulty of this task. A strategy which causes very little change and supports a vision that is already shared across the organisation will require less planning than one which puts everything into a state of turmoil.

The behavioural factors

Envisioning

Vision was one of the subjects of an earlier chapter, but there we were discussing the total vision of an organisation. This may be valid for certain implementation situations, although for others it may be too remote from how the strategy is perceived. For example, an element of the strategy which causes serious upheaval to a particular area of the organisation, may appear to be very remote from the overall vision by those affected. It may be a valid and widely accepted vision, but the connection between what is happening on the ground and what the vision says about the future of the organisation may be too remote. What is needed is a vision statement which nestles within the overall strategic vision, but which is specific to the situation and the changes that the strategy is causing.

Formulation of a credible and understandable vision statement, which attempts to show what this part of the organisation will be like after the strategy has been implemented is the first step in successful implementation. Think of the impact of a managing director's statement that the organisation is to cut total employment by 5%. It is a description of an action, not a statement of vision, and leaves everyone unclear about what the organisation will be like after it has carried out the task. It is not much help in motivation, and leaves the situation wide open to rumour. I am not privy to BMW's October 1998 actions to improve productivity at their Rover plant at Longbridge, involving a reduction of 2500 in the overall workforce. However, from the press reports it seems that a vision has been painted of a world-class operation, supported by major investment, and with new models of cars, which would follow once the productivity hurdle had been overcome. If this vision is seen as credible within the organisation, it is a much more effective start to the change process than just stating the immediate action. It starts to explain the why in addition to the what.

Activating

A vision that is understood and believed in by only one person is only helpful if the intention is to drive change rather than to lead it, and coercion can in many circumstances have a negative impact. The activating stage of the model is to gain the commitment of others to the vision, so that it becomes widely shared. The reasons for this are that a shared vision makes it easier to empower others so that they help make the strategy effective, resistance may be lowered because the process of gaining commitment is one of involvement, and there is likely to be a greater willingness to accept the adverse aspects of the strategy, if people believe that the cause is worth supporting.

The leader, who in this context is the person charged with implementation, should not expect to achieve commitment by posting a notice or issuing a memo. Commitment needs to ripple out from the leader, to the key managers who are needed to help implement the strategy, to their subordinates, and to all others affected.

The process might well start with a series of meetings at which the leader would explain the vision and the strategy that helps achieve it. In a very large change situation, these meetings might well cascade to several levels in the organisation. There is usually considerable scope for involvement at those meetings, both to deal with the concerns of people, but also to get their input into some of the detail of the implementation. It should be remembered that motivation can change as a result of behaviour, as well as the other way around, so actual involvement in making something happen can help to build a commitment to it.

There is a requirement for a clear communication strategy, using all the media the organisation. Much also depends on the leader, and ultimately other senior people involved in the process, who should live and breathe the vision, talk about it on both formal and informal occasions, ask others for their views on it, and above all behave in a way that is compatible with it. It is not difficult to see why dissonance was caused through the 1990s, by chief executives of newly privatised companies, who increased their own salaries dramatically, at a time when they were preaching cost reduction, higher productivity, and smaller work forces. Whether or not the increases were justified, the timing was wrong, in that behaviour seemed to be at variance with the vision.

Supporting

During the implementation of a strategy, particularly if it involves major changes for the organisation, a key role for the leader is to give support to those involved in the process. This involves emotional support, treating all concerns as important; resource support, so that genuine obstacles to progress are removed; and morale boosting, showing confidence in people's abilities to fulfil the tasks allocated to them.

The other side of this is careful selection of people for the various implementation roles, which takes into account their strengths and weaknesses, and providing additional coaching or training for those who need further skills in order to cope with the task.

It is also worth considering the value of training courses and workshops as an aid to the activating stage as well as to the support stage of the process.

The systems and process aspects

Installing

I have never been completely happy with this as my "I" word, but have found nothing better. It is less effective as a descriptive label than the others in the mnemonic. What is means here is the process of breaking down the strategy into the numerous actions that have to be taken in order to implement it, and building the strategy into other management processes. It includes:

- a means of converting strategies to detailed actions and goals;
- ensuring that the strategy drives all budgets and other short-term plans;
- mechanisms for measuring progress.

Project management.   Strategies may come in many different degrees of complexity. The description below starts at the most complex, and works on to the relatively simple. Whatever the complexity, the task of planning the implementation is critical, and often requires the involvement of many managers and specialists, both to identify the tasks, and to determine the best way to fulfil them. One element sometimes overlooked is the need to plan for the resources of money and time needed to implement the strategy. Implementation involves cost and the time of people, and may fail if adequate provision is not made.

Many strategies can be defined as projects, often with subsidiary projects within them. A strategy to break into a new market with a revolutionary product might be one large and complex management task. However, if the components of the strategy required the building of a new factory to make the product, acquisition of a distribution company, making an alliance with an organisation is South East Asia, further market research, and the negotiation of contracts with several suppliers, there are in fact a number of projects to manage, requiring different competencies, and of varying degrees of complexity.

Network analysis is particularly useful for complex projects. There are many forms of network analysis (for example critical path, PERT), but fundamentally they all require each task to be identified, its relationships with other tasks defined, and the length of time it will take estimated. In all major projects there are some things that can be done simultaneously, and others that have to be done in sequence. In the manufacture and installation of an elevator, it is possible to manufacture the major sub-assemblies at the same time. The machine can be made at the same time as the lift car and the architectural components. When each of these is started will depend on when the elevator has to be shipped, so although their production will overlap, the network analysis will ensure that everything is ready at the right time. (If we broke the manufacture down into tasks we would find that the sequential relationship did not apply to all of them.) What we cannot do is install the elevator in the building until it is made and reaches the construction site. We could install the guide rails before this equipment arrived, but could not do this before the contractor had completed the building to the required degree. Again there will be some tasks that can run in parallel, and others which have to be sequential.

Network analysis is a type of plan whose aim is to ensure that everything is done at the optimum time, and that critical tasks, which would otherwise delay the whole project, are given particular attention. Overall time can be saved by ensuring that tasks that can be undertaken in parallel are not treated as if they were sequential.

The Gantt chart also shows tasks and their start and finish date, and tries to organise them so that those that would otherwise hold up the others do not do so.

In many cases simple schedules and bar diagrams are sufficient. Sometimes, where each step will reveal alternatives for decision, a decision tree is useful. Whatever techniques are used, the main steps in this type of tactical planning must be the isolation of each task or event to be performed, setting a date for performance, and ensuring that responsibility for performing each stage is assigned to an appropriate individual. Whether the plan is for test marketing a new product, installing new machinery, or simply changing the location of the office, these methods will make sure that management's intentions become action, in a way that is positive and controllable.

The final degree of simplicity is when the strategy requires relatively few and easily defined actions, which can be written as a simple list, with a statement of who is to do it. Typically these actions will become part of an annual plan/budget, which is the next topic.

Annual budget/plans. If a strategy remains as a broad statement something that will be done over several years it will be unlikely to result in action. The conversion of the strategy into an action plan, possibly using critical path analysis, Gantt charts, or action lists of one kind or another, is a first step. These should then be used, together with the vision, objectives and general tone of the strategy, when annual budgets are prepared.

The annual budget should always be prepared in the context of the strategy and never as a document in isolation. It should never be a vehicle for the introduction of new strategies that have not been fully agreed by the people that set the strategy in the first place. To be fully effective, the budget should be supported by an annual plan, which includes all the actions necessary for the implementation of the strategy, and assigns responsibilities to organisational units, and under these to individual people. In concept, the budget should be seen as a vital part of the strategic implementation system, and not viewed as an accounting procedure which occurs in total isolation.

The action plan and budget provides an opportunity to involve numerous levels of management in the strategy process. Although the strategic plan is generally restricted to the more senior levels, with a certain amount of support from their subordinates, the implementation actions will involve managers at all levels. There may be little point in asking a regional sales manager to play a part in formulating overall corporate strategy, but a great deal of benefit may arise if the manager is asked to plan a course of action, in the context of that strategy, for the forthcoming year.

The budgets and action plans should show top management how the strategies are to be carried out. Where, for example, the long-range plan would deal with advertising in perhaps a broad policy statement, the annual plan will get down to detailed campaign objectives, media schedules and the like. The marketing strategy should end up as a blueprint for the coming year's activity.

Action plans should be prepared in advance of the budget. Having set out beforehand the course of action intended, it is possible to prepare the budget to show the financial results. If these results do not take the organisation to its targets, it becomes necessary to re-examine the action plans. The draft budget figures should never be changed unless the actions behind them are also. In this way the action plan gives the budget much more meaning than is the case in many organisations, because the need for any policy changes becomes fully apparent. Any changes must, of course, be seen in the context of the strategy and actions outside of the long-range strategy should only be taken if the full implications are appreciated.

Action plans and budgets should be subject to a review process before they are accepted. The process begins with top management. Staff support actions for the review should include making sure that actions in the annual plans do not cut across long-range strategy, and to see that elements of the strategy are not omitted from the appropriate tactical plan. It is very easy to "lose" the odd course of action, and although no organisation should implement a strategy which time has made inappropriate, no course of action should be abandoned by accident (or possibly sabotage).

Ensuring

The right actions do not happen just because they are written down and someone has said they will do them. The ensuring stage is about monitoring and control. The project plans and budgets provide a frame work which can be controlled, both to ensure that the planned actions have been taken, and to confirm that the results of those actions are as expected.

There are behavioural implications in the design of control processes, in that the way control mechanisms are applied, will have an effect on the way people behave. Some, such as a performance management system, may be inextricably mixed with the next stage of the implementation model, which deals with recognition and reward. Although the emphasis here is on the system and process issues of monitoring and control, the behavioural implication should not be forgotten.

How can the organisation make sure that actions are being carried out? The only answer is to have a system of monitoring and follow up. If an action is scheduled in the project or other action plans, the leader is entitled to expect that it will be performed: if the various individuals in the organisation know that a monitoring system exists, they will be less likely to fail for trivial reasons, since their sins will come home to roost.

The first part of the controlling procedure comes from the budget. Regular comparisons of performance against plan, and analysis of variance, give the direction in which the organisation is moving, and it is possible for all managers to see how close they are to profit targets, and to take action to correct disadvantageous situations. The principles of budgetary control are, of course, well known as a management tool and need no further discussion here.

What *is* important is recognition that the budgetary processes are not by themselves sufficient to ensure that the plan is being carried out. The right result can often be obtained for the wrong reason, and the budgetary processes may not necessarily reveal this. At the last moment a manager may take action which is against long-term interests in order to get the profit figure "right": figures may not reveal this. Most important of all, there may be actions which have to be taken which are essential to the implementation of the strategy, but which have no separate identifiable effect which can be measured by the accounting control processes.

Something else is needed. This is a means of monitoring the action plans, to make sure that actions are completed on due date, and that their effect is recorded. Some part of this was discussed above, and there was also relevant material in Chapter 3, where objectives and goals were considered. It is not possible to monitor actions unless they are defined in a way that includes timetables and where appropriate, their expression in quantitative terms. In parallel with the budget there is an action to monitor the various departmental and individual action plans.

In theory monitoring individual actions could be part of a performance management system, and success or failure in the various tasks is an important part of this. However this is inadequate for some of the needs, partly because of frequency of review, and partly because the strategy implementation actions may be a very small part of an individual's total job. It is of little help to the organisation to find at the end of the year that an essential task which should have been done months ago is still unfinished: this information is needed closer to the time when the task should have been completed, so that remedial action could be taken. So although there are key links with performance management, and the more the better, it would be unwise to rely on these processes to ensure implementation of the transient tasks of implementation. It is ideal for monitoring the permanent tasks, such as the way in which the individual behaves to customers, but not for the abnormal non-repetitive tasks. However, it is important to ensure that the existing performance management system is causing people to behave generally in the way the strategy requires, a point discussed in the chapter on human resource strategy.

Complex projects, are in a way easier to establish a control system for than the simple ones. They are more likely to be run by a project manager, to whom control responsibility can be delegated, the network analysis makes it clear where the priorities of the moment are, and the process would normally include regular meetings of the project team. Network analysis also makes it easier to report on progress, and to understand the impact of any delays.

Recognising

The final step in the process is to give recognition to those who have helped successfully implement the strategy. This may involve bonuses and salary increases for key people, interviews with their managers where the part they had played was discussed and they were thanked, or it can take the form of organisational events, such as a dinner for all key players, where the leader outlines the outcome and thanks everyone for their help. It is possible to express thanks to individuals and departments through the organisation's internal newspapers.

Recognition is an opportunity to close the loop, to say that this part of our journey to the future is now finished, and that it could only have been achieved with the active help and involvement of many other people, some playing a major and some a minor role. To work, it has to be genuine, and be seen to be genuine.

ARE WE STILL ON COURSE?

One of the issues is that the outcome of a strategy is not always known in the short term. It may be possible to measure that everything that had to be done was done, but often this is only the first stage and the situation has to be managed thereafter. Even if all targets are met in the first year, this does not mean that the strategy will achieve everything expected from it. Many things take a long time to work through, and in any case a complex strategy may overlap the financial year, or even several financial years. So there is also a need to measure progress against a longer term framework. Although it is possible to argue that all this is part of the ensuring stage discussed earlier, I am treating it separately because there is no easily definable end point.

One such monitoring procedure that should be instituted deals with the project plan involving major capital expenditure. Many organisations make very comprehensive investigations into capital expenditure appraisals, but few have any follow-up procedure to compare their studies with what really happens once the capital is spent. Some form of monitoring capital projects is important, to make sure that top management's wishes have been carried out, to ensure that no further action is required by management to bring the situation back to plan, and to improve planning ability in the future. The last reason is of greater importance than is often imagined. Many lessons can be learnt through a study of mistakes, and any project study is subject to a large number of areas for potential error.

The elements of a project proposal which require monitoring include the time span for implementation, the actual capital spent, and the benefits actually achieved. The comparison must, of course, do more than state variances, it must show the reasons for them. Management can learn no lessons from knowing that certain key forecasts are wrong, unless it knows why they are wrong.

It follows that if results are to be monitored, the accounting system must present them in such a way that comparison is possible. This may not be difficult in a multi-million pound project involving the construction of an entirely new factory for the organisation. It is not so easy when the project involves the modifications of existing plant, or where the capital is spent on a function which is indistinguishable from operations already being carried out. In extreme cases the total results may be immeasurable in practicable terms, and management may have to be informed of this, but even in these cases it will be possible to measure certain aspects, such as additional personnel employed and the capital spent.

It is also impracticable to think about measuring results for each of the years included in the original proposal, be they 5, 10, 15 or longer. Some compromise is necessary, and it is suggested that this should be to carry out a full comparison of results against the proposal, at the end of the first full period of twelve months trading, which of course may be much more than a year from the start of the project. If this seems to be too soon, do it a year later. The aim is to choose a time when a comparison is likely to be worthwhile, and which will yield results which will be helpful to the organisation. What is equally important is that it may not be too late for management to take corrective action if events are not proceeding to plan. If all is well, this may be the only monitoring action that is needed, and the project may then be considered as a true part of company operations which will fall within the overall management processes of the organisation. Occasionally, it may be desirable to continue monitoring results for the next few years, and this will be essential if the project is one which is expected to yield a loss for a number of years. The final decision will depend on the particular project; obviously the major new chemical works deserves more management attention than the new warehouse.

Among the many organisations which I have had dealings with, only a handful had any form of post project audit. Managers usually prefer to bury their mistakes, and in any case unless the need for monitoring is established up front, the accounting system often makes it impossible to make comparisons. One of the organisations which does undertake post-project audits does so as a learning exercise, although it is hard to prevent some blame attaching to a manager who makes a complete mess of something. But they try. In addition to the lessons that can be learned by those involved in the project, the audits have enabled some points of principle to be defined to prevent the repetition of the same bad points by other managers, and to ensure that what can be learned from the good points is applied in the future. Yet another use of the reports is a basis for case studies used on internal management training programmes.

Someone in the organisation should take on the task of continuously checking that strategies are still appropriate. Earlier it was stated that strategies should be flexible, and that they may require amendment if either they do not deliver the expected results, or if the external or competitive environment has changed. Ignoring these factors would deprive the organ-isational of a fast response to turn events in the outside world to the organisation's advantage.

What may also be desirable is the regular updating of the expected financial results of the strategic plan. Some organisations revise all these figures as a matter of routine at 6- or 3-monthly intervals, on the grounds that this forces managers to give attention to any changes in perception of where the organisation is headed.

The measures outlined will help bridge the gap between the strategic decision and an actual result. Although it may be possible to dispense with one or two of the measures and still retain a fair chance of success, the organisation which adopts them all will improve its chances of success. There are many things that can go wrong with a strategy which are beyond the control of the organisation. What the measures proposed here do is to ensure that everything which is under the organisation's control is done properly, and that there is as early a warning as possible of changes in the things that it cannot control.

REFERENCES

Alexander, L. D., 1991, "Strategy implementation: nature of the problem", in Hussey, D. E., editor, *International Review of Strategic Management*, **2**.1, Wiley, Chichester.

Kaplan, R., 1995, *Building a Management System to Implement Your Strategy: Strategic Management Survey: Summary of Findings and Conclusions*, Renaissance Solutions, London.

FURTHER READING

Bate, P., 1994, *Strategies for Cultural Change*, Butterworth-Heinemann, Oxford.

Hussey, D. E., editor, 1996, *The Implementation Challenge*, Wiley, Chichester.

Hussey, D. E., 1998, *How to be Better at Managing Change*, Kogan Page, London.

Pendlebury, J., Grouard, B. and Meston, F., 1998, Successful Change Management, Wiley, Chichester.

15
A Process of Strategic Management

Not every reader will want a process of planning in the organisation, and if your need is limited to the formulation of strategy, or the development of a strategic plan for a specific purpose, you may not wish to read this chapter.

A SITUATIONAL VIEW

There is no universal planning process that will suit every organisation. Among the many factors that affect the "right" choice for a particular organisation, the rate of change in the external environment has received most attention in the form of concentrated research. Ansoff, has demonstrated that successful organisations apply a process of planning which is appropriate to the degree of turbulence in the environment in which they operate (see Ansoff & McDonnell, 1990, Ansoff 1991).

Figure 15.1 summarises the five levels of turbulence identified by Ansoff, and what he terms strategic aggressiveness, which is the approach to strategic thinking that fits this level of turbulence. The optimum strategy process column is an interpretation of his views, and next to it are my own comments about what might be relevant in such a process. In a very stable environment, level 1, success comes from continuing an appropriate formula. Although environmental and competitor scanning would be advisable to spot changes in the turbulence level, the successful process is likely to be a form of bottom-up budgeting within the context of top-down

External Turbulence		Type of Strategic Response	Notes on the planning process	
Level	Description	Strategic Aggressiveness	Optimum strategy process	Comments
1	Repetitive	Stable, precedent-based	Procedures, budgets	Bottom up budgets, top down procedure
2	Expanding	Reactive, incremental	Financial control, extrapolated budgets	Tight performance targets, extrapolations
3	Changing	Anticipatory, incremental	Formal planning based on patterns of success	Top down/bottom up Planning formal process
4	Discontinuous	Entrepreneurial, expected futures	Strategic planning	Stronger top down input: scenario planning; issue management
5	Surpriseful	Creative	Fast reaction process	Scenario plans, early warning systems

Note: The first three columns derived from Ansoff; the last two are my interpretation of his concept

Figure 15.1 Ansoff stages of turbulence and optimum approach to strategy process.

policies and procedures. The aim is to keep the whole organisation following the successful strategy.

At level 2 the market is expanding but in a predictable way. Ansoff suggests that strong financial control with emphasis on performance improvement is appropriate. The forward planning is likely to be a form of extended budget, based on extrapolation. Again some form of competitor and environmental monitoring might be desirable. Although the budgets may be a mix of top down and bottom up, the degree of strategic freedom is small, with a strong emphasis on goals set from the centre. The organisation reacts to changes, instead of anticipating them.

Unfortunately there are comparatively few organisations operating under conditions 1 and 2. In level 3 the environment is changing faster but in a fairly predictable way, so that the changes, which may be of some magnitude can be anticipated. Ideal here, is a type of formal planning, based on past patterns of success, but with more effort devoted to competitor analysis and monitoring of the external environment. This is typically the situation written about by many of the early books on corporate planning, which normally postulated a top-down/bottom-up system, with very wide involvement of managers in the strategic debate. This would be followed by the completion of plans at various levels, which are gradually combined at the divisional and business unit level, and ultimately, with formal reviews at various stages, result in a plan for the whole organisation.

At level 4 the most concise definition of the level of turbulence is that the changes are discontinuous. Forecasting becomes harder, because past trends are less useful as a guide to the future, and it is not only the change that causes problems but also the timing of it. Nevertheless, there is still some stability in the environment. Ansoff sees the best strategic response as entrepreneurial, trying to move the organisation to an expected future, about which there is some uncertainty. My view is that strategy becomes of even greater significance, but more of the planning would go on at higher levels of management. This does not mean there is no lower level involvement, but that it is controlled. The planning process is tighter, and speedier than for level 3. Scenario planning approaches and contingency planning are options that could help the development of more flexible strategies. The regular study of key issues, their impact on the current strategies, and the development of new strategies when appropriate become an important part of the process. Although plans might be put together once a year, the organisation reacts much faster than this and manages its strategy on a continuous basis.

At level 5, the changes are so fast and furious, that the normal planning process cannot cope. Continuous analysis is needed so that the organisation develops early warning systems. The whole approach to strategic management has to be fast reacting and flexible, which is why Ansoff suggests that a creative response is important. Changing the industry boundaries may be important from level 3 upwards, but may be essential at level 5. Those organisations that can successfully do this at the least may cause some competitors to drop out, and at the best may give the organisation an advantage that is difficult to copy. Strategic management becomes a way of life in these organisations, although highly formalised planning systems are unlikely to be the appropriate tool to achieve this: it is not plans which are the problem, but systems which take too long to produce a plan which may be out of date before it has completed its review process. Planning as a once a year exercise is not the way forward.

It is very easy to look quickly at Ansoff's levels, observe how the business world is changing, and claim that we are now all at level 5. In fact we are not. While it is true that there are probably few organisations below level 3, the different competitive environments, markets, and degree of technological change mean that all organisations are not in the same position. For example, personal computer businesses are fast changing because of major technological developments, the consequent short life cycles of products, and the fact that the industry is driven by a major chip manufacturer, Intel, and a supplier of operating systems and other software, Microsoft. This industry as a whole is probably somewhere between levels 4 and 5. The retailers and mail order suppliers of PCs are at least a full point lower than this. Television sets have probably been on level 3.5 for at least two decades. This industry is about to move to level 5 in the UK because of the impact of digital television, for which there seems to be no single standard format, and where the market acceptance is an unknown. Within five to ten years it will have probably fallen back to level 3.5.

But few organisations do only one thing, and there are not many that make only television sets. Sony, for example has a vast range of product and business areas, which are operating at different levels of turbulence. This suggests that the process which some multi-nationals use of making all business units plan in exactly the same way is not the best way to achieve success.

Other factors which affect how a strategic planning process should be designed for a particular organisation include complexity (organisational, geographical and of activities), culture (although Ansoff also argues that there are appropriate cultures required for success at each of his levels of turbulence), and management competence.

In the description of an outline process which follows, I am of necessity taking a general view. It could fit organisations from levels 2 to 4, provided there was adaptation of the process at each level on the lines discussed above. I have also not attempted to modify the examples to fit every different organisational situation, but make the point that modification is always needed.

AN OUTLINE STRATEGIC PLANNING PROCESS

We should begin by defining three types of plan which are of relevance in a formal planning process. "Project", "strategic" and "operating" plans require definition because they are quite different types of plans, although all highly important to the company practising strategic management.

A project plan is a plan covering a particular capital investment or marketing operation. For example, an investment in a new factory would be supported by a detailed study of the expected results of that investment. Project plans are prepared on an "as required" basis. This does not mean they have no relation to the other plans, since they must fall within the framework of these plans. Obviously a company would be planning badly if it had to prepare a project plan for a major investment that was not mentioned in its strategic plan. It is of course possible to carry out project planning without embracing any other aspect of planning (Chapter 13 discussed projects at some length).

Strategic and operating plans become the heart of the regular planning cycle which is the basis of most formal planning systems. Put simply, the strategic plan sets out the objectives of the organisation and the means (strategy) by which it intends to reach those objectives. An operating plan is the plan of an established area of the organisation, for example, a division or a subsidiary.

Now we cannot leave the definition of strategic and operational planning hanging in the air, for there are other plans which are bound up with them and there are inter-relationships that must be explained. Figure 15.2 shows a generalised family of plans which an organisation might develop. I say "might" because practical application of the principles will often suggest changes to suit the particular situation. The whole system is described below to give a coherent picture.

The diagram is in circular form to indicate the fact that not one of these plans is an entity on its own. Each depends partly on the other plans in the system, and indeed, during the completion of the plans there is a feedback from one plan to the next.

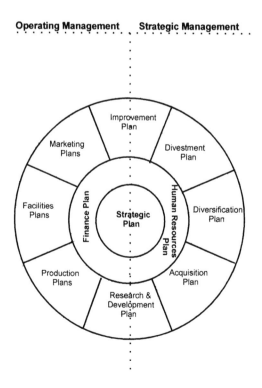

Figure 15.2 Generalised planning system.

In the heart of the system is the strategic plan. This really is the key to the whole process, and from this will come strategic guidelines to the operating units of the company. Surrounding the strategic plan is another circle, which is split between the financial and human resource plans. These, too, are master plans for the whole organisation, which show how the programmes in the strategic and operational plans are to be provided with the twin resource requirements of money and people. Naturally, these must balance with the total corporate strategy, since if there is a shortage of resources, there may have to be revisions to strategy.

All the operational plans are found on the left-hand side of the diagram. The dotted line has been positioned to emphasise that there is a direct relationship between these plans and the three master plans. The diagram assumes a simple one-division organisation, but it is easy to see how the plans shown on this side of the diagram can be repeated for additional divisions and departments, right down to the smallest unit to which the chief executive wishes to bring formal planning. The headings here are quite straightforward and fairly logical, covering marketing, production and facilities. Shown partly on this side and partly on the right-hand side are the improvement plans and the research and development plans.

The right-hand side of the diagram shows the family of plans, also descending from the master plans, which are the responsibility of the strategic management of the company: in other words, the chief executive's plans, although of course it is usually advisable to use staff assistance and involve the top management team.

Research and development, and the improvement plans fall under the influence of both strategic and operating management. The normal operating unit may use R & D to constantly improve its products, to produce new ideas in line with its current operations. On the other hand, strategic management may call on R & D to develop the product or technology which will take it into a completely new business area. Improvement of all operations is a total management task, and a striving for increased productivity and for greater profits through higher efficiency is such an important issue that it is worth preparing a special plan devoted to it.

The rest of the plans on the strategic side show the other major groups of options open to an organisation: expansion, acquisition and divestment. These three headings, plus the other two, really sum up all the types of action that management can take to reach an increased profit target. They can make their current operations more efficient, and reach it in this way. They can decide to expand capacity, open a business overseas, buy up some licences: hence the expansion plan. They can find new areas of activity through their R & D, or they can go off on a shopping expedition and acquire their way into new areas of profits. They may have to get rid of some of the areas in which they at present operate, hence the divestment plan.

At this stage, I must confess that the word plan still tends to suggest to me an image of a huge leather-bound document, perpetually locked, and hidden deep in the company archives. I do not think I am alone in this, for example, I once had a perfectly serious enquiry from an acquaintance who wanted to know what a strategic plan looked like, and how long it was. "Plan" must not be interpreted in such a way in the conceptual approach outlined (no corporate plan should ever gather dust in the archives!) and in many cases the whole "plan" may be only a few sheets of paper. In other cases it may be long enough to make up a file or a book. The objective should, of course, be to keep plans as concise as possible, but at the same time they must include enough data to make them actionable. There is some merit in having the various parts of the total package so that they can be lifted from the whole: because of its confidential nature, it may be advisable to restrict readership of the total corporate plan. In this case, various sub-plans may be taken from the whole, and passed to those people who have to take action on them.

The total approach discussed above is for an organisation which has embraced the corporate planning method. Just as it is possible to carry out project planning without corporate planning, so it is possible to do operational planning or strategic planning in isolation. But in the right situation, greater success may come from undertaking both.

Plans such as those described do not suddenly come into being. In fact, one might claim that they are the middle part of the planning process. Figure 1.2 showed the various steps which have to be followed in the development of a strategic plan, and to some degree these are mirrored in the various subsidiary plans. Earlier chapters showed what is involved in preparing such a plan.

There is much that needs to be done to move from a description of plans to a process that helps prepare them, but there is another matter to consider first.

HOW LONG IS LONG RANGE?

The difference between a long range and a short range plan is a matter of degree, and a planning system is incomplete if it does not incorporate both. In the previous chapter we saw how the short range plan can be used as one of the steps in converting a strategy to action.

Short range in this context means up to 12 months. The term "long range" is relative, and I see this as extending for a period of 3 years or more. The question of for how long a period an organisation should plan is often raised. There is no stock answer, and each organisation must make its own judgement. It is important for the period to be sufficiently lengthy for strategy to be developed: any period of less than 3 years is usually too short for this. Major capital investments in, say, a chemical plant may take a long time to complete and the planning period should try to cover a sufficient period so that a realistic picture emerges. A company in the forestry business must think many years ahead, since it may be a very long time before newly planted trees begin to yield. An orchard company may have to consider a 7-year planning cycle, since it may take this long for new apple trees to become economic.

The first principle that can be deduced is that the planning process should take into account any normal cycle of events that is pertinent to the business.

At the same time it is a fact that the shorter the period studied, the more accurately the organisation is likely to be able to forecast future events. This leads to the second principle, that organisations should not plan for a longer period than fits the business they are in. While it might be realistic for our forestry enterprise to plan for 20 years ahead, it is unlikely to be a useful period for an organisation in the theatre business.

I suppose the third principle is that no organisation should be dogmatic about the time period, but should make sure that it chooses a period which fits its business. Most organisations seem to opt for a 3-, 5- or 7-year period. There is nothing really magic about any of these numbers, and I would suggest that 5 years is often chosen simply because it seems to be a nicely balanced unit of time. I would be reluctant to take a period of less than 5 years for any business, because I think a lesser period tends to lack perspective. At the same time, it must be admitted that 3 years seems to suit some organisations very well.

Now setting, for example, a 5-year planning cycle does not mean that a plan is prepared at 5-year intervals, nor does it mean that the organisation should make no study of trends beyond the 5-year period.

What I understand by a 5-year plan is one that "rolls". It may be revised and updated once a year (or more frequently), and at every revision an additional year is added. So there is always a 5-year plan. The plans must be flexible, and the organisation must be prepared to reconsider the whole of its strategy if events show this to be necessary. What it must never do is write a 5-year plan, and then follow it blindly for the given time period.

The trends beyond the planning cycle will have an effect on the organisation's strategies. A simple example is the quarrying enterprise whose quarry has only a 10-year life. This fact may well be a major influence on the first 5-year plan, since it may restrict the investment the enterprise is prepared to put into the quarry, or cause it to search for some other area of activity so that this can be well established by the time the quarry is exhausted.

Both these points are really a statement that the far-sighted company will apply good sense and business judgement to its plans. Slavish attention to a set of rigid rules can well mean planning with defective vision. The fact that an organisation goes to the trouble of writing a document does not mean that it is actually planning! The act of planning is more important than the written plans themselves, provided the emphasis is strategic thinking, and it is not just a form-filling exercise.

It may be that the organisation will wish to have two or three planning time periods. It is often very sensible to consider a project plan for a period of much longer than the 5 years laid down for the strategic plan. Also, it may be wise to plan strategically for 5 years, but to only produce operating plans for a 3-year period. I would recommend in a multidivisional company that the planning horizon of divisions be chosen to fit the divisional business needs.

TURNING IT INTO A PROCESS

We are now very close to the design of a planning process. This takes Figures 1.2 and 15.2 and combines them in a way that will meet the unique requirements of the individual organisation, so that the resultant process clearly shows not only what analytical steps are needed and what plans will result, but *how* the organisation will tackle this task and *which* organisational units will be involved.

In addition, the complete process has to bring in the concepts of time, and the subdivision of the various tasks into steps to be completed by a defined date. Overall the process is continuous, and designed to lead to the formal revision and extension of the plan every year. Within the process provision must be made for formal reviews of the plan, and the dissemination and formal discussion of the strategic guidelines which enable operating divisions to make their plans.

The final links which complete the process are forged with other systems in the organisation: for example, budgeting control, capital budgeting, project and capital expenditure evaluation, personal appraisal and management development.

There is no universal flow chart which will illustrate the process in a way which fits every company. The best that can be done is to show a summary diagram of the process as it is applied in a particular company: this is illustrated in Figure 15.3. Variations on this theme have been successfully used in a number of organisations, but each time the concept has been re-thought in the light of the specific situation in the organisation.

Figure 15.3 is a three-stage planning approach. Phase 1 gets the head office and divisional top management teams into discussions about strategy. Detailed plans are not worked out at this stage, although this does not mean that no work is done in trying to think through what a particular course of actions might mean. At the end of this phase there is broad agreement over where all parts of the organisation are trying to go, and how they may get there. It is then possible to move into phase 2, doing all the work needed to produce a long-range plan in the knowledge that the only objection to the strategies would be if the detailed work showed them to be flawed.

The final phase includes the intermediary step of detailed capital

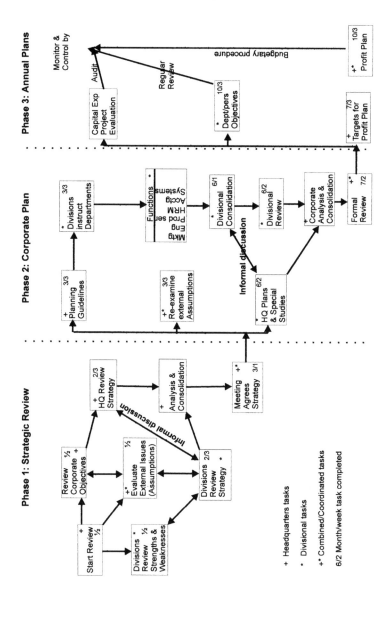

Figure 15.3 Outline planning process (from Corporate Planning at Rolls Royce Motors Ltd, R. Young & D. E. Hussey, Long Range Planning, April 1977).

expenditure appraisal, the final check on the sanity of a project and the returns expected from any expenditure. Most of it is about using the budget and other types of annual plan to help implement the strategy, and to ensure that the short-term actions are compatible with the strategy.

THE PRINCIPLES OF STRATEGIC MANAGEMENT

So far we have looked at planning and plans, but have not related these to the overall philosophy that is strategic management. Ansoff et al. 1976 established the idea of strategic management. It derived from an earlier conference at Vanderbilt University and was a response to the increasing complexity of modern business (Professor Ansoff states that he developed the concept in 1972). The differences of emphasis between strategic planning and strategic management are:

STRATEGIC PLANNING	STRATEGIC MANAGEMENT
External linkages	Adds internal elements
(e.g. products, markets, environment)	(e.g. organisation, style, climate)
Strategy formulation to solve problems	Adds implementation and control
Focuses on the "hard" aspects of the	Also concerned with social and
external environment	political aspects.

Thus strategic management may be seen as a more complete way of managing a business, concerned not only with markets and decision making, but with social developments, implementation, and the "fit" of strategy with organisational structure and climate. By the 1980s strategic management had become the most widely used term and remains so today.

If strategic management is a philosophy of management, it must have certain principles. These are not very complex, and can be superimposed on a variety of different theories of management. What they really do is give a particular slant to the way in which the organisation is run. The only thing with which they are incompatible is poor management (which is not, of course, accusing those organisations which do not plan formally of being badly managed). All the principles of planning fall within the definition of management given by Koonz, 1962, in a *Harvard Business*

Review article, a definition which I do not think has been bettered by anyone.

> Managing is the art of getting things done through and with people in formally organized groups. It is the art of creating an environment in which people can perform as individuals and yet co-operate towards the attainment of group goals. It is the art of removing blocks to such performance, a way of optimizing efficiency in reaching goals.

The principles of the strategic management approach are worth examining, because they are vital to the successful introduction of a planning process to an organisation. Acceptance of the principles means that planning should never become an empty exercise, and will mean that plans work, and that the carefully prepared long-range plan does not disappear into the files for a year, unread and unused.

In some organisations planning has grown out of an existing activity: the market research/forecasting function, the budgetary control function, or an *ad hoc* team set up to appraise a major capital investment. In fact these are all potentially flawed approaches to strategic management, which should be introduced as a deliberate decision by the top management that this is the way to run the organisation. Growing into strategic management is the wrong way to go about it, and can jeopardise its chances of success.

There is a body of research evidence which suggests that planning frequently is introduced as an answer to a crisis: either internal, such as a change in top management, or external such as the energy crisis. It is a pity that this is so, for an earlier introduction might well have avoided the crisis.

So this is the first principle: that top management must genuinely desire to apply strategic management, and must back these wishes by positive action. It must not only be wanted, but it must be seen to be wanted, which means making the senior management team excited over the idea. This means that top management should submit to the same sort of planning discipline as the rest of the organisation, for nothing is worse for the success of a planning process than the feeling that this is medicine that the chief executive reserves for subordinates, but which will never be taken personally. The chief executive's interest in the planned approach must be as obvious to the organisation as the edict that this is the philosophy by which the organisation will be guided.

Of equal importance is the principle that all managers must be concerned with the long-term results of all decisions. The shape of the organisation in the future years ahead depends on decisions made today. The planning organisation makes it a cornerstone of management that all managers look beyond the short-term results of their decisions. This goes far wider and much deeper than the mere writing of plans. It spans every management level in the company, including people who might not normally be involved in the preparation of formal plans. All managers are motivated to evaluate the total logical outcome of their decisions, and not to make them solely against the background of pressures of the day.

The planning system forces managers to accept that there is always a choice of actions possible, and that part of their job is to make the best choice. This enforces the consideration of options, and the deliberate definition of all the practicable ways of solving each particular problem. The solutions sought will not simply be the ones which spring first to mind.

This leads on to the next principle which is that all such decisions must be made objectively, after consideration of the available facts. This suggests that appropriate management techniques should be used in the decision process. It presupposes an effective management information system, and a flow of data on the environment, so that reasonable options can be considered. Above all, it calls for an attitude of mind that attempts to banish emotionalism from decision making. It also requires inclusion of "soft" factors, such as the fit of the proposed course of action with the culture and structure of the organisation.

As there is a proper evaluation, the results should be recorded. Wherever possible the expected effects of the decision should be quantified, to provide a simple model against which performance can be measured. This leads to the principle that as much as is reasonable in the management task will be written down. One of the reasons for a permanent record of the problem, the alternative solutions, and the reason for choosing the decided course of action is that the act of writing focuses the mind, and leads to clearer thinking. Too often, organisations make important decisions without ever setting down what they are hoping to achieve. If an organisation does not do this, how can it know when it gets there? And, of course, another reason for a written record is that it becomes possible to monitor results to confirm that the standards set *a priori* are in fact achieved.

Planning is a very important communication process. There must be adequate discussion between senior managers, so that plans have both the involvement of those responsible for them, and the approval of the person whose duty it is to set the overall pace of the organisation. It follows that if management is a team approach, there must be a naturally healthy atmosphere for the discussion of problems and the development of ideas.

The planning process should try to encourage the growth of ideas from all areas of the organisation, and the open approach so necessary for good planning stimulates this result. Good, sound, business opportunities can come from many corners of the company, and are a diet needed for the continued well being of the body corporate.

Perhaps the last principle is that the spread of the planning approach throughout the company must be total. You cannot claim that this way of management includes everyone except Bill Smith ("who is difficult"), or the Human Resources Department, or Production, or whatever other departments spring to mind. The planning philosophy must go all the way through the organisation, and everyone in the organisation must learn to approach problems in the ways described. But this also means that sufficient data must be made available to enable everyone to plan. This does not mean that no secrets may be withheld from the office junior; but it does mean that the Human Resources Department (for instance) must be aware of the major developments taking place in the organisation. The principle of communication again.

The task of planning the progress of the company lies squarely on the shoulders of the chief executive, just as the task of planning their own operations is part of the job of all line managers. These cannot be delegated.

WHY ORGANISATIONS APPOINT PLANNERS

The preparation of formal plans involves much detailed work; even more important is the time needed to study the trends in the environment, to make sure that the company can take advantage of all opportunities. In all but the smallest companies, the volume of work in organising and preparing plans and in the evaluation of options is such that the chief executive just does not have the time available to do the task justice: indeed there should be priorities in the rest of the work task which would put much of the *routine* of planning in a fairly low position. This is why most organisations that have a planning process employ the services of a planner. Now this does not suggest that the chief executive delegates the task of planning; nor does it mean that line managers can throw up their hands and say that as the future is now being looked after they need give no more thought to it. A good planner will never try to take the chief executive's decisions, but will certainly ease the burden by objective analysis of alternatives; illuminating opportunities; and taking over many of the problems connected with making planning happen. Similarly the planner will never try to do the planning for line managers, although certainly there is a duty to help them, and the processes the planner gets working will ensure that they are able to take more factors into account when they do plan. In all this activity the planner is nothing but an extension of the chief executive.

This is not to suggest that the planner should be a "yes man". He or she should present personal opinions to the chief executive, and should make suggestions that will improve the way in which the company moves towards the attainment of its objectives. The role must be an active one, and must never fall into the passive situation of being nothing more than the master's letterbox. But at the same time the planner has no right of position to impose personal schemes on to the organisation.

The optimum-sized planning staff is one, and that any increase in numbers over this represents a degree of relative failure: my only exception to this principle is where the complexity of operations makes it worthwhile attaching additional planners to major subsidiaries, particularly important in an organisation operating in a number of countries, or in a very diverse field of activity.

It may happen that the sheer size of the planning problem in a large organisation makes it imperative for the one-person principle to be left behind, and that additional people will be required to study opportunities and environmental factors. If this is really justifiable, then it has to happen: but this is a far cry from the over-large planning departments built up by many companies, on the assumption that as planning calls on many disciplines, you have to try to have an expert in each. What sometimes happens, is that functions which exist elsewhere in the organisation are duplicated in the planning department: an empire is created which is justifiably resented by line management, and there emerges a form of ivory tower planning which becomes more and more remote from the real affairs in the organisation. It is usually more effective to use consultants to help cope with such a temporary bulge of work, rather than to build large internal departments which subsequently have to be disbanded.

Of course planning calls for expertise in more than one area, and no planner can be a leading expert in every one of the disciplines or techniques that may have to be called upon. But there is a good deal to be said for the designing of a planning process which makes use of existing talent from within the organisation, such as a "task force" approach which establishes a team from different areas of the organisation to perform a specified job. Examples are a task such as the corporate appraisal, or a capital expenditure evaluation. The big advantage of the task force approach is that it is possible to include representatives from the operating areas of the organisation that will be concerned with the outcome.

One thing that fogs judgement about the size of planning departments is the habit which some organisations have of attaching other functions to the planning manager: marketing research, operations research and general trouble-shooting. In principle this is incorrect, because apart from giving the appearance of an empire, it means that the person in charge has a number of administrative duties which restrict the amount of time available for the all-important task of planning.

By the nature of the position as an extension of the chief executive the planner should report to no one but the chief executive. Anything else is wrong, and puts a blockage between the person who carries the responsibility for planning and the person recruited to help. It follows that the planner must be of a calibre suitable for the position held. It is very damaging for the chief executive to claim to be too busy to have the planner as a direct report: all this suggests is an attempt to abdicate from the responsibility of planning, and the chief executive can only do this if he or she surrenders their position of chief executive. The planner should be able to communicate on equal terms with the most senior managers of the company, and reporting to the chief executive helps this to happen.

The selection of the planner is a very important step in the planning process. The person chosen must be able to make objective evaluations and must be numerate. This indicates an ability to "sell" ideas to people, and the planner must therefore be a good communicator both verbally and in writing, and, of course, must be of the calibre to inspire confidence in line management.

Planning calls for the use of many skills, and it is highly improbable that any one person has expertise in all of them. This

---

1. Faults of the Chief Executive
   A. Does not believe in it, but has a planner because it seems the thing to do.
   B. Insufficient backing by chief executive leads line managers to underestimate its importance.
   C. Instructs staff planners to take no interest in current activities and to avoid upsetting line managers.
   D. Gives planner too low a status to enable discussions with general managers to take place on equal terms.
   E. Creates a planning committee rather than give planning task to one individual.
   F. Allows some managers to opt Out of the system.
   G. Spends too little time on planning.
2. Faults of the Planner
   A. Tries to do all planning personally.
   B. Planner of low calibre.
   C. Planner has only a part-time interest in planning and has to spend too much time on other activities.
   D. No control mechanism or other procedures to convert plans to action included in the system.
   E. Planner a narrow specialist who lacks ability to see full scope of the task and views planning only in terms of a personal own disipline (e.g. OR., accounting).
   F. Lack of attention to one or more of the basic steps.
3. Faults of the Organisation
   A. Organisation as a whole does not understand the corporate-planning process (not all organisations with "planning departments" carry out formal planning).
   B. Managers judged on current results only and no account taken of their future plans.
   C. Organisation tries to move into an advanced management area before it is ready (e.g. companies with no management accounting function).

Figure 15.4   A check list of reasons why planning may fail.

means that the basic discipline in which the planner is trained is not of vital importance: it can be as an economist, econometrician, mathematician, or virtually anything. As wide a knowledge of techniques as possible is a desirable feature, but the planner should never be a narrow specialist, appointed *because* he or she is an economist, OR person, or the like. The other qualities required outweigh the narrow skill, and of course are found in a very wide range of people.

The planner should preferably possess, or at least be able to rapidly acquire, an expertise in strategic management. It takes a certain skill to design a system of planning for a particular company, and much wasted effort can be avoided if the planner is knowledgeable.

PLANNING THE PLAN

What happens when the planner has been appointed into an organisation where the chief executive has been at pains to create the right climate for the success of a planning process? It is worthwhile thinking about some of the steps which the planner will have to take to make planning happen. This is when the chief executive's decision to undertake the corporate planning approach begins to move very definitely into the action phase.

A number of things have to be done before a planning system can be set into motion. This really is a pre-planning stage, when time must be taken to "plan the plan". As I see it, there are four basic steps to take:

1. Self-education.
2. Management education.
3. Design of planning system.
4. Issue of planning instructions.

The only problem with writing down a series of steps is that there immediately appears to be a neat ordered sequence. In practice the steps all have blurry edges: some will be started before others have finished and in the middle of it all the planner will be beginning those elements of the planning process which have to be carried on, regardless of the final shape of the system. Objectives will be set, the corporate appraisal begun, and, because the planner will be walking into a dynamic situation, there will be *ad hoc* situations which will require attention. Only in a company that begins planning before incorporation is it possible to prevent anything happening until the planner is ready for it! So there will be capital investment decisions, new products and a thousand and one other decisions which will make claims on the planner's attention, long before it is possible to help the organisation to produce its first plan.

With this in mind, it is possible to interpret the four steps in the way in which they will occur in the hustle and bustle of the normal business environment. And, of course, order will gradually appear out of the apparent chaos.

If the appointment has been made from within, and the planner has no planning expertise, the first task must be to acquire some. If recruited from outside the first priority is to learn enough about the organisation to begin the other steps: but in this case the learning can be linked with the preliminary moves towards the corporate appraisal. In any event, step one should not last more than a matter of weeks (although this does not suggest that the planner should then have a closed mind and assume perfect knowledge of everything!).

The next stage is a vitally important one. Something new is happening in the organisation which will affect the work of each and every manager. It is only fair that a determined effort is made to explain what is happening: it is not only fair, but it is prudent, since many misunderstandings can be avoided if managers are shown what a planning process is before any other demands are made on them.

The development of managers' knowledge of methodology can be approached in two ways. Firstly, in the first few weeks the planner should meet as many managers as possible, to "sell" planning to them, and to establish good interpersonal relations. At this stage the planner may still be eyed with suspicion, but at least will have shown that he or she is flesh and blood, like everybody else.

It is also useful to hold an internal seminar (or series of seminars) to explain to managers the full implication of planning, and the theory behind it. The handling of these meetings is important, for they can shape line managers' future attitudes to the planner and to planning. Depending on the requirements of the company, it may be worth holding seminars for different levels of management: each should, of course, be pitched to appeal to the particular responsibilities of the managers attending. A professional approach is important in the holding of any seminars, for all managers will be giving a little of their most precious resource, time, and this must not be wasted. In many situations it may be necessary to develop a more comprehensive course or programme. A development from the training seminar is a workshop, at which managers both receive instruction and work on their real planning problems. Specialist outside help is usually advisable to ensure that any training or workshop approach is professional and effective.

During the whole of this educational process, the chief executive should by personal behaviour show full support for the planner. It would be a very bad start to planning if the chief executive were to be "too busy" to attend the seminar. The chief executive's presence is vital to convince managers that the intentions are serious. In a large company, where many training sessions have to cascade through the organisation, it may not be practicable for the chief executive to attend every session. Other signals of commitment may have to be devised. One may be the attendance of the top management team on the first session of the training seminar, which is a very powerful way of stressing the importance of the activity.

The second worst mistake a planner can make is to give the impression of an intention to do, personally, all the organisation's planning from now on, and that the managers are the little chess-men whose function is to put the plans into operation. (The worst mistake a planner can make is to *really* try to do all the planning personally! Unfortunately, some do.)

There will be many decisions to be taken on the design of the planning system. The unique needs of the organisation must be taken into account, and the ultimate scheme should slide as neatly as possible into the company's way of doing things.

Every organisation is likely to have in existence some semiformal elements of planning, and there is almost certainly bound to be a process of budgetary control. It is worthwhile using these existing elements as building blocks where they are suitable. Similarly, the basic organisation chart should provide a framework for establishing the exact contribution required from each person, although, of course, it must not be forgotten that the corporate appraisal may show the need for changes in the structure. Do not think the planner can expect that the first system designed will be absolutely perfect: there should be an expectation of the need to make changes as time progresses, both to meet the needs of a dynamic organisation and to improve on the original ideas. In this way the system will be a flexible part of a living organisation.

It is considerate if the process can avoid the making the busiest planning periods at the time of year when managers are most stretched. Of course, this is not always possible, but where a clash can be prevented it will make for the smooth running of the system, as well as giving the managers more time to think.

There is one very real danger in the formalisation of planning. The standardisation of plan layout can bring the risk of a standardisation of thought, which would be disastrous to the organisation. If planning ever becomes a form-filling exercise in the eyes of managers it will be well down the path to failure. To be successful it must stretch the imagination of managers, and must force them to think into the future.

Any plans that have become dreary "form-filling" will have little value to the organisation. This is an avoidable situation and action starts with the planning instructions issued to managers, which should stick to essentials, and avoid petty detail. The managers should be given a certain freedom of choice. For instance, it is worthwhile providing a conceptual guideline for market planning, so that all can see the sort of approach required, and the areas of decision to be covered: but it might be unwise to insist that this framework was adhered to rigidly. Having given the guideline, the planner should encourage managers to approach the problems in their own way. So long as all points are covered, it does not really matter in which order the manager records them.

A sensible system of control, and of standards of performance, will also help to make plans worthwhile, especially if the chief executive lets it be known that planning ability is one of the factors against which a manager's success is measured.

Over all, the planner must resist the temptation to be pedantic, or to collect data which is only of academic interest. Attention to the appearance of plans might reveal a professionalism which is to be encouraged, so long as it is remembered that good prose and pretty diagrams are the means not the end. A gold plating does not change the characteristics of a base metal, and some base metals are not worth plating. In marketing research there is always the danger of the researchers becoming hypnotised by their own project, so that they spend money finding facts which are of interest to them, but which do not contribute one iota to the solution of the marketing problems they are studying. A first-rate researcher guards against this: I think a planner has to beware of a similar tendency. A good plan will never be cluttered with trivia.

The planner must always remember that not all operating managers have the literary skill to write a plan with the style and quality of the professional (and neither do all planners!). Again, it should be stressed that it is the thought content of the plan which is important.

If there is any overriding message about planning, it is that the processes involved must have a certain flexibility, so that they do not break at the first crisis. Planning is a total process. And we should never to forget the very important relationship that each part has with the whole.

REFERENCES

Ansoff, H. I., Declerk, R. and Hayes, R., 1976, *From Strategic Planning to Strategic Management*, Wiley, Chichester.

Ansoff, H. I. and McDonnell, E., 1990, *Implanting Strategic Management*, Prentice Hall, Hemel Hempstead.

Ansoff, H. I., 1991, "Strategic management in a historical perspective," in Hussey, D. E., editor, *International Review of Strategic Management*, Vol. **2**.1, Wiley, Chichester.

Koonz, H., 1962, "Making sense of management theory", *Harvard Business Review*, July–August.

Index